Trisha

THE FAMILY SURVIVAL GUIDE

Trisha Goddard with Dr Terri Van-Leeson,
Peter Gianfrancesco and Billie Gianfrancesco

Illustrations by Madi Gianfrancesco

Vermilion
LONDON

1 3 5 7 9 10 8 6 4 2

Text and illustrations © 2003 Trisha, Peter, Billie and
Madison Gianfrancesco and Dr Terri Van-Leeson
Programme Material © 2003 Granada Media Group

This book gives an account of real life case studies originally
featured in the *Trisha* series of programmes, although the names of
people, places and events have been changed to protect identities.

Trisha is an Anglia Television/Universal co-production for itv1.
Published in association with Granada Commercial Ventures.

Trisha, Peter, Billie and Madison Gianfrancesco and Dr Terri Van-Leeson
have asserted their moral right to be identified as the authors of this work
in accordance with the Copyright, Design and Patents Act 1988.

First published in the United Kingdom in 2003 by Vermilion,
an imprint of Ebury Press
Random House UK Ltd., Random House,
20 Vauxhall Bridge Road, London SW1V 2SA

Random House Australia (Pty) Limited
20 Alfred Street, Milsons Point, Sydney, New South Wales 2061, Australia

Random House New Zealand Limited
18 Poland Road, Glenfield, Auckland 10, New Zealand

Random House (Pty) Limited
Endulini, 5A Jubilee Road, Parktown 2193, South Africa

Random House UK Limited Reg. No. 954009
www.randomhouse.co.uk
Papers used by Vermilion are natural, recyclable products
made from wood grown in sustainable forests.

A CIP catalogue record is available for this book from the British Library.

ISBN: 0091887704

Typeset by seagulls

Printed and bound in Great Britain by
Mackays of Chatham plc, Chatham, Kent

From Trisha

I dedicate this book to my parents in recognition of the struggle and tremendous sacrifices they made to give my sisters and me what they never had. In honour of that, I promise to continue and build on what they did for me, so that like a snowball on a hill, my children and generations to come will go from strength to strength.

From Trisha and Peter

We also dedicate this to those we've loved and lost because in dealing with their passing we've been given a chance to grow.

From Terri

I dedicate my part in this book to the late Alison Wade (née Tupper-Carey). She was a great inspiration to me professionally and I feel privileged to have known her.

Acknowledgements

Thanks to those who work flat out on the *Trisha* show who still found time to gather the information for the case studies used in the book: Deputy Editor, Lucy Price along with Supervising Producer, John Redshaw did most of the hard slog and my Executive Producer, the amazing Ms Jackie Heffer helped out.

We have nothing but respect and thanks to the *Trisha* guests who let us use their stories to illustrate important points. May they continue to inspire those around them to realise happiness is a journey, not some pie-in-the-sky destination.

Without Trisha's totally switched on Personal Assistant, Gaile Lee, the juggling acts involved in co-ordinating publishers', programmers' and publicists' requests would have gone balls up!

Our sincerest gratitude to Susanna Wadeson of Granada Media who possesses an almost surreal aura of calm, yes even in the face of virgin, time-challenged writers like us!

Thanks to the Random House clan, Kate Adams who was so on our wavelength, followed by Aussie Amanda Hemmings who didn't bat an eyelid when she bumped into Trisha and Peter at an Elton John Concert the very night they'd told her they'd be staying in, writing like mad to meet a deadline! Miren Lopategui – our praise for making the editing both painless and pleasurable.

Trisha and Peter would like to thank their daughters: Billie for writing and thinking about stuff in greater depth than 'coolness' dictates, and Madi for the way her drawings capture the spirit of each chapter! Terri would like to thank her husband, Nick, for his constant support and patience, and her son, Tom, for being quite simply the best....X

Contents

Introduction   ix

1. Working Out Where You Come From...   1

2. Losing and Choosing a Partner   21

3. Unconditional Love – and Other
   Myths About Parenthood   55

4. Is *The Brady Bunch* Just a Bunch of Lies?   101

5. The Power Game: Bullies and How to Detect Them   141

6. Fighting Fair: Conflicts and Discipline   169

7. Down or Depressed?   191

8. Fit for Life   241

9. Choices and Changes   301

10. Help   313

   Conclusion   341

Introduction

I'm a passionate believer in getting people to challenge the status quo – in not putting up with 20th best when they'd be a lot happier with 15th best, if you know what I mean. Not only is that the philosophy behind my show, *Trisha*, but I guess it's been the driving force of my life. Don't get me wrong. I don't pretend to be one of these lifestyle gurus whose whole existence is naturally based on achieving personal best, and, lo and behold, seems to fall in poo and come out smelling of roses. As with most people, it's sometimes taken the feeling of hitting cold hard rock-bottom to make me reluctantly realise things can't go on in the same way. I freely recognise the greatest encouragement to change is often based on anger, hatred, sorrow and general unhappiness. Thanks to a boyfriend who came home to find a 13-stone me, sitting watching videos and gorging on chocolate in the middle of a hot, sunny day and voicing his total disgust ('Look at you! Sitting there with your stomach hanging out, stuffing yourself with chocolate. What a repulsive sight'), I've made a good diet and keeping fit a crucial part of my life for the past 20 years.

What I'm saying is that if you even have the teeniest feeling that things could be better for your family, then this book will help you identify what you need to change. If things keep going wrong and the same arguments keep coming up, then here's a chance to challenge the patterns that are making your family less fulfilled than it could be. Our purpose is to get you to rethink patterns and behaviour you may have so far taken for granted.

And who are 'we'? I guess we're a slightly unusual bunch of authors. Our ages span from nine to 45 years old. As befitting a book about families, a large part of it has been written by a family: mine! Obviously, there's me, there's my husband, Peter Gianfrancesco, our eldest daughter, Billie (aged 13 at the time of writing) and the illustrations are by eight-year-old Madi.

I've nicked the idea of everyone speaking for themselves from my television chat show. You know, we have Mum and Dad coming on and having their say. Then the kids are allowed their voice, however controversial to the parents that voice might be. Often we'll then have an expert come on and give everyone an overview of what could be happening in the family and how they can improve things. Sometimes that person is me alone. Sometimes, I'm joined by a professional whose particular area of expertise is the topic of the day. In the case of this book, our expert happens to be a friend and colleague, Dr Terri Van-Leeson.

Terri deals day in day out with what most of us would label some of the most damaged young people around. But she never does the smug professional thing. She is totally aware that if she doesn't keep one very sharp eye on the way she brings up her son, the career thing will pretty much be dust in her mouth. She's gone through the difficulties of a painful divorce and intro-ducing a new partner to a son who wanted to protect his mummy from every potential dragon on the horizon. But I'll leave her to go into more details about herself and the challenges she'll set you later.

So why write a book about improving family life in the first place? Living in Australia back in the late 1980s, as a mental health activist I was invited to contribute to drawing up that country's health goals. What things were killing Australians and making them unhealthy? What needed to be tackled as a matter of urgency? Heart disease, cancer, drug and alcohol dependency, car accidents. Sure, I said, but what's behind drug and alcohol dependency? What is vital to someone's recovery from major surgery? Why was suicide one of the major causes of death for young men aged 18-25? Easy – what was happening in their *minds*. In other words, people's mental health.

I spent ten years chairing the National Community Advisory Group on Mental Health, steering both Conservative and Labor Governments with regard to how they needed to improve existing mental health services and create new, client-focused ones. My youngest sister (now dead) had battled with schizophrenia and the stigma that surrounded it for years, but I suspect there were deeper reasons I kept banging on about mental health in those days. Research quickly worked out what many of us had already suspected, that for mental health problems – just as with physical ones, such as high cholesterol or cancer – getting in early stopped them from robbing people of valuable years of their life. Most mental illness starts in teenage years, so it tends to rob young people of the whole experience of dating, leaving home, getting a job and making mates – which makes what we call 'early intervention' even more important.

Then we asked ourselves the obvious question: 'What is one of the most important ways we can strengthen people? Shit happens – how can we best prepare people to deal with it? We looked at what the research was telling us about why some people could handle some situations and why some fell at the first hurdle. Why did some people go through their lives forever thinking they deserved every disaster they stumbled into and why did some draw the line and refuse to put up with another person's inhumanity? What has the biggest, earliest impact on each and every one of us? What's our first source of influence, which has the power to dictate how our minds work for years to come? Families. We're not just talking about mental illness here – we're talking about mental health. Families are the targets of healthy eating messages. Parents are the ones who need to be convinced of the benefits of a good all-round education, sex education, telling kids not to get into cars with strangers, safely using the Internet, inoculations – the list goes on. But rarely do you see how to strengthen your child's mental health included in all of this.

So here's the crunch point. Three people who've spent over 50 years between them, passionately involved in giving people information about how to be mentally healthy without terrifying the poo out of them and doing it in a way people can relate to. Three people passionate about doing a Julie Andrews in *The Sound of Music* – you know, starting at the very beginning... With the Family. I guess one of the things that attracted us to each other is the fact that we don't do the infallible expert thing. We don't do this 'Listen to me – I'm the expert. Tell me about your problems and there's no way I'm showing you my humanity, mate. I'm the expert here' stuff.

Professionals out there, put your fur down. Someone has to do the dispassionate professional thing, and I know from experience and the in-depth research I was involved in with the Australian Government that the most successful way to get people to think about their attitudes to mental health is to be honest about yours. You'll quickly discover that we all do that in the course of this book.

In his job as Chief Executive of MIND (the mental health charity) in Norwich, Peter was impressed by his colleague, Terri

Van-Leeson, for the same reasons. She's passionate about youth and adolescent mental health issues (trust me, professionals in that area are as precious and rare as diamonds), while at the same time, sticking to people-speak and being gloriously free of jargon. Terri isn't afraid to include her own experiences and, like us, she doesn't have a problem admitting that parenting skills are a kind of 'work in progress'.

One thing we all feel is that we have no right to ask people to look back at how they experienced childhood with a view to checking out whether it's affecting the kind of parents they are to their kids without being prepared to open up a little ourselves. It's like on my daytime chat show, *Trisha*. Other people in the media constantly ask me how I 'get so much stuff' out of my guests. My secret? There isn't one. I hope it's more of a trade-off. I don't have a problem saying that I'm human and I stuff up (okay, sometimes it is uncomfortable for me, and maybe that's part of it) and I guess it's that which makes my guests feel I'm less likely to judge them. I don't take lightly the fact that people choose to talk to me so personally. Journalists ask if I'm in a position to give advice to my guests because of what I've been through myself. Well, yes and no.

Yes, because I know what it's like to go through stuff that makes you not want to be around. I know what it's like to fight addictive tendencies. There's always some flipping obsession going on with me. As a teenager it was about cleaning teeth and touching the taps a certain number of times, then it was about starving myself and secretly swigging sherry before I went to school. Then it was smoking the strongest cigarettes from the minute I woke up...it took a spell of hospitalisation with bronchial pneumonia for me to switch to light ciggies, and another bout of illness to frighten me off completely. I've been hooked on hopeless relationships with even more hopeless men. I've been thrown down stone stairs and bashed... And put up with it because he cried and said sorry...till the next time. I confused being 'smacked' by a man with being cared about by a man... And I learned that one from an early age. I slipped into a life where I had more of a relationship with marijuana than with a man. I had a man cheat on me while I was pregnant with his baby. I've had two major suicide attempts – one that's left me with a minor disability. I went through a phase of trawling through the seediest kind of nightlife and sexual behaviour and, no, it wasn't during my teens! And until I landed up in a psychiatric hospital, I was blundering from catastrophe to catastrophe, playing the part of 'Why does this happen to me?' victim.

Blimey, looking back at that lot, I could be a guest on my show. Well, I'm not a victim, and I absolutely cringe when people feel sorry for me. I can't blame my experience on childhood for ever. I can't bury my head in the sand about my mental health problems for ever. And I can't avoid the reality that, however awful, I *chose* to get into many of the situations that ended up being so bad for me.

Hitting rock-bottom was the biggest and best wake-up call I could have had. I had to stop and look at the destructive patterns I kept on repeating, and when I ended up as a single mother of a newborn and a four-year-old, I had to seriously consider everything I had ever preached about not passing on poor mental health and coping skills from generation to generation.

Without going into details, I remember a fraught argument with my parents during my single mother days, the bottom line being, 'Okay – the shit stops here!' I am one of those people who has to work at things. If I mess up a lot, it's because I love learning about anything new, and in the old days I did a hell of a lot of leaping and precious little looking before I sprang into action.

Peter is the real adventurer, though. I so admire him. He pretty much brought himself up from an early age, and had it not been for his big sister letting him stay in the caravan at the bottom of her garden (her house was too small) when he was 14 years old, he would probably not be where he is today. Had his sister's then partner not been working in psychiatry and had he not recognised that spark and hunger for learning and self-improvement in Peter, Peter's the first to admit he could well have landed up on the wrong side of the tracks. Peter seems so strong, but every now and again, I see that vulnerable little boy still not understanding why his father didn't want to know and why his late mother ran away from that man.

One of the best things about writing this book has been reading Peter's 'take' on commonplace family situations. I have been constantly taken aback by him. There have been times when I felt completely sure about what he thought on certain issues, only to find that I've been way off-centre. He's said the same about reading my versions. So, if two people with mental welfare backgrounds can misread so many everyday things their partners feel and think, be my guest and take Terri's end-of-chapter challenges to see how you measure up.

And then how many times did Peter and I read the things Billie's written, raise eyebrows and realise we needed to talk more to her about certain things? What can I say about my eldest daughter Billie? I could spend an awful lot of time feeling guilty about what she went through during my acrimonious marriage break-up with her natural father and my subsequent hospitalisation for depression, but guilt isn't worth mentioning unless you're prepared to work damned hard for the future, rather than spending your energies beating yourself up about the past.

Billie is very emotionally astute and intelligent for a 13-year-old. She has an awareness of mental health that most kids twice her age couldn't come to grips with. She's experienced moving from one side of the world to the other and has learned the lesson that every journey to heaven involves patches of stumbling through what seems like hell at the time. As with most people who've been children of single parents, she had to go from extreme closeness with me to sharing me with Peter. In many ways now, though, she's closer to Peter – you know, Mummy's Number One in some aspects, Daddy reigns supreme in others. She's not my best friend, and I'm not hers, and that's the way it should be. I'm her mama and best friends often cop out of doing the more yucky mama duties to do with discipline and guidance.

Peter and I have a style of parenting that involves debate and discussion, but we're the first to admit everything's not always family heaven, thanks to being knackered, crotchety, exasperated or just realising that the time for debate is over and here comes discipline. Billie often sees us as ogres because at her age if there's a chance of getting her own way by 'debating' until we're literally on our knees, then, hey, she's all up for that. In the true interests of democracy, however, her unedited and uncensored views on all subjects appear in this book. Don't think my bottom wasn't clenching as I read some of it, but if you encourage children to be emotionally honest and listen to their voices when they are, get ready for a really tight butt!

Madi has only ever known our family to be the way it is now because she was just a few months old when her natural father left. Although she knows who he is, her emotional ties are firmly with Pappy (as the girls call Peter). She's drawn the pictures that appear at the beginning of every chapter.

Madi and Billie are like chalk and cheese. Billie is Miss Heat, Light and Energy. Madi is more Cool Reflection and Studious Caution. They've always got their arms around each other – it's either a death-grip or a cuddle. They love each other some days and other days Peter will take Madi out to play golf with him and I'll take Billie clothes shopping or vice versa, just to give them breathing space from each other.

Like any family, same surname or not, we are made up of individuals and the fact that Billie may have a totally different view of what happens at home, that Peter may wonder what the hell I'm on about with some issues and I sometimes come across as overzealous about other things, is perfectly 'normal'. (I hate that word. 'Normal' is a cycle on a washing-machine. Full stop!) I guess that's the importance of being a family: enabling individuals to live together in relative harmony and happiness with minimal pain and chaos. It's not about agreeing all the time. It's often about agreeing to disagree. But mainly it's about working with your family to create a sanctuary for each and every one of them: somewhere they know they'll be emotionally and physically safe. Somewhere it's okay to be themselves, whether they stuff up or succeed. Somewhere that promotes working together instead of fighting or competing which ultimately keeps everyone apart. Family is about allowing and encouraging members to leave the nest, not because they feel they need to run away to survive, but because they feel they can walk away having been taught valuable lessons in how to survive. It's not about using guilt as an excuse for being bogged down in old destructive patterns, it's about learning lessons about how our pasts can colour our children's futures, and making changes if need be.

None of this is done overnight, as well I know. None of us gets everything right first time. There's usually a lot of trial and error involved. Again, that's something we authors admit to.

Between Terri, Peter and I, like so many 30- to 40-somethings, we've done maybe more than our fair share of living, but we're the first to admit we haven't sampled everything, or anything like. That's why we've included case histories of some of the guests I've been privileged to meet on my show. We've yet to experience the 'teenage' thing in all its glory, if we're to experience it at all. Neither Terri nor I have had to deal with being a stepmother when it comes to blended families. Difficulties that may occur when the chicks have flown the nest we can only guess at. Doing a bit of fun detective work about who your teenage son or daughter may or may not fancy is very different to absolutely hating who they decide to set up home with some years later.

I was a single mum to my babies, so I've drawn on the experience of guests who've had difficulties single-parenting teenagers. I learn from the guests on my show all the time, and I'm grateful that they have allowed us to learn from their experiences. Problems are universal: How do I get over the past? How do I have good relationships? How can our family successfully face the future? How do I learn to be happy? How do I give my *children* the best chances of being happy? How can I make our home the healthiest place I can for mind, body and soul?

There's no way this book covers it all. When our editors first gave us an idea of how much we'd have to write, I think we all went into shock. But when we actually started writing, we freaked out for another reason. Blimey, we thought, we've only just scratched the surface of things. What we've tried to do is to get you to question, question, question. That's because curiosity is the key to discovery. There are some parts you may feel are bloomin' obvious, but that's your experience – not everyone else's. Remember, one person's 'normal' is another person's 'weird'.

Funny, isn't it? Guys spend hours tinkering about on their cars. Women spend ages reading about the latest fashions, gossip or television celebrities. We spend a whole heap on improving our houses with DIY. We may spend ages practising karaoke or doing exercises to get a flat tummy. We'll really research the latest mobile phone or computer. We'll read the small print on a microwave meal or readily consult a cookbook. We're not prepared to leave any or all of these kinds of things to chance. We so want to get the look, the car, the body, the recipe right. But do we even spend a fraction of that time getting our mental well-being and our loved ones' introduction to life on this planet right? Looking hip, having the latest accessories, eating the yummiest meals and driving the flashest car…. It all means sod all if your head, heart and soul is messed up.

Convinced? Good…get reading!

A Note from Dr Terri

The philosophy I work from in life, both professionally and personally, is very person-centred. If you are looking for a high-powered psychological definition of how I work, then get ready to be disappointed. Fundamentally, I believe that we are all lay psychologists (i.e. thinking about what is going on for us in our everyday lives, even if it doesn't always make sense!), and that we all have the potential to make sense of, and change, the things that are happening to us in our lives. I also passionately believe in the emotional power of people, no matter what they have done or what they are faced with; that everyone has a right to be respected and understood in the context of their own personal lived experiences. That is my starting point, and from there I believe that, even if it's sometimes through professional support and encouragement, everyone can face the most difficult challenges in their personal lives, overcome them and actually emerge stronger as a result of these experiences. Also, that life is an ongoing process, never static, and so we are always learning.

The second point I want to convey is that I (again) passionately believe that knowledge is power – and that no one ever has the right to abuse it. By this I mean that quite obviously there are a great many different and diverse people who are *professionally* trained in the respective fields of family work, mental/emotional and physical health, but that does not mean they are experts in *your* feelings. No one has the right to tell you how you feel. Rather, they are merely there to help you to try and understand how *you* think you are feeling, and why this may be the case. Their job is to empower you. They can volunteer various hypotheses, but their ultimate aim is to explore possibilities with *you* taking centre stage. That's where this book comes in. Together with Trisha, Peter and Billie, my intentions here are simply to give you access to ideas and information that may be useful to you in some way. This book is written in a reader-friendly style so that you, hopefully, feel comfortable with its language, without feeling you have to consult an encyclopaedia all the time.

To get the most out of this book, we have written it in a way that encourages you to start thinking about some key areas of your own personal life. At the end of most chapters I have included a small task or quiz for you to complete. The purpose behind this is to get you to self-challenge, by thinking about your own situation and the way you think and feel about certain aspects of your life (e.g. parenting or personal relationships). You will also find some Top Tips to help you. Our overriding aim is to empower you enough to go forward in your life, to feel brave enough to start making changes that could improve the way you live. It may be that you are someone who has already reached a point in your life that is very satisfying. If that's you, we simply want to encourage you to reflect, so that you can really appreciate and enhance your everyday lived experience.

Finally, we have included case studies at the end of each chapter. The purpose behind this is to show how people cope with experiences differently, reflecting diversity in lived experience. Some of the stories have been taken from a real-life perspective, but we have also changed some aspects of the experience (as well as names) so that they become hypothetical. So, you'll have Trisha's experience of life to reflect on, Peter's life experience and advice, Billie's experience as a young person, together with some case study material – all giving you a variety of perspectives to think about. Overall, though, life is for living and experiencing, so read on.

Chapter One

Working Out Where You Come From...

A Note from Dr Terri

Have you ever wondered why your life is the way it is? It's a complicated question with any one of a number of answers, but one that is essential in any discussion about family relationships. In this chapter we're going to focus on what I believe to be the main determining factor in all our lives: the past. Research has overwhelmingly shown that past experiences, both good and bad, will influence the way you feel, think and behave in adult life. The way you are brought up by your parents (or whoever else had the responsibility of caring for you as a child), combined with your life experiences, will form the sum of your whole – the real you.

This will be a recurring theme throughout the book. But for now, let's start with hearing the first-hand stories of the lives of Trisha, Peter and Billie and look at how their past experiences have shaped their lives. As you will see, they've all had difficult times, often battling against tremendous odds along the way. Let them speak for themselves...

Trisha

Right up front, let me say, just as Billie's recollections about parts of her childhood differ from mine, so my memories probably differ in detail from my parents'. Obviously my youth is written from my perspective, sometimes with the help of diaries I kept – emotion–fuelled and all! Let me also state for the record that my parents worked practically non-stop to scrape money together to give me and my sisters what their childhoods could ill-afford. Mum spent hours sewing outfits, doing our hair; encouraging us to do well and look good at a time when the colour of your skin was even more likely to colour your chances of success than today. Without the plethora of parenting manuals and advice, they did their best and are honest enough to admit that given another chance, there are things they'd do very differently. I'm sure your parents are pretty much the same – so let me start my story...

I was born in 1957. My parents were both student nurses back then. Mum was amongst the first wave of West Indian immigrants encouraged to come to the UK in the 1950s to bump up the falling number of medical staff (Enoch Powell's idea). Dad was from Norfolk and had moved down to the Big Smoke of London, having done a stint in the army medical corps. They got together when they were both studying nursing.

Mixed race couples were pretty rare in those days, but then Dad has always been 'adventurous'. Yeah, well...two nursing students earning almost zilch. And obviously with no telly, because they had four kids (all girls) in horribly quick succession. Poor Mum never got past having a six-month-old before falling pregnant again. In fact there are only 366 days separating two of my sisters. In 1962, when I was about five, we went to the then newly formed Tanzania in Central East Africa, where Dad worked as a psychiatric nurse, and we ended up spending a couple of years there. By then, many of Dad's family had gone Down Under as part of a massive emigration scheme to boost that country's population, but not us. (Australia had its White Australia policy then and it's worth noting that I was 21 before it was repealed.) Although I was a keen traveller, the thought of such institution-alised racism made me unwilling to go there.

My years in East Africa had a profound impact on me, and Tanzania remains etched in my memory as being absolutely idyllic. It was tough, wild and exciting, and always a bit 'on the edge'. It hardened us all up, although not enough to withstand the hell that was to await my next sister down and I when we left. In 1965, when I was around eight or nine, Dad's contract in East Africa ended and we returned to his native Norfolk for a few months – and school bullying so awful that it's fair to say it affected me for years. I thought I'd coped with it all until I had a breakdown in my late thirties and it all came back. I had nightmares about that teacher-condoned bullying until I was in my late twenties. (More of that when we talk about how I dealt with Billie's being bullied when we first arrived back in Britain.) We didn't stay long in Norfolk, as Dad got a job in Virginia Water, Surrey. Very affluent. I passed the 11-plus exam and got a place at a 'posh' grammar school in Chertsey and willingly took on the mantle of a total snob. I learned how to talk the talk. As perhaps only the second 'coloured' child ever to have been to the school in its 200-odd-year existence, I was treated as a coveted, welcomed novelty. I was already bright, talented, chatty, opinionated – and probably a complete pain!

It was an all-girls' school – Sir William Perkins' Grammar – and it shaped my life. We had this English teacher, Mrs Millard, who really made a big impact on me. Among other things, she introduced me to Simone de Beauvoir's book, *The Second Sex*. One phrase from that book is a cornerstone to how I see life: 'The World and everything in it is the work of men. They see it from their own point of view which they confuse with absolute truth.' You can take the word 'men' out of that philosophy and replace it with 'the West' or 'upper classes', but, for that matter, it might just as easily apply to each and every one of us who's too scared to deal with life's complicated greys instead of just the simple black and whites.

Mrs Millard was resolute in her belief in me and my talents. Her face would light up at my essays and she'd actually clap her hands and laugh in absolute glee when I tried something new either in drama or English lessons. In other words, she unequivocally *believed* in me. Alison Millard was also the only shred of left-wing conscience in an environment that was otherwise heaving with the philosophy of the True Blue. Understand that my dad at this time was involved in nursing union politics in the large psychiatric institution in which he worked and that we lived in hospital employee housing with both parents working all the hours God sent just to keep our heads above water. Hardly a breeding ground for baby Tories.

I really don't recall a hell of a lot about my parents being around much for me during those years back in England. Don't get me wrong: they provided heat, warmth and, thanks to Mum's excellent sewing skills, we were always smartly decked out. But my memories don't include my ever feeling I had much of a relationship or particular closeness with them. My main recollection of those years was the feeling of being held responsible for my younger sisters.

I left school with above average O level results, having taken some at the age of 15. I loved exams, just as I now love doing live television. I work best under pressure – adrenalin plus! But when I started Sixth Form I absolutely hated the emphasis on personal responsibility. I already felt that I had enough of that in my personal life, thank you.

Having played the piano since I was about six, I'd been in an all-girl rock band called Eve for 18 months or so and when I was given the chance to leave school and 'gig' in West Germany with them I jumped at it and dropped out of school.

Leaving Home

By this stage, I was desperate to leave home. It wasn't so much about having something important to run to, but, rather, about things I wanted to get away from: four teenage girls sharing two small bedrooms, the likelihood of having to shoulder more and more responsibility at home, and the feeling that I had practically no relationship with my sisters (who were all at another school) or my parents. So I became a professional musician for a couple of years and discovered the folly of smoking the hard way at the age of 18 when I became so ill with bronchial pneumonia in Holland that I had to be repatriated to England.

For a couple of years I lived in a squat in Notting Hill Gate and grew up fast, surrounded by prostitutes, street kids, rough types and more than a few rogues. Then I got myself various up-market shop jobs and met a colleague who became my close friend – a wonderfully regal, loving lady called Frances Marcus, who mothered me at a time when I was struggling with living alone in London. 'Fozzy', as I called her, would just seem to *know* when I was broke, although I was way too proud to admit it. Somehow money would mysteriously appear in the bottom of my previously empty handbag. One Christmas, I had such little money that I couldn't afford to have the heating on in my tiny little London flat, let alone festive food. Crying with self-pity, I think I was about to open a can of baked beans when the doorbell rang. In true, regal Fozzy-style, the dear thing had sent over a Fortnum & Mason's Christmas hamper. It was the first time in my life I had ever tasted caviar.

Fozzy never sweated the small stuff with me. She mothered me in a way that allowed me to hang on to my stupid, stubborn teenage pride... When she asked me how I felt about things she didn't even freak when I told her the gory bits! She saved my emotional and financial ass on more than one occasion.

A job as a Hovercraft Hostess followed in 1978, when I read about the amazing Cross Channel invention on the No. 7 bus ride home one day. Then, after two years in Dover, I read about veil-swathed air stewardesses in a place called Bahrain. It rang a bell, because a lot of war correspondents were writing their stories from there at the time. I was still looking the place up on the map when the plane landed. I had five crazy, exciting, hedonistic years as a Gulf Air stewardess living in Bahrain. I grew to love the Middle East and still have a healthy respect for Islam. While there I had a boyfriend who was probably my first love, but I ended up running away and hiding out from him because of his violence. Even so, it took a couple of things to force me into making the choice to get away: the embarrassment of other people witnessing him being violent to me, plus my mother's outraged reaction when I told her what was going on. When the violence was no longer secret and I had to find words and explanations I didn't have in order to stay in such an awful situation, I stood back, took a good look at myself – and legged it.

I was about 28 by now and, ignoring the standard air hostess's rule of never hooking up with a seat number, I met my first husband, Robert, on the plane. It was a whirlwind situation – I won't use the word 'romance' or even 'relationship'. Put it this way, I married an Australian man I barely knew and ended up living Down Under. The marriage lasted three months.

Moving Down Under

Down Under, Robert was involved in Conservative politics and my arrival as his fiancée caused a fair bit of interest. We made a handsome couple and it wasn't long before we graced the pages of newspaper gossip columns. Thanks to that publicity, Robert's contacts and the fact that black Englishwomen were few and far between, I rather fell on my feet as far as employment was concerned. I worked in public relations for a dynamic woman called Jan Murray, wife of the then Australian Government Minister for Tourism, and one of my colleagues was Sue Pieters-Hawke, daughter of then Australian Prime Minister, Bob Hawke. I was immediately plugged into the country's movers and shakers. Around this time I also worked for the woman who was to become my very closest friend, Clarrie.

As a result of my PR connections, I often worked with people in the television industry and once confessed to a News Anchor acquaintance that I'd spent time doing radio and television courses for a couple of years when I was working as an air stewardess. In fact, I had been successfully short-listed from 7000 applicants to do a BBC traineeship – an opportunity I walked away from when I got married to Robert. My News Anchor friend practically bullied me into applying for a job as a television current affairs journalist with Australia's SBS TV. (By this stage my marriage was over.) I got the job and worked longer and more obsessively than just about any other reporter. Talk about learning curves and in at the deep end! I did interviews with the PM, covered Aboriginal Deaths in Custody and Filipino Brides in the Outback and later, a few months after his release from prison, worked on a fund-raising concert with Nelson Mandela.

Eighteen months later, I was head-hunted by the Executive Producer of rival ABC TV to be a presenter on their flagship news and current affairs programme, *7.30 Report*. It was only at the press conference to announce my appointment that I (and the rest of Australia) realised that I'd become the first black prime time Anchor person on Australian television. The country went mad. I became the topic of every radio talk show, and countless newspaper articles about 'token blacks' and why wasn't I Aboriginal? I attracted every racist element and virtually went into hiding for a while. I have Michael Parkinson to be grateful to for damping things down by a major article he wrote in the British press about the reaction in Australia. He still vividly remembers the whole episode and always seems pleased to see me and the progress I've made on television.

By then I had also been chosen as a presenter of the children's educational programme, *Play School* – a role I filled as a 'side job' for 12 years. If you can't change the adult racists, I thought, infiltrate children's minds by making a black face totally un-noteworthy.

Mark was a colleague I met in the early days of my television career. He'd pursued me relentlessly. My relationship with him was one that followed a familiar pattern in those days: men chased me and, flattered by their attention, I did a kind of 'What the hell! If they like me *that* much, I might as well be caught and go out with them.' A big factor in our getting together was the fact that I had to move into a new flat and Mark wasn't happy in his place. We ended up living together more out of convenience than choice. I was so immersed in my fledgling television current affairs reporter's job that we didn't really spend a lot of time together. Not being as career-obsessed as me, I'm pretty sure Mark read far more into the relationship than I did – that was, until my youngest sister Linda (or 'Winnie', as we nicknamed her) committed suicide. She'd been diagnosed with schizophrenia when she was 19 and at the age of 27 died as a result of burns and injuries, six weeks after sitting in my mother's car and setting fire to it. I dashed back to England and the six weeks I spent by her bedside in an intensive care ward made me arrive at one of the most important decisions of my life: to speak out about mental illness and the injustices surrounding people's treatment and the associated stigma of the condition.

Dealing With Mental Health

I joined mental health advisory groups and became such an activist in mental health issues that I was one of the most powerful and key people on the subject in Australia, eventually becoming a Government Advisor in the field. My reputation in mental health even spread overseas and a few years later, I was invited to work with the World Psychiatric Association based in Geneva. Obviously, this was all a way of working through the feelings of guilt and anger I had about Winnie's death.

Another crucial way I dealt with this loss was to come round to Mark's suggestion that we have a baby. He had wanted this right from the beginning, but I had always chosen not to listen. Then, when Winnie died, the time somehow seemed right – I wasn't the first, and certainly won't be the last, person to want to fill the void of loss with a new life. The singer Billie Holliday was a favourite of Winnie's, which is why I called that baby Billie. A new life was everything to me at that time. I got out of the dope-smoking, hard drinking, partying television workers' scene, embarked on a tough fitness regime at a trendy Sydney gym with clients like Nicole Kidman, and basically took on the guise of a born-again nun. So I now had motherhood and ambition to focus on. Looking back, that was really where the separation from Mark began. During all this time I was on fairly friendly terms with Robert, my ex – once I left him there was no animosity. In fact, I continued to be involved in the international charity organisation he'd run when I was married to him.

A month after Billie was born, a friend rang to tell me that Robert had died. I was saddened but not shocked. He had, after all, told me that he had cancer a year before (I felt sorry for him. I sure didn't wish that on him). Then the bombshell: I was tipped off, and later told by doctors, about the real cause of his death – AIDS-related illness. I was immediately called in for tests. It took ten days for the results to come through, and, miraculously I did not have the disease, despite the doctors' counselling me in the belief that it was highly likely both Billie and I were HIV-positive. How did I cope with all that? I don't know if I did – I more or less survived in limbo during those ten days of waiting. But, as far as my mind was concerned, something went awry during that Christmas wait in 1989.

Things got to the stage that about four years later, when waiting to cross the road, I recall I often used to be overwhelmed with a compulsion to walk under the next car – I couldn't understand the bouts of total and terrifying emptiness I was going through. By this time I already had one major suicide attempt under my belt from my early days with Robert, when I slashed my wrist badly. I still have a physical disability in my left hand as a result.

By then, my marriage to Mark, Billie's father, was going nowhere. We were like flatmates more than partners. I had made the age-old mistake of thinking that marriage would kick-start some kind of emotion that had never really been there from the start. Then I decided there was no way I wanted Billie to be an only child, so I more or less plotted to have Madi and fell pregnant first go. (Both girls were two-hour-no-painkiller-and-back-to-work-hours-later-type births.) I found being a mother really natural and easy. I breast-fed Billie for almost two years. Madi was different. She nearly died of respiratory failure when she was seven weeks old and I spent several days and nights in an intensive care ward willing her to live minute by minute.

Unbeknown to me, my husband took this as an opportunity to be with his girlfriend of several months, one of my trusted researchers. When it all came out, I had nothing in my reserve tanks and it was on to suicide attempt no. 2. Actually, I saw it more as an 'I can't take this shit anymore', a 'This hurts too much' action. A new baby is all about sleep-deprivation. Running your own company and being on television is all about time-deprivation. My 'relationship' by then was all vitriol, recriminations, lies and broken promises. Put those circumstances together and if I'd been in prison I'd have been put on suicide watch. I was sleeping three hours a night, having panic attacks and talking to myself non-stop. Go figure. Something had to give – and it was my sanity.

I spent five weeks in an acute psychiatric ward, totally terrified of absolutely everything, from the leaves on the trees outside my window to every human being that came near me. Mark and I split up in the most acrimonious way possible. It took almost two years of therapy to make me realise the impulsive, obsessive, destructive patterns of my life. During that time I experimented with everything, from men and mind-altering self-medication to sex and the seedier side of life. Stuff I was way too sensible and 'responsible' to do when I was a hard-working teenager in a band obsessed with making money. The combination of psychotherapy and controlled abandon was the making of me.

In the years following my breakdown I was so ill I couldn't work much, except for the stuff I did in mental health, which is where my unlikely knight in shining armour appeared – one Peter Gianfrancesco…

Peter

I was brought up in Geelong, a semi-rural town near Melbourne in Australia. My mother was Australian – a reliable and stolid working-class woman with an incredible ability to learn, despite not having had much of an education. She never travelled in her life and, like many Australians of her generation, had a very narrow view of the rest of the world. I remember once hosting a slide show evening, which showcased my latest European odyssey as a young backpacker. I put up a slide of a well-known leaning tower, and my sister, a well-travelled woman, named the tower for Mum's benefit. My mother, however, was having none of this. There was no way she was going to be shown up by her own daughter, so she corrected my sister, confidently saying, 'Don't be stupid, he didn't go to Paris!' This was typical of my mother – she never let a lack of knowledge get in the way of an opinion. She was a strong and independent woman – and clearly not a Europhile.

It was perhaps surprising, then, that she married an Italian. My father was one of many Italian immigrants who came to

Australia to boost the labour force in the post-war period. To my mother, he was a charming and exotic catch. Apparently, he used to slay the girls with his dancing (boy, I missed out on that gene). When I came along, the first (and only) son of an Italian, my mother's two other children from an earlier marriage were neglected and, at times, treated very badly by my father. Fortunately, being much older than me, they were able to leave home. My father's clear favouritism of me over my brother and sister, along with his generally poor treatment of my mother, resulted in their separation when I was six – my mother took me 'to stay with Aunty Mona', but neglected to tell me it was forever. I didn't see much of my father after this but as I grow older I can feel his influence rising within me and this does not bode well for our eldest daughter, Billie, who is approaching teenagedom like a runaway train...but more on this later.

My mother, a single mother, maintained and nourished my memories of my father as a loving and decent man. It was not until fairly recently, when my mother was dying, that I learnt the truth and by then, of course, it was difficult to accept. (I'll talk more about all this later in Chapter 3, page 78.) My mother entered into a relationship with another man when I was nine and we went to live with him. (In fact, another thing I learnt as my mother was dying was that this was essentially a housekeeping arrangement and there was never intimacy between them.) However, I did not like this man. He seemed weak and pedantic and by the time I was 14 it was clear that I couldn't stay with them any longer.

From this point on in my adolescence, I stayed with my sister, actually living in a caravan in her backyard. This was great from my point of view as it afforded me a lot of independence from a very young age and also taught me to accept responsibility. I lived on campus at university in Melbourne when I was 17 and while I was there probably learnt more about life, politics, women and just about everything except what I was there to study. After university, where I studied Recreation, I moved to Sydney and built a life for myself there. I qualified as a nurse, and later on in social welfare, and began my career in mental health. I travelled extensively and it is still one of the things I enjoy most. So, what did my childhood contribute to who I am today? I would say the key things I learnt are:

1) It's okay to rely on yourself
2) Travelling puts everything in context
3) I have the 'Italian gene'
4) Don't be afraid to make big changes
5) When in doubt, give an opinion

When I met Trisha in 1995 she was fiercely independent. There were two ways of doing something – her way, or not at all. She was like this because she had to be. As a single mum, as she was when we met, she couldn't afford the luxury of relying on anyone else. Perhaps one of the hardest things for single mums to deal with is partnership and sharing. I mention this because it was a really difficult part of our early relationship but something which helps us greatly as a family now.

In fact, I used to equate Trisha with an Amazon warrior fiercely guarding her tribe with a large spear. In the early days I felt the spear was always close by and that it could be picked up and used to put an end to this new love (me) and the threat it posed in her life at any time. Perhaps many of you who are single parents can understand this. I have always understood and accepted it.

Trish's spear also served as a caution to me as a new member of her tribe, which, of course, included Billie and Madi. My entry into the family was a very gradual and natural process. It was essential that I understood I was the newcomer here; it was me entering the lives of three people who already had very happy and secure relationships with one another. I was also aware that I had very little experience of parenting, or being parented to bring to the equation, so I was happy to go slow, step back and learn.

In my view, Trish was (and is) a wonderful mother who placed a lot of emphasis on explanation and fairness in her parenting. I simply watched and learned. In many ways this has enabled me to be a better parent and a better partner in parenting because I didn't assume a legitimate right or ability to be a stepfather. I am happy to say that over the years my relationship with Billie and Madi has flourished, my skills as a parent have developed and the spear is now in the cellar.

Oh, by the way, did I tell you how we met? I was encouraged to apply for a job with the Australian Government and Trish was on the interviewing panel. I didn't really care whether I got the job or not so it was one of those rare times when you could be completely honest with the interviewers. I was mesmerised by Trish, but thought, 'She's famous, she's married [she wasn't] and she lives in Melbourne' (I lived in Sydney). I was later to learn that she had been attracted to me, too, but felt that the physical distance between us was a real problem. The reality was that we lived just a few miles from each other in Sydney. Anyway, two weeks later she rang me and invited me to a mental health function. I agreed to go, not knowing whether it was meant to be a date or a semi-professional get together. I was fortunate (or unfortunate, depending on your viewpoint) to be surrounded by psychiatrists at work, so I asked their opinion and the advice was, 'If you feel something more than friendship then she almost certainly does too' – good advice, as it turned out. We went out, dispensed with the mental health element of the occasion, went to a café at midnight and talked over copious quantities of peppermint tea until dawn. The rest, as they say, is history. Oh I didn't get the job, by the way, but who's complaining!

Billie

I reckon I've had some pretty big changes in my life – moving from Australia to England, going from a city to the countryside. Although I can't remember much about life when Mum was married to Mark (my natural dad), I can remember some of the changes from when it was just Mum, Madi and me. Then, of course, Mum met Pappy (the Italian nickname for Daddy). Here's my story up to now…

So far I have spent most of my life in Sydney. One of the first things I can remember is being down on the floor crunching cat biscuits from one of our cats' bowls. I think I was about three. Maybe I was curious. Mum came downstairs with the laundry basket and cried, 'Get up! Get up!'

I had a nanny called Lindy from just after I was born and Mum would take both of us wherever she was working in Australia. She's always telling me how she breast-fed me for nearly two years. When I was about two years old, I used to go to childcare. I can remember quite a bit about my early child-hood, but not with my natural dad in it. I can remember more about him after Mum and Mark were divorced. If you ask me what I remember about Mark and my mum splitting up, it's Mum crying, and his blue Mazda driving up and down the drive. A lot of this is still too painful for me to talk about.

I recall being so upset that I found a packet of seeds in the cupboard and stuffed one of them up my nose. Maria (our nanny at the time) took Madi (who was a little baby then) and me to visit Mum in the psychiatric hospital. I told her about the seed up my nose, and she took me for a walk to the doctor's. I think I sneezed it out before we got there, though.

When Mum and Mark split up, Madi and I lived with Mum and used to go and see Mark in his flat. I remember feeling awkward every time Mum dropped us off; it felt like I was betraying her by going to his place.

I don't remember Mum going out with many guys before she met Pappy, but I do remember being in the car on the way to school one day and Mum saying, 'What would you do if Peter and I got married?' I said something like 'No way'. But, over time, I came to look up to him because he was one of the first men I ever respected. He didn't just barge in. He came in slowly, and my cats liked him, so I started to like him too.

I remember when Mummy and Pappy got married in Cortina, Italy. Everything was covered in snow and the sun was shining. When we left the town hall, after the wedding ceremony, the local people cheered and threw rice and some went down my knickers and down the front of Mum's dress. We laughed so much.

A New Country

Moving to England was difficult. I missed everything about Australia; my friends, school, our little house. My new school in England was small – about nine to 11 children in my class. In Australia there were 30 and the school was a massive inner city building that used to be a perfume factory. Suddenly I was at a school where the teachers could see what you were up to all the time! It was pretty hard trying to fit in when all the other kids had known each other since Reception class. I used to make up stuff in those days to make people at school like me. I wanted to seem interesting. I didn't think it was a big deal that Mum was on television.

There was a time when I got into a fist fight with a girl and it ended with Mum and Pappy going to see the headmaster. As a result I was told that if I had any more problems there was one special teacher that I could go and talk to.

I really liked being in Year Six, even though I was one of only two girls in our class of ten. I won a Drama scholarship to my Independent High School and at the time of writing this I'm in my second year there. It's quite confusing because it's so much bigger than my prep school, but so far I enjoy it and have made some good friends. I actually find the schoolwork easier than when I was in prep school, even though we have the same amount of homework. Mummy is pretty cool about schoolwork, but Pappy is quite strict about it. He says it doesn't really matter if I get a high mark in exams as long as it's an improvement on the last result.

I'm expected to do jobs around the house. I clean out the fireplace after it's been used, and every other morning I unstack the dishwasher. We have a very big garden and I have to make sure all the wild birdseed holders are full. I don't think I should do so many jobs, but, hey, I need the cash. Excuse me while I roll my eyes, but Mummy and Pappy say, 'If you want to be a part of this family, we all have to work together and you have to play your part.'

We go on really good holidays: from the hot sun in Bali, Florida and Mauritius to skiing in Colorado and Italy. They're wicked! Mum and Pappy are really keen that Madi and I see the world.

One big change is that now that we live in England we see much more of Nanny and Grandpa. They used to come out and see us in Australia. Either that, or Mum would take us all the way to England to see them. But even though we saw them every year and talked to them on the phone quite a bit, it was hard to really get to know them back then. We see them quite a lot now. Whoever said old people were boring and slow haven't met my grandparents. Nanny is full on. She buys all the latest pop CDs and dances to MTV even though she's 70-something. Grandpa goes on the longest walks, whatever the weather, and is always really interested in what Madi and I are up to. It was scary when he had his heart attack and it made me want to spend more time with him.

If you asked me to sum myself up, I'd say I think of myself as bold, stubborn, bitchy (sometimes), chatty and always up for a laugh. Mum says I'm pretty confident. I guess she's right. Since I was little, when my natural dad left, Mum's taught me to be an independent person. In some situations I'm glad of that. In others, I'm not. For instance, if I spend my own money on something I really want, I use it and look after it more. Sometimes I feel trapped because I feel too proud to ask someone to buy something for me. Then I have to save up for ages. Meanwhile, my sister buys sweets and scoffs them in front of my face!

Actually, even though some of the stuff that changed my life was painful at the time, I'm really glad things changed. Although I would never have believed that when it was happening. As a kid I don't have as many choices as I'd like but Mum and Pappy always say that whatever I choose to do, I have to deal with the results.

In this book I will call my step-dad (Peter/Pappy) Dad. I'll be giving a kid's point of view all the time, so when my parents tell you how they feel, I'll tell you what the side-effects on me are. See you in the next chapter!

Dr Terri's thoughts…

As you can see, Trisha, Peter and Billie haven't always found things easy. Each of them, in their own way, has had to confront difficulties in their past – none more so than Trisha, who, amongst many other things, has had to battle against a problematic childhood, bullying, racism, unhappy relationships, the death of a much-loved sister and bouts of recurring depression. They've also all had key turning points in their childhoods – changes that have shaped their lives and views. For Trisha it was having to adapt to England after an idyllic childhood in East Africa; for Peter it was being forced to fend for himself at an early age. Even Billie, young though she is, has already had to face the disruption of leaving Australia and all her friends, and coming to England – not to mention her parents' separation. But, crucially, no matter how hard some of these experiences have been, they have all contributed to making Trisha, Peter and Billie the people they are today.

Change is a key factor in all these stories, and it's an important theme that we will be returning to throughout this book. As you will discover, change is an important part of all our lives, whether it comes from external factors that are beyond our control, or from within. We'll be exploring this subject in more detail in Chapter 9, where you will see how, despite their difficulties, Trisha and Peter learnt how to make the right choices to make their bad times work. By the time you've read this book we hope that you too will learn how to change your life in the ways that matter, and how even changes that seem bad at the time can be controlled to you and your family's advantage. For now, a useful starting point may be just to look at the stories you've read, and see how they relate to your own life.

Chapter Two

Losing and Choosing a Partner

A Note from Dr Terri

Relationships are fundamental to living – some form of relationship is essential for survival, whoever you are. The very first relationship most (though not all) of us have is with our mothers. A baby demands constant love, comfort, security and attention (for example, being fed every two to four hours), and on the whole some form of mother figure will be present to meet these physical and emotional needs. As time goes by we grow, forming relationships with significant others within a family. Also – and very significantly – as human beings, most of us have a tendency to want some form of intimacy with someone else. This is a normal part of human need; we can flourish with intimacy, and falter without it.

Through childhood we are exposed to many different kinds of relationships, and so learn how to interact and be around other people in given roles. This is known as social learning and, loosely speaking, means that we learn how to interact by observation, direct experience and copying/modelling ourselves on others. So why am I telling you this here? Well, because for many of us, the way we grow up and engage in adult relationships will depend on our *childhood* experiences with relationships.

Let me explain this further with an example or two. If you are a little girl who is brought up in a household where your mum is constantly bullied and/or beaten by your dad, you may come to internalise a belief that men should dominate women and that this is normal. Okay, you may also go the other way and start to resent your dad when he kicks off, which strengthens your resolve when you are older not to put up with such experiences. But the former reaction is very common. The way it may affect you as an adult is that you may subconsciously *choose* men who are dominant, so that the power dynamic in your relationship is not an equal one. Your perception of a man who is normal or satisfying will be a man who is dominant and possibly aggressive towards you at times, and any other kind of man may somehow seem weak and undesirable. So you can see how this might begin to affect the way you relate to men in interpersonal relationships, and what you will be prepared to put up with in a *normal* sense. The knock-on effect is that your past experiences will have some bearing on the *choices* you make in adult relationships. Trisha goes into this in a lot of detail, so, bearing in mind what I have just highlighted, let's focus on what she has to say.

Trisha

If you've ever wondered how come you end up with such losers as lovers, get ready for a shock. It's not bad luck. And don't waste time with the victim's cry of 'Why me?' Knowingly or unknowingly, we *choose* our partners. What? Those of you who've had more than one dominating or abusive partner put it down to fate? Women who've had a succession of violent partners, you think that was a coincidence? Don't tell me you honestly thought there were sinister forces at work that led you to forever end up with the wimp or the gold-digger? What's the link between every dud partner you've ever hooked up with? That's right – *you*! That's what I mean when I say we seek out or attract our partners because of the way we are. We might as well have a sign plastered across our heads, saying 'Violent/abusive/wimpy/angry/emotionally cold/aloof/gold-digging/philanderer, etc – this way to heaven.'

If You Don't Like the Fish You're Catching...

There was a moment in my painful post-breakdown therapy after rotten relationship no. 6284 when *ping!* the light came on and a saying of mine was born: If you don't like the fish you're catching, change the bait. After something like two-and-a-half years of the most painful soul-searching under the guide of professionals, I finally worked it out: I had to take some responsibility for all the hellish relationships I'd had with men, because there was a big something about me that they found irresistible. I had no right to whine about them when I had (albeit unknowingly) been part of the problem in the first place.

Yeah, yeah, great theory, you say, but where's the proof? Well, shock of shocks, after I'd done some serious work on myself – changed a lot of damaging behaviour, rearranged my priorities, experimented with a totally different approach to sex and who should be in charge, thought about what was attractive in the male sex and a whole lot of other stuff – guess what? The very men who'd come flocking to me in the past virtually ran away screaming. Over time, very different guys were coming my way. It certainly wasn't sudden. In fact, I can trace my post-breakdown boyfriends all the way through to Peter and if I were to illustrate their personalities and qualities, the picture would resemble that Ascent of Man poster that goes from the ape, through to *Homo sapiens*, then to a regular modern-day fella.

When I see women on my show describe some horror-story of a man and then shrug their shoulders and say, 'Well, men are all the same, aren't they?' it reminds me of how I was in the 'relationship beginning'. For starters, I went to a highly competitive and successful all-girl grammar school that reinforced the mantra: anything a man can do, a woman can do with less fuss and far more quickly. Remember, this was the 1970s and teenage girls were the targets of full-on feminism. Many of our mothers saw this as an opportunity for their daughters to break free of the things that had hindered them. The thing about being in an all-girl situation at home (bar my father, even the cat was female) and at school, is that you start to regard men as something from *The X Files*. You sit around wondering how 'they' operate and what 'they' think of you. Too many break-times to count were filled with outright lies of lost virginity, discussions on snogging, or reading the dirty bits out of overblown romantic trash where the hero got his willy out over the course of two chapters. If the book described a man as 'wildly, passionately throwing her to the bed' then, as far as the girls at school were concerned, that's what they did, and, I kid you not, many a girl in our school got herself into a sticky situation by confusing this crap for a credible situation. I guess you were slightly more informed if you had brothers, but they invariably went to boys' schools and were equally mixed-up about girls as sexual creatures.

Maybe I've overreacted a tad but, fabulous though my school was, this is why I was adamant my girls would go to a co-ed school. Never mind the bleating about boys being disruptive or holding the girls back from achieving academic nirvana. Co-ed schools more than make up for any of these stereotypes by teaching girls a far more important lesson: how to get along with approximately 50 per cent of the population in a normal, down-to-earth way. For Billie the trauma of being only one of two girls in her prep school turned into a triumph of cool. It's so great to hear her talk about boys as personalities and characters and not solely in terms of their snogging potential.

The Relationship Stew

As with the vast majority of girls' school issue who had no brothers, I swung from chasing anything remotely male to allowing anything remotely male to chase (and catch) me. Add to that my relationship with my father, who gave me a mixed message of love, apparent disdain (which is how I interpreted a virtual lack of praise and lots of criticism), bursts of a temper I feared, a wicked sense of humour and perpetual boyishness, and you've pretty well summed up every relationship I chose before I fell apart and was forced to see the pattern. Then there was my mother's input, which gave me a subliminal message that men were not to be relied upon financially or emotionally. Add to that my own impulsive/compulsive nature and it's no wonder I had so many relationships.

From my kid's-eye-view I saw the most intimate part of my parents' relationship as being about joky point-scoring and humorous teasing. I don't remember them ever holding hands, cuddling or kissing in front of me. During my mid-teens, Mum used to say, over and over, that I would be like Elizabeth Taylor: married and divorced loads of times. Okay, so I'm married (happily) for the third time, so what are we talking about here? Eerie prediction? Or self-fulfilling prophecy? She also said that men would find me too hard to live with and I believed it. On the one hand I always expected to be dumped and it was almost a relief when I was. On the other hand, thanks to my father, I was (and, to a lesser degree, remain) so touchy about being rejected or criticised, that I was quite histrionic and over the top when it happened.

So those are the major ingredients in 'Trisha's relationship stew'. Let's not forget to add in to the pot my highly strung, obsessive, high-octane personality and my ability to shut out the world at whim.

I was popular with the boys, which took me by surprise. It was certainly far more about personality than looks. When my daughter recently complained that the popular girls were the blonde babes and she couldn't compete, you know what I told her? I said that being a pretty adolescent was a curse because there was no pressure on you to fall back on other things such as raw intelligence, humour, personality or resilience. Those poor pretty bitches had everyone take one glance at them, go all gooey-eyed and let them get away with every social faux pas, and the inability to crack a joke, hold a conversation or entertain. We plain ones, on the other hand, had the opportunity to find another way of dazzling the crowds. Oh yes, I was plain. So plain that I seem to recall the local vicar once congratulated my mother on a fine family of three sweet little girls and a strapping boy. I remember frowning and looking at my (then) petite sisters and wondering, 'Who does he think is a boy?' I knew I was nothing special right from the start. I was no fool. Like I told Billie, 'No, you're not the totally gorgeous type – yet. Neither was I. But, you know, "gorgeous" isn't just looks, it's a whole lot of other things that won't fade like conventional beauty will.'

Men and Other Mistakes

I won't trawl through all my pre-Peter relationships, I'll just do the headlines:

First sexual encounter: Being sexually assaulted, which, for obvious reasons, I describe in the chapter on depression (page 197). Gave me major sexual hang-ups for longer than I realised.

First longish relationship: Bev. Why? I'd lost my virginity to his best mate, Steve. (Yucky business, done in true Capricorn style: waited till I was over 16 and on the pill and with military precision thought, 'Tonight'll do'. All over in seconds. Thought, 'Phew that's that over and done with.' No even vague pretensions that love had anything to do with it. Certainly no enjoyment, more 'Is that it?' It was more curiosity than anything else.) When Steve went off me, I wanted to make him jealous – hence Bev. Bev cheated on me with a member of the girl band I played keyboards in. I did an 'Either she goes or I do' number. *She*, a single mother of one, went. Screaming, shouting hysteria from me, together with a determination to keep the relationship going even though it was dead. Bev was in a band too and ended up running off with some girl he met at a gig a few days before Christmas and my birthday. I spent Christmas phoning hospitals and Missing Persons. He spent it in bed with a groupie. I lost weight and went to pieces and ended up running off to Dover to be a Hovercraft Hostess.

First real love (and violent relationship): Let's call him Kevin. Charismatic, charming, dark, sexy and *very* violent. A journalist who sparked my interest in my present career. My main memories of Kevin are staying with his folks on a tropical island. The house had walls that didn't go up to the roof, so you could hear everything. Us lying in bed, he with his hand over my mouth, so his parents wouldn't hear me scream while he punched me in the side and stomach. Then there was the time he accused me of looking at another man in the bar. (Rubbish – by this time I'd learned never to look anywhere but at him or the floor.) On the drive home, he steered with one hand and punched me with the other. In desperation, I opened the car door and half-rolled/half-fell out. Luckily he was driving slowly in order to give me a good hiding.

We were living together in Bahrain where I was a Gulf Air stewardess. He was a damned fine journalist and the violence started right at the start of our dating when we went to a party and one of my fellow Bahraini cabin crew members put an arm round me (the fact that he was gay didn't matter). The result was Kevin throwing me down some stone stairs and smashing my glass front door to smithereens. I was flattered. He cared. Like Dad. Anger/aggression=care/love. No Battered Women refuges in Bahrain. I was living in a small village where the very fact we were an unmarried couple would've been frowned upon.

I know it sounds dramatic, but after about three years of this I ran away. At night. In my nightie. Through the window, while several of his mates struggled to hold him down and yelled at me to run. A fellow stewardess gave me cocoa and let me hide out in her flat (thanks, Maddie!). I arranged a van and some mates and when Kevin was at work, moved all my stuff out of what had been our flat.

First husband: Here's a pattern. The nice guys I treated abominably and labelled wimps; the jerks I lusted after and allowed them to walk all over me before they dumped me. There were a few relationship-ettes from then until I met Australian Robert on a plane (all together now – *silly cow*).

Robert wooed me all around the world, and I ended up agreeing to marry him, even though I knew nothing about him and hadn't even slept with him. He looked like Robert Palmer, the pop star. I kid you not. It was the main reason I thought, 'Why not?'

I can understand why Robert was such a control freak. He was obviously sitting on a great deal of confusion and guilt about who he really was, while having to maintain the veneer of a credible Conservative politician (he had been Leader of Australia's Young Liberals).

It's hard to go into the details of this relationship – my weirdest ever. Was I in love with him? No. I thought maybe I could grow to love him, but that didn't happen. Did I like him? It took me a few weeks to realise I didn't particularly. Did we have a lot in common? He was politically conservative, I was as far the other way as could be. We both believed in International Aid and that was pretty much it. He was a man who worked hard at keeping people at an emotional arm's distance. I've had the odd opportunity to use my investigative journalist skills to delve into what he was about, but was always scared off. Either by myself and my memories, or by people who were then in Australian politics.

Things became so dangerously fraught with Robert, that one night, for probably the first time in my life, I lost my temper. The result was a total lack of control as I turned the anger in on myself. I ended up having micro-surgery for four hours to mend the slashed nerves, muscles and tendons in my wrist and virtually lost the use of my left hand for a year. Thanks to my dearest girlfriend,

Clarrie, and her television journalist husband Peter, I escaped. Literally. And went into hiding to get away from a man. Again. Clarrie had known Robert way before I did and had thought me mad to be with him, so it beats me why I didn't listen to her when she took an instant dislike to...Mark.

The natural father of my children: Mark (a television colleague). Basically, Mark chased me and even though I didn't initially fancy him, I got to like him. I was a dope smoker in those days and he was one of the key players in that scene. Come weekends, we'd binge drink and, yes, you've guessed it – get stoned. Thus I have no clear recollections of what the early days of my relationship with him were like. But how's this for true head-in-the-sand behaviour? When he started chatting me up at a television industry ball, he was there with two girlfriends at the same time, one giggling on each arm. But did stupid me hear any alarm bells? No.

To be fair, right at the beginning of the relationship I told Mark that my new television career was practically everything to me. He was a mate really and should have stayed that way, but things got serious (in that I finally gave into him and agreed to have a baby) just after my kid sister Winnie committed suicide (see page 217). Having kids and celebrating life suddenly became very important for me. In hindsight, it became such a yearning that it eclipsed everything else, including examining whether I was in a relationship that was strong or good enough to be 'family' material. There had to be more to life than working and getting stoned every evening. I was, after all, 31.

If Mark thought a baby would slow me down a bit, it did...for about a week. The problem was I never really saw spending time and energy with Mark as being worthwhile. I nagged him into being a good, hands-on dad, but he didn't seem to be into family outings at all. I'm sure he found me as boring as I found him, especially when I transferred 90 per cent of my emotional energy and involvement to Billie. Sure, I loved breast-feeding her. But for two years? And once Billie was at school, Madi took up the emotional slack.

Not long after Madi was born, I discovered Mark had been having an affair with a researcher I'd taken on and who I had been quite 'mother hen-like' with. When she came crying to me about a lump in her breast, I pulled strings and got her an immediate mammogram at my private clinic, knowing she had breast cancer in her family. When she had boyfriend trouble and confided in me about it, I gave her advice. I could empathise with her. After all, her boyfriend Mark was so like my husband Mark. (When I discovered she'd actually finished with *her* Mark some time before and that when talking about 'Mark' she could have been secretly asking me for advice on how to handle *my own husband*, it was another shove over the cliff of sanity, I can tell you.) Apparently, she and my husband had 'got together' while I was six months' pregnant and on holiday, visiting my parents in England with four-year-old Billie. (It tells you something about our relationship that we took separate holidays and didn't think it was that big a deal to do so.)

About seven weeks after Madi was born, she was rushed into hospital with respiratory failure. I slept on the floor while she was in her little Moses basket on the bed, hooked up to a respirator and monitor in the intensive care unit. During that dreadful time Mark would bring Billie in to see me and the baby. He would look dishevelled and be in the same clothes as the day before and I'd hold him and comfort him. It was obvious he was taking this far worse than I was – he was too overwrought to shave or change and looked a complete mess. A couple of times, when there was a real possibility we could lose Madi and I thought I was going mad with terror, I phoned at night. The phone rang and rang and then the answering machine kicked in. I thought he was so exhausted, what with running our production company and looking after Billie and dealing with the stress, that he was literally out cold. It was only much later, when I got my itemised mobile phone bill, that I saw that the telephone number of this researcher kept cropping up continuously. He'd been ringing her at 4 a.m. from the City on one of the nights that I'd tried to call him from the hospital. Eventually, torn with guilt, our wonderful nanny told me how Billie had slept at her place while Mark went out for the night. By that time, I'd gone straight back to work, while breast-feeding all night, and doing school runs – generally being the sort of woman certain tabloid newspapers go to great lengths to demonstrate collapse in a heap under pressure because they would be so much happier playing the little woman at home.

The fact that Mark had been having an affair was one bombshell. *Who* he was having it with was another. I almost felt more betrayed by this slip of a girl who'd spent so much time telling me how wonderful she thought I was, and how much she'd give anything to be like me. Hello?

In Mark's defence, he must have been damned unhappy to go for such a revenge affair, and in many ways, I'd given him *carte blanche* to do so. I'd always said, 'If you must sleep with someone, do it when you're far away from home, do it with someone I don't know and never let me find out about it.' I'd actually always assumed he would be unfaithful. When/where/with whom were almost minor details.

At that time, I was breast-feeding a three-month-old baby who had only just come out of hospital. I was also looking after a four-year-old while Mark was out most evenings seeing his girlfriend. Professionally, I was fronting a television show, part-owner of the company making it, co-producing the programme, doing National Mental Health Strategy work, and working as a *Play School* presenter on ABC TV. I'm sure there was more. Oh yes, hellish screaming rows. I had absolutely nothing in reserve – which is what led to suicide attempt no. 2 and five weeks in a private psychiatric hospital. So next, the husband went.

Divorce no. 2: Actually, I made him leave because our marriage guidance therapist and my psychiatrist could see that I was in danger of lapsing back into mental illness. I was left as a single mother of two (Billie aged four, Madi a babe in arms) and thus, praise God, my life began.

The word I think best describes how Mark and I related to each other, is 'antipathy'. Until the acrimonious end, there were no major clashes or rows. There was no passion, no fluttering heart stuff, no major concerns…it was all just a sort of nothingness. It only bothered me on a few occasions. One was the morning my mum rang me in Australia and told me that my kid sister Winnie had died just minutes ago, after weeks of being in a coma. I put the phone down, curled myself up into a ball and screamed like an animal. I remember Mark watching me from a distance and having the overwhelming feeling that he seemed almost frightened of me. In hindsight, I think it was the raw emotion he was frightened of rather than anything else. I don't think he knew *how* to be there for me. He had the same reaction when I'd just had Billie and discovered that my ex, Robert, had died of AIDS. I was going out of my mind, terrified that Billie and I had contracted the disease. I couldn't sleep, eat, or think. Again, Mark just couldn't connect with me or support me emotionally in the way I needed. It just wasn't what our relationship was based on –

all that mentally intimate stuff or being needed. We were two singletons living together. I don't think we were ever really a 'couple' in the true sense of the word.

And some others: In the years before I met Peter, I felt I went from 'emotional knuckle-draggers' to increasingly emotionally intelligent and caring guys. At one stage I was going out with three men at once. They all knew about each other and knew in no uncertain terms that if they didn't like it, they could go. First, there was Anderson, a total lovable rogue – heart in the right place, a warped sense of morals, and totally unreliable, but, oh boy, did he show me Life on the Wild Side. There was one memorable morning after a show business do where we went on to party all night. It was sunrise – about 5.30 a.m. and there was I leaving a nightclub, barefoot, in ballgown and with shoes in hand, walking down the middle of a deserted Sydney inner city street, the sun in my face and all danced-out. After the confines of a psychiatric ward, trust me, that was a feeling of pure freedom and the moment I realised I had been doing too much. Now I wanted to *experience* life. Steve was an upper-class English single dad going through a divorce that was even messier than mine. I could spout legal venom and exchange stories on 'bloody exes' till the cows came home, with him nodding and finishing sentences for me. Then there was pretty boy computer-whiz, Chris. Purely a handbag. I got rid of the sexual side of those three simultaneous relationships when John came along.

John was a senior airline pilot and Peter's fore-runner. He was a single dad of two. His daughter, Alice, went to the same New Zealand ski-school as Billie (we were there on a Frequent-Flier point holiday). The two six-year-olds decided to get John and I together and plotted until they did. I went out with him for a year and we had great blended-family type holidays and outings together. He was a hands-on, devoted single father and made me realise that (a) hey, there is a chance of finding a fabulous lover who adores kids after all, and (b) I was worthy of romance and respect from a man with an awesome IQ who was actually grown-up. John was really the first man I dated after years of being attracted to responsibility-avoiding boys. But I still enjoyed the fact that he was away a lot of the time and that he actually lived in New Zealand and only popped over to see me or flew me over there to see him. He wanted more; I didn't. He finished it; I was pretty upset, but didn't self-combust as I would have done in the past, because this time I didn't see it as a personal rejection.

I'm still friends with all those guys I dated during those three years. They were part of a very important journey for me – as, indeed, I was for them. They were around when I was going through intense therapy and each one of them either learned how to help me through panic attacks, or just to be amazingly supportive emotionally. For the first time in my life, I awakened sexually because the therapy helped me to come to terms with my first sexual experience: an assault in my early teenage years.

But there came a point when, although I still went out with these guys as mates, I decided to become celibate and stayed that way for eight months. I was now ready for a 'proper' relationship, I felt. It's a long story, but basically there was a moment when I was lying alone in bed, in front of a roaring log fire in a little cabin apartment in the middle of the Colorado mountains. The girls were tucked up in the big double bed in the bedroom. Outside there was four foot of snow and it was still silently falling. It was Christmas-time and all we had was a six-inch plastic Christmas tree on the window-ledge. And I thanked God. 'If

I can keep in touch with how I feel at this moment,' I thought, 'I need never have another relationship again. I am whole without a man. I am happy without a man. I am alone, but not lonely and I'm well at last.'

My soul sang. It was right after that holiday that Peter came into my life. What does that tell you? I had finally changed the bait. That's why I caught such a beautiful fish, when I hadn't even bothered to unpack my rod!

No More Kissing Frogs...

Peter Gianfrancesco: a long, romantic-sounding foreign name and an exciting rebellious voice in the field of mental health. He hates me saying this, but I used to read through Peter's papers on how he thought the mental health system should change and I used to think, 'Wow! This guy writes this stuff for the Minister to read and doesn't give a damn about politics. He's totally for the rights of those with mental illness and their families.' To say he's a passionate man in every single way is an understatement. To cut a long story short, I phoned him up after interviewing him for a job – and noting to a startled interview panellist that 'I wouldn't kick him out of bed for eating biscuits'.

Peter was the first man *I* pursued. He is the first man whose mind and soul turns me on. He's definitely the most comfortably 'male' man I've ever known. Other guys I've dated have postured, pontificated and acted macho. Peter just *is*. He's the first man I came across who could talk my knickers off without using a single cliché (oh-oh, Billie's got to read this!) But Peter has been a part of our lives since Billie was just over seven and Madi was two. In fact, he has been in the girls' lives more constantly and for longer than their own father. That is not to say the girls don't know who their father is. Peter has been the main instigator of ensuring their ongoing contact with him, problematic though that often is. More on that later...

I'm amazed that having been together for six years, having experienced the 'I-want-to-make-you-a-star' discovery and been enticed to England to make my own television show, I love the guy even more now than when I first met him. Before Peter, my record for being in love was about ten months. By the first anniversary in those earlier relationships, I was doing the 'I've made my bed, so better lie in it' speech to myself. So, I made a conscious decision to stop kissing frogs and chose instead to check out a prince. But up until that moment of realisation that if I didn't sort myself out I'd be dead, I was choosing to be a bit of a toad myself...

Looking back, I realise I drifted from relationship to relationship. It was as if a lot of the time I didn't really make a conscious decision to have them; they chose to have me. I seemed to swing from one extreme to the other, falling either for men who were control freaks and favoured violence, belittling, intimidation or emotional aloofness; or I was into men who seemed to have no boundaries, who couldn't even start to talk about their emotional needs because they were too busy doing stuff (or *taking* stuff) to block out as many feelings as possible.

At the time I was with Mark, I knew I could be without him. In fact, I often bitchily told him so. When he first left, I was more scared of being a single mum with a baby than of being without him. After a while, it hit me as weird and quite shocking that I never actually missed him being around. Did I miss talking to him? No – we didn't really have conversations as such, unless they were about our shared business interests. Did I miss sleeping with him? No, because in those days I didn't particularly enjoy sex and it seemed to be more about him than me. Did I miss his help? No, because I'd become a one-woman show – partly through my perception that if I didn't do it, it wouldn't get done, and partly because of his detachment from the family. My workload didn't actually increase much at all after he left, but I slowly, but surely, became more mentally healthy and content.

The thing that makes my personal commitment to Peter so strong is that I know my mind, body and soul would ache without him around. He is so involved and fiercely proud and protective of both me and the girls. I love talking with him about everything and anything. Making love with him is as much about my head as my heart. I love the way we go through new challenges together and constantly reassess things. What was it I read Madonna had said about Guy Ritchie? That he was the only man who stood up to her? That rang a bell. I love how Peter is so emotionally upfront. He doesn't sulk, he just *talks* – be it about sex, something that I've said, or whatever. He explains rather than complains. No, he's not perfect but I can nearly always tell him when he's pissing me off without ending up having a row. He has taught me so much about being emotionally honest. Scary, sometimes, but that's what real intimacy is. He hardly drinks and doesn't do drugs. He's too passionate about reality.

So What Have I Learned Not to Choose?

Trouble always starts if there's a huge difference between what you want in a relationship and what you need. Put it this way, if you're hooked on booze, you'll spend a lot of time looking for, *craving* for your next drink. Boy, do you want that scotch. But what you *need* is to find out why you're drinking in the first place; to dry out, be in a supportive environment, etc etc. It's about breaking the habit of seeing contentment in the bottom of a bottle, or, going back to relationships, about breaking the habit of being comfortable with an uncomfortable situation. Once you work out why you keep going for and attracting the very relationships that are eating away at your soul, you can start choosing relationships that *add* something to your enjoyment of the world.

One thing I've learned, through sheer experience and from guest after guest on my show is: you *either* have a relationship with drink or drugs *or* you have a healthy relationship with a human being. I've learned that when someone uses violence, it's about trying to force someone to stay with them when they feel unstayable-with. They're the ones who know they'll be weaker without the person they're beating up or slapping. And they're right. But it's *their* problem – unless *you* choose to make it yours too by staying. Plus, if you've got kids, you're choosing to sacrifice their future happiness and mental health, all so one emotional cripple can get to feel temporarily safe. Put it this way, if one family member was very ill, would you purposely poison the rest of your children and yourself, just to make them feel okay about their illness?

I've learned that daughters of alcoholic fathers can often hook up with alcoholic men. Sons of emasculating mothers who put them down often end up being partners of women who do the same. Girls with violent, smacking or dominating fathers often end up with husbands who do the same.

Wouldn't it be great if we studied relationships in high school? I'd start the lesson by asking each child to work out what they *don't* want in a relationship, write it down and then refer to this throughout life. How many of us would end up listing the very qualities we despised in a parent?

Peter

I will never forget my first love, Stana. She is etched into my memories for several reasons and most of them are bad. Firstly, she had a difficult father and brother. I was 13 and she was 16 (I've always had a thing for older women!). We were in the same year at high school because she had failed to progress and I was always the youngest in my year.

Believe it or not, I was one of the first boys in my year to have a proper girlfriend – you know, the type that you actually kiss and write poems to. We were crazy about each other and weren't allowed to see each other. Her parents were from Yugoslavia and they wanted her to marry a fellow Yugoslav (she eventually did), so the idea of her seeing an Aussie boy was a total no-no. I spent most of the three years that we were together literally running away from her father, fighting with her brother and finding new and even more secret ways to spend time together.

I actually missed quite a lot of my penultimate year of high school by 'wagging' school to spend time with her. We even went through a period of about six months of meeting by the river at 2 a.m. every morning, each of us sneaking away from home. This ended when my mother caught me returning home at 6 a.m. with a blanket. God knows how I'd react if Billie did the things I did and I have to remind myself that I was a total fool for love when I was younger.

This relationship finally ended when Stana got run over on the school crossing and suffered horrific injuries. I remember I was by her bedside in hospital when her parents turned up. This time I didn't run, instead thinking 'Surely they have to accept me under these circumstances' and, sure enough, they were pleasant and her father offered me a lift home. On the way home he stopped the car and started ranting and raving and told me that if I ever saw his daughter again he would kill my dog. I believed him and that was the end of that.

Later Loves

I have always had girlfriends since then. I have never stayed single for long. This was because I found being single boring and I guess I had a need to be close to someone. My next big thing was Suzan. I met her at university about two years later and we went out for about four years. In fact, I followed her to Sydney from Melbourne. She was Lebanese and came from a well-known Sydney family. Her family were fantastic to me but they tended to want a commitment that I wasn't ready to make. I recall once being taken to the family's jeweller and being encouraged to buy an engagement ring 'just in case' Suzan and I wanted to wed. She was a very intelligent and vivacious girl and looked about five years older than me. In the end our relationship just sort of drifted apart and she ended up marrying an accountant – he was just the sort of person her family wanted for her and I always thought she would end up with. We stayed in touch for many years and had one or two flings along the way but this all eventually came to an end when she started dating my best friend, Dario. Unfortunately, this led to my friendship with Dario falling apart which, for me, has always been a very sad thing. It just goes to show that you need to keep past and present parts of your life separate at times.

I then met a woman (she was 30) called Wendy and she seemed the opposite in many ways to Suzan. She was earthy, worldly and practical. She was more interested in horses than fashion and I really enjoyed growing up with her. However, the age difference was too great from my point of view and I ended the relationship after two years.

By this time I was in my early twenties and had established my life and career in Sydney. At the time I was working in a psychiatric hospital and I met a young nurse called Billy (short for Bilyana – another Yugoslav). She was the girl all the guys fancied. She was pretty, drove a sports car and was suitably dizzy. We actually met while changing an incontinent old man – not the most romantic start! Billy and I dated for several years and had always planned to spend a year backpacking around Europe. Then, just as we were ready to leave, she told me that she had changed her mind and would be staying. I travelled anyway, rather naïvely thinking that we would both remain faithful to each other. I actually did remain faithful to her (much to my regret) but while I was away she started dating a good friend of mine and they actually slept together in my bed. She rang me in London two days before I was due to come back to Australia and told me. I was devastated. I returned to Australia and two days later (Christmas Day) my house was burgled. This was probably one of the lowest periods of my life. Ever since this time I have brought a touch of cynicism and distrust to relationships – something that was never there before.

After Billy, there were a number of short-term relationships but nothing serious until I met Jo. She was just like me. She liked the things I liked, shared the same sense of humour, played tennis pretty well, worked in mental health like me and being with her was really easy. We spent seven years together and during that time we dated, travelled, lived together and bought a house. The one thing that was missing for both of us was a sense that it was for ever and that it would lead to marriage and children. We were like really good friends. We had a great social circle. In fact, life was like an episode of *Friends* – lots of fun, but in many ways very shallow. I can only recognise this in hindsight, whereas Jo gradually came to see it while we were together and eventually had the courage to break away. She met and married a guy and they now have a little girl. When I examine this part of my life and the decision that Jo made I realise that you have to constantly assess the relationship you are in... Are things the way you think they are? Are you and your partner travelling alongside each other? Are you ignoring the warning signs of a problem? And, most importantly, do you have the courage to act if there needs to be change? This experience helped make me more analytical and more willing to change the status quo if necessary. Armed with this lesson, I am less likely to settle for second best in my relationships.

Meeting Trish

So, here I was, single again, and knowing what I wanted in a woman but being unclear of what I wanted in a relationship. When I met Trish all that started to change and for the first time in my life I had a sense that I was with a woman, a person who satisfied me on all levels, and who gave me reason to start thinking beyond just comfort, familiarity, fun and 'friends'.

Her call came totally out of the blue. I was working as a Director of a mental health service in Sydney. I had met Trish a few weeks earlier at a job interview. Prior to that, we had met a few times in our respective roles in the field of mental health. I wasn't particularly aware of her as a television personality, but I respected her greatly for her mental health work. I had flown down to Melbourne for the job interview with Trish and her colleagues and left thinking, 'Wow...she's all right'. I assumed that she lived in Melbourne so didn't give this any more thought. Besides, I was more concerned about whether I had done well enough to get the job.

I was in a fairly casual relationship at the time and I wasn't

really looking for anyone. I had only recently ended my relationship with Jo, I had no plans or ambitions to get married or
have children.

Anyway, back to the phone call, which went like this...

TRISH: *Hi, this is Trisha Goddard.*
ME: *Hi [did I get the job?].*
TRISH: *Ummmm...I was wondering if you might be free next
   Friday.*
ME: *Sure [the job?].*
TRISH: *Would you like to come to a mental health dinner with
   me?*
ME: *Sure [oh, I see....this is about work].*
TRISH: *Great...see you next Friday.*
ME: *See you then [what's going on? Is this a date? A work
   thing?].*

I didn't think twice when Trish asked me out even though (a) I
was seeing someone (sort of) and (b) I didn't really know what
it was about. I just said yes before thinking too much about it.
Anyway, we had agreed to meet, so it was a case of 'take a step
and see what happens'.

Trish was late (she said she couldn't get a cab but, knowing
her as I do now, I am sure she was trying on outfit after outfit).
I waited, then walked up and down the street, wondering if I had
imagined it all. Had I got the details wrong? I was literally about
to leave when she turned up. She was apologetic and looked
great, so all was quickly forgiven, but I often wonder where my
life would have taken me if I hadn't waited as long as I did –
would she have called again? Would our lives have come together
in some way? Somehow I doubt it.

The 'date' was fun but bewildering. I didn't know whether it was work or not. It wasn't till it was over and we got some time together that it became clear that it was more than work and we spent the rest of the night talking and listening to each other – we've been together ever since.

Ever Since

This is a very different relationship for me. If I look back through all my previous relationships I can see the swing I make each time between the following categories:

- *sporty/feminine*
- *homely/adventurer*
- *tomboy/girlie*

This is the first time I have found someone with all of these qualities. I must admit until now, I always had a sense I was looking for something more or something different. My relationship with Trish is an exciting mixture of all the things I've ever had, plus some wonderful new qualities that I love in her – like her maternal side, her intellect and her personal strength.

Our relationship is a strong one, characterised by very good communication, a shared passion for our family life, travel and, to a lesser extent, our respective careers. It has its ups and downs like everything else. It has its own unique pressures arising from Trish's fame. However, every relationship has its challenges and areas of compromise, so there is nothing special in that respect. What makes this relationship so great is that we genuinely respect each other and admire each other's intellect as well as personality. I know that with Trish we will never run out of conversation, never get completely set in our ways – and never stop laughing...both together and at each other.

My approach to relationships has been typified by a willingness to jump in, explore and think about it later. I am not particularly analytical and tend to let my heart lead my head. In many respects, as Trish has described, she is the opposite. She approached our relationship in a very considered and deliberate way, allowed it to develop at a pace that suited her and the girls and, even now, uses her head to articulate her feelings far more than I do.

To me, relationships are adventures and opportunities, which offer a chance to explore another human being and to examine yourself in the context of that relationship. No other relationship has compelled me to challenge myself in the way this one has, whether it be adjusting to parenthood, living with someone else's fame, leaving my country, or just being with someone who insists at every turn that I should be healthy, live long and prosper.

Dr Terri's thoughts...

It is not that unusual to find yourself divorced, separated or single after being in a long-term relationship. For some people, it can be an exciting challenge to find they are out fishing in that big sea of love and dating once again. However, it can also be very daunting. Ending a long-term relationship can be a very painful experience, and it can take some time to find someone who can replace what you've lost. It's not unusual to go on a number of dates, and have a number of fleeting relationships before finally finding Mr or Mrs Right. As in Trisha's case, however, this process can often pay dividends, because you certainly come to find out about what you *don't* want in a relationship. This is why many people who marry for the second time have far more successful marriages. Learning from experience can be the strongest way of growing.

The other issue to contend with when becoming single is that even though you've started seeing someone else you may find yourself still emotionally affected by the experience with your ex. The *emotional* aspect of breaking up can be completely consuming, and you may cope with your emotional pain in any one of a number of ways – going out a lot, having multiple sexual partners for a while, or staying in and feeling like you can never face the sun again. Emotions can feel very muddled for a while, making you do things you wouldn't ordinarily do. You may be looking for relief in others, and it may not necessarily be forthcoming. It can take a considerable amount of time to start to feel less emotionally fragile.

The best position to be in is one where you finally come to the point of working through your emotional hang-ups (whatever they may be) and find the confidence to start valuing life as someone in your own right again. Many of these emotional problems stem from *change*. Most significantly, when you separate/divorce from a partner, many facets of your everyday life can be affected, right down to who you eat and sleep with. It can't get any more personal than that. So the *changes* that occur can be difficult to adjust to. Common emotions experienced around a break-up are rejection, hurt, jealousy, anger, denial, betrayal, loss, grief, and sometimes relief. Some or all of these can be experienced at once, which is why we can feel really confused and emotionally flooded. We often think that emotions are black and white, and that we are either happy or sad and can't be both. Not so. You can feel extremely sad about ending your marriage, and feel relief at the same time.

The final aspect of separation/divorce to consider, which Trisha has emphasised so well, is that people often go out on the hunt for a new partner without stopping to think about *why* they are now alone, and you might want to think about this. Were you in a violent relationship before, for example, or with someone who was constantly unfaithful? Why did you put up with such a difficult relationship for so long? Did you ever stop to think about it, and have you always thought that you simply didn't have any choice? Think about what I said at the beginning of this chapter, and your past affecting the way you might subconsciously be making choices in your adult relationships.

What you need to be doing now is to start to reflect on previous relationships and see whether you merely 'fell into them', or whether you could have actually chosen not to engage with some of the factors you were presented with. In order to learn from previous relationship experiences, and to start making more informed choices about your relationships, you need to become more consciously aware of the things that influence your choice of partners. For instance, is it purely looks or a macho/feminine weakness that you go for? Are there any particular qualities you look for, or have you never actually consciously looked for anything?

The question to ask yourself is 'What can I learn from that past relationship?' No life experience is ever wasted. You can always take something from the most horrendous times in your life, although it may be a while after the event(s) before you can reflect on them. So now I am going to encourage you to do just that. Work through the questions below, which are intended to guide you through your thoughts on any significant relationships (past and present) in your life. This can apply even if you are now happily married.

Quiz

First, take a few minutes to *identify* an earlier relationship – it doesn't matter who ended it. Once you have thought about it, answer the following questions:

- Where did you first meet your ex-partner?
- What were the circumstances?
- What was it that attracted you to this person? Was it something about them, or was it to do with the feelings you were having about yourself at that time (e.g. low self-esteem, feeling that you needed to be loved)?
- What were you seeking to gain from this relationship? What did you really want?
- What was the most important thing about the relationship, and did/does this match up to what you wanted or needed?
- Why did you choose to stay in this relationship? What was the main reason?
- Under what circumstances did this relationship end?
- On reflection, what have you learned from this experience, and what could you do differently now or in the future when approaching a potential new relationship?
- Finally, are there any beliefs that you would like to adjust slightly, such as 'men are all the same' or 'sex means he/she loves me'?

Write down your answers, then take a few minutes to think about whether there is anything you can learn from your past that will help you in your future.

Top Tips

1) If you think it's just bad luck that you end up with Mr or Ms Wrong, get real! Realise you're the honey that keeps attracting these bees. If you want to change the sort of person you have relationships with, start by changing yourself.

2) You won't get what you want unless you know what you're looking for in a relationship. Spend time working that out.

3) People who panic when they're on their own are like drowning non-swimmers, i.e. they'll grab onto the first bit of driftwood within grasp. *Priority*: Learn to live happily for a good amount of time on your own.

4) Know you may slightly influence a partner by example. *You* will not change or rescue them. Only *they* can do that.

5) If you're a single parent, keep your love life away from your kids for as long as possible, and even when you bring the two together, don't allow love to blind you when it comes to the way your new partner treats, looks at or talks about the children.

6) A happy relationship is not the only thing that can provide life fulfilment. You are more likely to find happiness with another person if you can put the relationship into a life context that involves lots of other positives.

7) Learn to love yourself – others will then find it easier to love you!

Case Study

The Cast
Susan (37 years old)
Jim (31 years old) – her husband

The story so far...
Susan has been married to Jim for nine years, and they have two children. This is her second marriage. Although at first both Susan and Jim were very much in love, over the years Jim has suffered with a serious alcohol problem. This has put a huge strain on the marriage, as Jim readily admits that the drinking led to him becoming violent towards Susan; culminating at times in him beating her up when she challenged him about it. He also readily admits that it was only because Susan stood by him during the most difficult times, and her love and patience, that he was eventually able to stop drinking.

Jim would spend up to £100 a day on alcohol, and he began gambling to fund his drinking habit. He was ashamed of his behaviour, but reached a point where he couldn't seem to help himself. He would constantly lie to Susan to try and hide his problem and the fact that he had no money. Even then, he would ask her for cash, and she would give it to him. He would stay out all night, sleeping at friends' houses because he was so drunk, which aggravated the situation. Eventually all he and Susan did was argue, and their marriage became a cycle of drinking, rows and violence. He even had a one-night stand during the worst times, which resulted in another child. Because of this and his violence toward her, Susan now finds it difficult to trust him. The lies were the thing that upset her the most.

Now Jim is off the drink, and readily acknowledges that he gave Susan a terrible time in the past. He just wants things to go back to how they were before he started drinking, when they were both very happy together. Susan wants this too. However, she now suspects that he is returning to his old behaviour of drinking and lies, and she doesn't know what to do. Jim, on the other hand, says that he is looking for work, and not out drinking. He is getting fed up with Susan nagging him all the time.

Help!

There are two key issues here: Jim's past abusive behaviour, and the complete lack of trust on Susan's part. It seems that both parties have now become polarised in the way they see things, and it doesn't matter what each of them says, as neither are relating to one another. The one area that they both agree on is that Jim's drinking caused a serious problem in their relationship: it led to him becoming violent and abusive toward Susan. She found it difficult to cope with the lies but stuck with Jim through it all and helped him come off the drink, when she could have just walked away. However, Jim needs to realise that trust will take a long time to rebuild, and that he has to display alcohol-free and non-abusive behaviour for a long time to prove that he has really changed. In addition, they would both benefit from marriage counselling. This would enable a neutral party to mediate between them so that they could begin to share their feelings, and start really listening to one another again.

In terms of losing and choosing partners, this case shows how people can, and do, choose to put up with abusive behaviour from their partner. This can be for a variety of reasons, and in Susan's case it was about her valuing her marriage and wanting to stay with the father of her children. It may also have been about the familiarity of her role as Jim's wife, and that to change this would have seemed terrifying until now. At least she knew how to function as she was, even when being hit by Jim. To leave a familiar situation, even when abusive, can be potentially so frightening that many people choose to stay with it. However, life is never static, and over time people's feelings change. In this case Susan could no longer trust Jim, and eventually she did file for a divorce. The one thing she learned from this relationship was that she was no longer prepared to accept a man who might be lying and unfaithful. The key to this would be in how Susan goes forward in life, and if she eventually seeks out a new relationship, the *choosing* aspect should become really important for her when making decisions about any new men she meets.

Chapter Three

Unconditional Love – and Other Myths About Parenthood

A Note from Dr Terri

For many of us the theme of this chapter – parenting – signals interest, joy, love, pride, frustration, defensiveness, controversy and – perhaps most significantly – something we have all some experience of to a varying degree. You may be a parent yourself, or you may simply have memories of how you were parented to think about when reading on. Even if you were adopted or cared for by a relative other than your mum or dad, this chapter will still apply to you because it is essentially about how *adults relate to children*. One thing we have no intention of doing is providing you with a template of what equals the perfect parent, because there is no such thing. Instead, we're going to give you Trisha's thoughts and feelings about the way she parents Billie and Madi, together with some useful general parenting tips.

It may sound obvious, but in any discussion about this subject, we need to be completely clear about what we mean by the terms 'parents' and 'parenting'. In the *Chambers Pocket Dictionary* (1992) the word 'parent' is defined as a mother, father or adopter of a child, and 'parenting' is used to describe the activities and duties of a parent. Depending on your individual life experiences, the definition of parent for you will depend on who occupied that role for you when you were growing up. For me it was my genetic/natural mother and father for the earlier part of my childhood, and then it became my maternal grandmother during my teens. For Trisha, it was her genetic/natural mother and father, and for Peter it ranged from his genetic/natural mother through to his sister. Peter's experience of being parented is particularly interesting because he lived with a stepfather for a short while, but there was a great deal of ambiguity surrounding the position this man held in relation to himself and his mother (see also Chapter 1, page 13). As this chapter unfolds, you'll be able to identify the consequences of maintaining secrecy, and will learn how not informing children of what is occurring in their everyday lives can breed confusion and contempt. Also look out for the way Billie defines her parents. She refers to her genetic/natural father by name, and her stepfather, Peter, by the affectionate term 'Pappy'. She certainly defines Peter as her father figure. Finally, I want you to think particularly about the *doing* part of parenting.

Trisha

Before you roll your eyes, let me explain why I also feel we all need to make sure we're talking about the same thing.

In my experience (both personally and when I talk to guests on the show), everyone assumes that when we talk about being a parent we all mean the same thing. No way. You talk to the vast majority of people who were parents, say, 60 years ago and they'll give a pretty different view of what made a good parent than people do now. Back then, Mother probably had a large number of children and parenting was about 'doing' for the family: cooking, cleaning, washing, etc. Discipline was usually physical and often meted out by Father. In many cases, this was just about the only contact the children had with him, so he ended up being this lofty, idealised and inaccessible character. Now throw in another variable. Money. If the family had lots of it and had people to 'do' for them, Mother was probably more likely to have the luxury of having time to develop a personality other than 'skivvy' or 'saint'. Most of the parenting might have been done by a nanny. In some countries even breast-feeding would be left to someone else – a wet nurse.

Then again, if one or both of your parents was born and raised in another country, their culture may have an entirely different set of values and methods when it comes to parenting. This might mean large doses of culture clash when you, as a child, go to school and start questioning what happens at home. And if you think all this 'what happened in the past' stuff has nothing to do with now, think again. Let me give you an example of how past experiences can impact on what sort of parent you are to your children.

If, for example, you come from a long line of families that sent their children off to boarding school, being at the tail-end of generations of people who spent practically their entire childhood *away* from their parents is going to have some impact on you. If you felt boarding didn't do you any favours, you may swing the other way and opt for a very hands-on role as a parent, but if the only friends you've had are ex-boarding school chums, maybe you've never seen how a non-boarder's family operates and know no other way things can be. So, come the right time, you pack your little one off as well.

Likewise, the way you discipline your kids. I'm constantly being made aware of how one generation's definition of discipline is the next generation's definition of abuse. So often what you get is one generation insisting they were brilliant parents because they kept their kids in check, and the kids never wanted for anything thanks to Mother and Father working their fingers to the bone. But when these people's kids become parents themselves, they enjoy the love, close contact and *time* they have with their children so much that they look back on their childhoods with regret. For instance, as a kid, I had no idea how old my mother was and because there were four of us children, I can vividly recall the only outing I think the two of us had by ourselves. She took me to the pictures to see the film *SWALK* (Sealed With A Loving Kiss), starring child actor Mark Lester, and I absolutely relished having her – and a whole chocolate bar – to myself! And from what I've heard about my mother's childhood, she and I had ten times more connection than she and *her* mother did.

And another thing. I never ever saw either of my parents without clothes. Heaven forbid! Nor do I recall seeing them kiss or hug – I guess that was the sort of stuff that happened behind the bedroom door. I was a child of the 1960s and early 1970s and, despite it being the age of so-called sexual liberation, I thought maybe that's what was normal at home. Then I started going round my school friend Sue's place and her parents were always kissing and cuddling – at first I was shocked.

But compare this with the relationship I have with *my* daughters. We have baths together, and unselfconsciously walk around naked. Having only two children five years apart means that I spend a lot of time with them, together and separately. We talk about just about everything. We use anything, from song lyrics, pop videos on MTV and newspaper stories to discuss everything from sex to terrorism. The girls get really fed up with Peter and I kissing and cuddling, and we frequently have 'group hugs' when we all kiss and cuddle each other together. We make time to play with the girls. What I love about the way things are now is that there are no taboos. If the girls get angry with Peter or myself, we're not averse to going along to their bedrooms later and chatting about what happened. If we, as adults, were out of order, we'll apologise. We discuss discipline issues. We sometimes say, 'Enough already. I'm pulling rank!' But we never, ever, *ever* smack.

'Smacking'? Forget It!

On this point, let's go back to the generational factor I was talking about. If you were brought up in a family where discipline often came in the form of a beating, and in an age when few questioned that, you may automatically adopt the same way of parenting yourself. Okay, it may be a toned-down version because society lets you know that all-out thrashing isn't on anymore. Or maybe you don't go to the same extreme as 'was done to you as a kid' because at *some* level you accept it caused more anguish than it was worth. I've often heard people say, 'I was belted as a kid and it never did me any harm.' I guarantee you that if these people are challenged with the right questions, they'll contradict themselves without even realising it. One elderly gentleman in my show's audience followed up his 'It did me nothing but good' statement with calmly stated sentiments about how he was never close to his father ('the thrasher') and how he in turn wasn't that close to his kids. 'But that's not the point,' he continued. 'At least I know right from wrong.' Full marks in the Good Citizen column. But how much of a rating as a parent capable of showing children love and of being loved in return?

All this is a pre-amble to just about the most difficult passage I will write in this book. If you smack or hit your child and vigorously defend your right to do so, read every word of this. It is written bearing in mind the anguish for all involved.

The fact that the subject of 'smacking' is still brought up in our family and still causes pain and tears some 30-odd years after it happened speaks volumes. I have put the word 'smacking' in inverted commas because that's the word my parents use when talking about certain aspects of how they disciplined me and my sisters. I guess that compared to the punishments *they* received as children, they did only 'smack' me. Time for a definition again. My generation's understanding of 'giving a child a smack' comes from this model:

1) Adult gives child a warning about child's behaviour.
2) Adult gives other warnings and adds that if behaviour persists, child will be punished with a smack. All done very calmly – no anger, just firmness.
3) Child misbehaves again. Adult tells child what they are about to be smacked for.
4) Child is given one or at most two smacks.

This is certainly not how I remember being 'smacked', or how any of my diary entries recorded it, but then I was on the receiving end. I only associate the 'smacking' I received as being accompanied by what seemed, from a child's point of view, to be uncontrollable anger. I was never told how many smacks I was going to get and it seemed to go on until my parents' anger was abated. It didn't deter me from whatever it was that I wasn't supposed to do and my diaries only recorded something akin to temporary blind hatred for the smacker.

During very painful therapy after my breakdown, it emerged that I have a powerful coping mechanism when it comes to pain. I just go somewhere else in my head. Totally. It's like the body is there, but the mind disappears. Having seen me do this, Peter says it's uncanny. My eyes glaze over, I disconnect and I turn into an emotionless android that hears and sees nothing and stops reacting to anything and everything. Remember, I went through childbirth twice with absolutely no pain relief. I just went somewhere else in my head.

When I'm in this kind of state, I do very heavy weight training and actually enjoy going somewhere else and zoning out the pain. I can run for 12 miles and get through any pain the same way. If I 'zone out' while running on a treadmill and connected to a heart monitor, my heart rate actually drops in spite of the vigorous exercise I'm doing. A good technique? Yes, often, but here's the downside. This pain-coping mechanism is so powerful that I'm prone to exercising even with injuries, so if my personal trainer doesn't keep an eye on me I'm capable of doing myself some serious damage.

When past relationships were in trouble, even though I was in immense emotional pain, I would again go somewhere else in my head. This 'unavailability' would drive partners mad. So what's this got to do with 'smacking', you ask? Well, I perfected my 'zoning out' technique to cope with what was happening when my father smacked me. If I 'wasn't there' I could ignore the pain. I could tune out his anger, which terrified me then, and even now, all these years later. Somehow it was different when my mother smacked me. Female-to-female anger I could cope with, even though I still hated it. But a physically intimidating adult male? That was an altogether different thing.

If you're a father who smacks his daughters, ask yourself about the possible outcome of a girl learning that love and being 'smacked' are all part of the same package.

- *Dad is there to look out for you, Dad provides, Dad loves you.*
- *You 'do something wrong' or 'piss Dad off', Dad smacks you.*
- *That doesn't mean Dad doesn't love you though, does it?*

In my early twenties, I found myself in a violent relationship. Well, that's what I call it now, but back then I saw it like this:

- *This man is there to look out for you, this man helps provide, this man loves you.*
- *You do 'something wrong' or 'piss this man off', man smacks you.*
- *That doesn't mean this man doesn't love you though, does it?*

I don't know if there are any studies to back this up, but I have found a recurring pattern in the numerous women I've spoken to who have been in physically abusive relationships. They've either grown up seeing Mum being belted by Dad, or, when I've questioned them about how their fathers behaved towards them when they were little girls, thay have memories of being hit or verbally intimidated or learning to 'cope' in the face of Dad's aggressive manifestation of temper. I'm sure there are many women who don't fit into this pattern, but is it worth taking the risk of Dad teaching daughter to allow violence into her interpretation of male love, and worse still, maybe teaching her how to 'cope' or 'put up with it'?

And what else does 'smacking' teach a child? That physical intimidation forces an opponent to 'respect' and fear you? Here's a very good example of this. My sisters and I used to get into some pretty horrible physical fights and acts of bullying with each other. It's ironic to note that we often ganged up on the one we thought wasn't being 'smacked' at home as much as we were. Somehow we seemed to think it was our right to give that one a good 'smacking' in lieu of what they had missed.

Here's another 'side-effect'. I've been in supermarkets or in the street and seen a parent shouting at or smacking a child. It's all I can do not to vomit there and then. I start shaking and sweating and I usually can't hold myself back and have to intervene. One notable time this happened was when we lived in Sydney, Australia, in the late 1990s. What I saw affected me so badly, that after a night spent crying in his arms, Peter suggested I sit down and write about it in the form of an open letter. At 6 a.m. I faxed what I'd written to the Letters page of the *Sydney Morning Herald*. A few hours later, the newspaper's editor contacted me and asked me to write up what I'd experienced as an article, which they printed a couple of weeks later.

About a year later, an American delegate at a mental health conference I was attending in London approached me, and congratulated me for my 'paper' on child violence. When I explained I didn't know what she was talking about, she told me her professor had handed out the following article as recommended reading for their social worker's course!

A Street Scene in Chatswood One Struggles to Forget
by Trisha Goddard
From the *Sydney Morning Herald*, Aug. 18, 1997

I still feel sick to the stomach by something I witnessed a couple of Fridays ago. I was shopping in Chatswood when I saw an extremely well-dressed mother ask her small son whether he wanted to go to the toilet.

'No, Mummy,' said the boy, who looked to be about four. Not 10 seconds later, clutching his little bottom, he changed his mind and said he wanted to go. I smiled to myself. As a mother of two littlies, I well know the 'no, I don't, yes, I do' syndrome.

But the mother wasn't having it. 'No, we've passed the toilets and I asked you and you said "No". So now it's too late.'

'But I need to go,' the child persisted. 'No, too late,' the mother countered, and so it went on. I took notice because I was thinking, 'Why sweat the small stuff, lady? Kids change their minds all the time. The loo's a few yards away. Take him.'

But no, she wouldn't, and the conversation seemed to go on and on as we all walked along. When we got outside the shopping centre, I heard her tone change and so turned around, realising she was really going to have a go at him. What I witnessed is something that has invaded my dreams every night since and had me in tears every now and then throughout the day.

The only way I can describe what next took place is that this immaculately dressed North Shore woman beat up her little boy in the street. With clenched fists she punched him around the head and shoulders with all her might. Picked him up by the neck of his little blue sweater and threw him against a lamp post.

All the time she was screaming: 'I told you it was too late. I asked you if you wanted to go and you said no.'

People on the crowded pavement froze in horror. I couldn't stand it and before I knew what I was doing I was screaming 'Stop it! Stop it! Leave him alone.' Without looking at me, she seemed to gain some control and in a terse voice continued admonishing him, then turned to me, all seething aggression, and barked: 'You were talking to me?'

I was in tears by now and just kept saying to her: 'You didn't have to do that. I'm just so distressed by what you just did.'

My tears seemed to have a tiny effect on her. She grabbed the child's hand and walked on. One of the shaken onlookers, a teenage girl, said to me: 'Good on you. That was horrible.'

I explained that the woman needed as much help as the boy did. I have seen children being smacked before. They howl, they react. This child was being beaten full-force with fists. He did not react. He took it. Maybe he was used to it. I'm glad my children weren't there to witness it. If you're not safe with Mummy in a crowded street, then where on earth are you safe?

I am involved in helping to determine the direction of the second phase of this country's National Mental Health Strategy. I am one of a group which pushed very strongly for the focus to be early intervention in mental health: working on the needs of children and adolescents, and their parents. Who the hell is stupid enough to think that good, safe parenting comes as naturally to us as sex and conception do?

Abuse usually has a domino effect through generation after generation and, although we no longer automatically connect mental illness with abusive parenting, who are we kidding? What we need to remember is that bad parents aren't necessarily bad people; they're just people who probably had bad parenting themselves. Get rid of the blame and treat some of the situations that lead to suicide from the day that little baby is born. From the moment that sweet, sad little boy was attacked by his desperate mother a couple of Fridays ago.

Lady, if you are reading this, I do not judge you. I beg you to get help for yourself and your little boy. And if you're reading this and you're not that lady, but feel as a parent you're not coping, if you have a small needling suspicion that something is beginning to slide, there is no shame in getting help. Indeed, it will be the bravest thing you've ever done.

So, okay, nothing like that ever happened to me. But it doesn't take a genius to figure out where I was coming from when I wrote that piece. That said, I don't want to paint my parents as 'monsters', or anything approaching that. They taught me a lot of brilliant things as well. Mum had this habit of waking us up in the morning with the most effusively cheery 'Good morning'. That greeting made you feel that each day was special and exciting. She made you want to get up, go out there and embrace the day. A small but powerful way to stoke up the fires of optimism. Mum also taught me stuff about the importance of appearance, spending hours tirelessly sewing beautiful outfits for me. Yeah, yeah, we'd all love to believe that saying, 'It's not what's on the outside that counts. It's what's on the inside.' But every bit of research going shows that, just like the rest of the animal kingdom, we sum up people in just a few minutes. We're still out in the wild, trying to work out which animal will attack, which is friendly and which one we wouldn't half mind mating with. Through Mum I learned that even if you feel rough, if you fake it with good grooming and a smile (albeit forced at first) the world will start smiling back at you and people will want to be around you. Before you label that as a superficial quality, let me tell you that I have triumphed in the face of racism many times, not through aggro and militancy, but by using good grooming, good manners, a radiant smile and sharp wit.

I learned the power of words and debate from my mother. I also learned to 'Shoot for the stars. Then if you miss, at least you'll hit the tops of the trees.' I learned never to give up trying. I learned to be a brilliant dancer by watching and dancing with Mum.

Dad taught me the importance of having a social conscience and fighting for the underdog. I also picked up a wicked sense of humour from him. I learned not to be afraid of damned hard work. And I learned from both parents never to rely on anyone but myself, which was a bit of a double-edged sword when it came to relationships.

The one punishment that taught me the most didn't involve even a raised hand. I went through a phase of petty theft. Each week, four sets of school dinner money would be left on the mantelpiece in my parents' bedroom. It was so easy just to start nicking the odd 5p or 10p at first. Then, as I grew bolder, I started stealing 50p here and there. I can't even remember what I spent it on, but I do recall that I got a bit of a buzz about getting away with it. I'm sure that at first my parents put it down to their miscalculating the amounts, but cash was anything but abundant in our household and they quickly smelled a rat.

I'll never forget the time Dad came into my bedroom immediately after one of my 'nicking' ventures. I was just congratulating myself at avoiding a sticky situation, when he confronted me about my stealing. Naturally, I indignantly denied it. The money I had was all mine. Then he demanded to see my money and explained that he and Mum had suspected what was going on and had deliberately marked the dinner money. That was it. I was caught. 'My' coins had biro crosses on them. I then got a stern lecture about the slippery slope of theft, but I don't really recall the words. What I do remember was the terrible shame I felt, along with the crushing embarrassment and guilt.

It was the most effective punishment my parents ever meted out. No amount of temptation has ever made me pocket anything that's not 100 per cent mine, thanks to that one powerful lesson. On the other hand, I couldn't give a toss about what I was 'smacked' for – not washing up when it was my turn or some such relative trivia.

I feel I should point out something here – namely, that our parents resorted to smacking us for only a few years of my childhood. But I'm sure it's no coincidence that even then, as a child, I had a deep sense of all not being well between them. Since then I have discovered that in the end, the 'smacking' caused them – and my father especially – about as much emotional pain as it caused us. Even so, as a kid, it had a devastating effect on me. You only need to check out places like the NSPCC website to read that reactions like mine amongst children who have been smacked are not at all unusual. You'll also find mental scars on the parents who did the 'smacking'. The vast majority of them would now beg other parents to find some other, less damaging form of discipline. I'm willing to bet my dear parents would be at the head of that queue.

Parents Are People Too!

It's all too easy to blame our parents for the past, but, as I said in the newspaper article, they may have come from a time when introspection was seen as ugly self-absorption or where pride in one's achievements was seen as boasting. In other words, your parents could just be the last people in a long line of behaviour that was taken for granted and therefore perpetuated.

There comes a time in life where, I believe, if one is lucky, one comes to see one's parents as people first and foremost. As people, they have good traits and bad – the same as anyone else. They make good and bad choices. Perhaps they shouldn't even have been together. Maybe the social pressures of an unwanted pregnancy in a different era threw them together and they've spent their one existence on this planet 'making the best out of things' while being secretly resentful. They mess up. It doesn't make them bad. It just means they're fallible, like each and every one of us.

Once you start seeing your parents as people first, you stop expecting them to make things better: you can even appreciate that you might not particularly like one, or even both, of them very much, even though you may respect and be hugely grateful for the hard work they did or sacrifices they made for you. Now I know you're not meant to say things like that. It's taboo. How many times have I had audience members stand up during the *Trisha* show and say, 'Blood is thicker than water!' 'You should respect your mother.' 'You should love your father, no matter what.' 'Bullshit!' I say. I've seen that kind of pressure destroy people. I've met women and men who've been horribly abused by a parent and what destroys them almost more than what they've gone through is society's blind bleating on about how they should put years of hell aside, simply because of an accident of birth. This is what I mean when I talk about the 'myth of unconditional love'. Might it just make us strive harder as parents, or brothers and sisters, if we were taught that birth is a lottery? You are under no obligation to like or respect those people who happen to have been born into your 'circle'. And there is no reason for them to like or respect you. Therefore, if you want a unit that thrives and nourishes both you and them, you'd better set about learning to *actively* love and respect each other – and respect is not just what a child *must* feel towards a parent; it's what parent *must* feel towards a child. Both need to earn the gift of respect from each other.

So Does the Past Make Me the Perfect Parent?

Ha! What you've just read was written with the Benefit Of Hindsight.

Like most parents, for me it started just after I had Billie. That moment you first get back from hospital, brand new babe in arms, sums it all up: 'What the hell do we do now?' You go from 'This baby's gonna have to fit in with *us*' to feeling like you're only just hanging on by the skin of your teeth! There are so many parenting books these days, each of which seems to contradict the last. I think I had at least one bookshelf full of them. Actually, with Billie, I learned a lot from the nanny I hired – well, the practical stuff anyway. After all, I thought, she'd looked after far more babies than I had.

When I had to fly all over Australia filming stories for my health and lifestyle television show, Billie and the nanny came everywhere with me and I breast-fed Billie. I'm not going to harp on about the massive health benefits of breast-feeding here, because if you don't know about them by now, you must be from another planet. But I do want to mention the psychological benefits – to the mother. If you persevere and relax, breast-feeding can bring you closer to your baby in seconds flat. If you're a stay-at-home mum, you probably don't need that instant shot of intimacy, but if you're a working mother, it's a godsend.

My parenting style has changed enormously from the days when I employed nannies, through the three years I was a single mother, to after my breakdown, and then when I met Peter. I thought I was a brilliant mum when I had nannies working for me. But back then, in the early 1990s, I bought into that 'quality time' theory someone came up with to salve the consciences of working parents. We were told that it wasn't how long one spent with a child that mattered. It was all about making the minutes spent together count.

Tough news, everyone. Having tried co-parenting with nannies (well, that's what it is really, isn't it?) and single mummy parenting 24 hours a day, three guesses which kind of parenting brought me a million times closer to my kids? You don't pick up subtle behavioural nuances in seconds flat when, as often or not, the child is 'performing' in order to bring you up to speed on the last 22-and-a-half hours of their lives that you've missed!

As a single mum, I developed a very 'co-operative' way of parenting. The girls and I invented a song called 'Do You know The Goddard Girls?', which we used to sing at the top of our lungs. We were a team and each team member had to pull their weight, as we had no one to depend on but ourselves. It worked brilliantly, except in certain circumstances. I noticed that when we visited my parents in England, and they told Billie to do something, she reacted very stubbornly. She was used to a 'Bills, it would really help me if you did such-and-such' approach. She was used to being one-of-the-team and not a 'minion'. Her reaction was to rebel, but I explained it was different in Nanny and Grandpa's day.

Parenting With Peter

I've always thought of Peter and I as two people in search of a family, albeit for very different reasons. I emerged from my childhood experiences of 'family' and from my experience of being a parent with the girls' biological father, craving, well, what I have now. Mark, my ex, just wasn't into doing things together as a family in the way that I was, and he made his feelings plain right from the start. I don't have any recollection of parenting *with* him.

It was more tag-team stuff, where one of us would be handing Billie over to the other on the way out of the door to go to work/the gym/do the shopping, etc. I used to look at families walking along hand in hand, hugging and kissing each other, and dream. I used to see families together, sisters and brothers playing and laughing, obviously close, and I'd wish and wish.

I remember Peter telling me he'd sit on a wall opposite a friend's house and daydream about what would be going on inside because that boy had a dad to be doing stuff with. And that dad would be interacting with the mum. 'What would that be like?' he'd wonder.

Peter always says that one of the reasons he wanted to be with me was because of the way I was as a mother. That just blows me away. I know I'm not perfect, but I work damned hard at being a mum – not just a financial provider and do-er. In fact, I keep telling myself that time spent doing housework will never reap the same rewards as time doing stuff with the girls. I see being a parent as a work in progress and Peter and I have no qualms in steering each other if we think one of us is on the wrong track. He's better than I am at a lot of stuff. He'll come and tell me, for example, if Billie needs time 'hanging out' with me. Or he'll sit me down and firmly tell me if I'm coming down too hard or too softly on one of the girls. Similarly, I can tell Peter if I think his stress is having an effect on the girls. We often discuss issues and decide together how to tackle things with them or which punishment is appropriate – and that's before an act of 'naughtiness' has even taken place.

Naturally, we don't agree on everything. I'm more into not sweating the small stuff; for instance, Billie is at that age when she's into giving you one of her 'looks'. They send Peter up the wall but I tend to ignore them, because I remember doing the same thing with my parents and the worst thing for me was when they *didn't* respond.

Here's a snapshot of parenting, Trisha and Peter style!

To dictate or discuss: Yep, that is the question! I remember I loved it when my parents actually talked about things with me. What with having had four kids in four years and working all the hours possible (my mother worked for virtually all my childhood), that was pretty rare. If the logic behind a rule was explained, I was far more likely to take it on board. I figure the same with my girls. I try to explain rules before the situation even arises. For instance, even though Billie uses her mobile phone primarily as a way of keeping 'in' and up-to-date with her crowd, Peter and I make sure she knows that the reason we succumbed to buying her one was for her personal safety. She has quite a way to travel to school in the countryside and is reliant on a bus service with Peter and I collecting her from the bus stop, and should one of us be delayed in traffic or the bus break down in the snow, it's vital that she has enough credits on her Pay-As-You-Go phone and that it is switched on while she's travelling. Should she use her phone in school or run out of credits (bought with the pocket money she's expected to work for) she knows the phone will be confiscated.

As I write this, she's minus mobile phone for a weekend because Peter caught her sending text messages to friends from under the bedcovers after lights-out. It's a punishment that hits hard. No phone = not being in with the crowd and what they're up to. She also has to explain to them why she's out of the loop. More embarrassment. Sure, she could use the house phone, but then she has the parents monitoring how long she's tying up the line.

In general, rules are established with varying amounts of

discussion. After that we go into 'dictate' mode. I actually don't subscribe to this treating-each-kid-in-exactly-the-same-way thing some people are into. What works with one child may not work with another.

For instance, I recognise that Billie and I have similar personalities. We're both pretty high octane and, therefore, combustible. I'm expecting us to clash when she's a teenager and we've already had a couple of humdingers, but I don't take it personally. I'd rather she communicated her anger and frustration with me than not communicate at all. It's how I was with my mum and it was sometimes easier for me to convey how I felt about things at the top of my voice. That way I got instant attention as I felt she was always too busy to have the time to sit down and simply 'shoot the breeze'.

With Madi, I tend to get her to repeat back to me what I've just told her. She's *soooo* much like Peter. All cerebral and in her head. With both of them you can never assume they've heard what you're on about, simply because they nod and say yes.

I use a lot of humour in parenting. I think being able to laugh with your kids is a must. I think laughing *at* them stinks. But having said that, I sometimes mimic their behaviour back to them so they can see how it feels to be on the receiving end. Here's a typical scenario: I ask Billie to give me a hand unloading the dishwasher, then...

BILLIE *(giving me one of her made-to-annoy-looks)*: Mum, I can't be bothered. Just chill. Do it later.

ME: Oh, okay, Bills. Now, what time am I meant to be giving you a lift into town?

BILLIE: Well, drop me off around midday and pick me up at four.

ME (copying the look Billie gave me when I asked her to help me):
Oh, Bills, I can't be bothered giving you a lift into
town. Just chill. Go another day. Hey, Bills, if that
attitude is okay for you, I guess it must be okay for me
too! Give me a shout when you've done the dishwasher
and the other jobs you need to do and I'll get the car
out of the garage.

Let me say here – and this is what I love about parenting – having read Billie's bit of this chapter, I've really got to work hard at not nagging. Mainly because it obviously isn't a good way of getting the message through to her.

All in all, I guess it's obvious why Peter and I are so hot on talking things through with the girls: neither of us really felt we knew what was going on in our families when we were growing up. I also think that if you want to make things that bit easier for yourself, you should start talking things through with your children as *early* as possible. Of course, it's a lot tougher if a child can 'appeal' a punishment and you have to go through again why this is how it's got to be. But, believe me, it's tougher still if you have to apologise for stuffing up. So many parents feel they need to be seen as omnipotent and infallible – a bit like demi-gods. Thing is, if you come over all god-like, the only place your kid can go to rebel (and they need to do this in order to become fully-fledged adults) is down with the devil. In other words, an extreme reaction is the only alternative they're left with. I try to let the girls know that if they do wrong. I'll be cross with them, providing they know what they did was wrong. If they don't, I see initial 'stuff-ups' as an opportunity to acquaint them with the 'rule' and the 'reason' behind it. Example: 'I don't want you to play with that ornament because it means a lot to me. It reminds me of a very special time when I first travelled overseas on my own. I know you've got special stuff you'd rather I didn't touch, so it's the same with that ornament.' So, say I catch one of them playing with that ornament again, I'll 'bark' (as the kids call it). I'll let them feel the heat of my anger and include how it upsets me that they're choosing to ignore how much that particular ornament means to me.

Choices: Oh, how did I ever parent before I discovered the power of this word? Choice. Peter and I are really hot on the girls realising that just about everything involves choice. For instance, at the moment we're trying to get Madi to start attaching some value to money. She'll blow her hard-earned pocket money on the first bit of rubbish she comes across and then start whining and niggling at us to buy her something she really wants. So now when that starts we say, 'Madi you can choose to buy this now or you can choose to hang on to your money and see if there's something you want more in one of the other shops.' Okay, she opts for a bit of tat. Come the toy of her dreams a couple of shops later, and the whining begins, we react like this. 'Hey, but you chose to buy what you saw first. If you're cross with yourself for doing that, so be it, but don't make all of us suffer.'

If the girls do something they know full well they shouldn't, we always remind them that they knew what the rules were and that they chose to ignore them. That's okay. You always have a choice, but with that choice comes a consequence. Your choice just landed you in a heap of poo!

Leading by example: The kids seem to be going wild. Screaming at the tops of their voices. You go to the bottom of the stairs and yell up at them, 'Shut up, you lot! Stop all that shouting. It's driving me mad!'

We're all guilty of the 'Don't do as I do! Do as I say!' method of cop-out parenting at some stage, aren't we? I know we'd often like to pretend it isn't so, but the fact is that a lot of our parenting is done without even opening our mouths. Those little eyes are watching us all the time. If you treat your partner like dirt, do you really have the right to get angry with junior when she picks up the message from Mum that boys are useless and starts treating little brother the same way? Say Dad slaps Mum. Are you seriously going to get cross with the kids when they slap each other or kids at school? Where do bullies learn to bully? How does a child differentiate between your 'little white lies' to a traffic policeman who notices your tax disc is out of date and their looking you straight in the eye and telling you they didn't take that £5 note from the sideboard. Do we think children can't spot a hypocrite at a hundred paces? There aren't many hard-and-fast rules in parenting, but I'll stick my neck out and throw this one at you: If you want to keep an orderly house put your own house in order.

Okay, so Peter and I haven't hit the teens yet, although Billie is sidling on up to the starting line. But we're already discussing different situations with her and will continue to do so. She knows it's okay to disagree with us and she's welcome to debate her cause, but when it comes down to the line, we'll do what we think is in her best interest, even if she doesn't like it. Like I tell her, every place has rules in order to keep some kind of order. We're just giving her the opportunity of experiencing what it's like in a safe environment. Out there in the Big Exciting World, there may be no debate, no warnings and no apologies. Sure, you have rights, but with every right comes a responsibility. In a family unit, we each have those rights, but we have to safeguard each other's rights as well in order to make the team work.

I aim to teach our girls that our love for each other is like looking after a plant: we need to emotionally feed and nourish each other just about every day. If I neglect, mistreat, 'smack' or do something we class as truly, terribly evil to dishonour them, or they do the same to me and/or Peter, there's nothing to say that love won't begin to dwindle or die. Sorry, nothing in life comes without terms and conditions. At least with household goods they come attached. Kids certainly don't come with a 'How to...' rule book and if that's what you expected in this chapter – bad luck! It ain't that easy. If you're thinking about buying a cooker, a house, a car or a fridge, you do your homework. You talk to each other about the features you feel are necessary in each item. You check out what maintenance it'll need. You don't put diesel in a petrol car: if it makes a funny noise, you'll investigate. You'll look into insurance to cover things that may go wrong in the future. What I'm saying is this. If only we prepared for parenting half as much as we prepared for taking on the relatively minor responsibilities of home, car or household appliance care, we'd greatly improve the lives of our children, wouldn't we?

Peter

I never had any aspiration to be a parent, let alone have children. Before I met Trish I was in a long-term relationship and we had a content but typically 'yuppy' household – shopping for furniture at IKEA satisfied most of our nesting needs. When this ended I met a woman with two teenage sons. They disliked me, I disliked them (so too, I suspect, did their mother), and reinforced to me that I would always be a bachelor type of guy.

Then Trish came into my world. I knew she had two young

daughters but I never really expected to meet them, let alone develop a relationship with them. Things developed fairly quickly between us and before long I was sitting in her lounge awaiting an introduction to Billie and Madi – no job interview ever felt so nerve-wracking.

It was really clear to me straight away that (a) I liked the girls and (b) they were first in Trish's life and therefore a major element to any relationship that might develop. I was amazed at how cool these kids were. They liked all the same things I did. We'd hang out together watching *The Simpsons, Ren & Stimpy* – cartoons I happened to love but that Trish wasn't into. This gave me a sort of 'cred' with the kids that I'm sure made my entry into their lives a little easier for all of us.

I really admired the way that Trish parented. She was protective and gentle with the girls. They had a dialogue that, in many ways, was very adult – they talked about stuff all the time. Billie and Madi were the most important parts of her life. I was third in line for her affection and love and this seemed totally right to me. In fact, it was her obvious love for the girls, and the fact that she was able to separate herself from the role of mother to enjoy her relationship with me as a lover, that I found to be one of her sexiest and most attractive qualities.

Gradually, I became more and more involved with the life of the 'Goddard Girls' and increasingly found that I wanted to exert my influence on the lives of the children. Trish, understandably, had a lot of trouble letting go of her role as *the* parent and sole protector, but, to her credit, she allowed me to test and refine my newly-acquired parenting skills. During this time I likened her to an Amazon warrior fiercely standing guard over her tribe with a spear ready to slay any male threat to the status quo. I have always said I think Trish is a great parent and, in the early days, I watched her and started to emulate her parenting style which involved a lot of explaining, discussion and negotiation. It was important for us that I did not assume that just because I was a man I knew how to be a father – this is simply not true. Parenting, while instinctive, involves new skills and understandings, and I had a great teacher. Eventually, she put down her spear (or, at least, stopped pointing it in my direction) and I started to grow into my new role as a parent in my own right. This journey is described in more detail in our chapter Is *The Brady Bunch* Just a Bunch of Lies? (page 101).

Parental Influence or Confluence

One area where Trish and I disagree is the extent to which our past influences how we act in the present. While it can't be denied that we are all, to some extent, the product of our experience and upbringing, I strongly believe that the way we act in any given situation today is more about the forces at play right now. The idea of confluence differs from influence in that it acknowledges that all of the factors influencing us at any given time (e.g. the traffic, the weather, health, work) converge to determine how we might think, act or plan in relation to our life. Confluence also frees us from thinking that we are trapped or destined to simply repeat or respond to the mistakes our own parents made.

Trish has already mentioned how her parents brought her up and how that influenced the choices she made in life and the style of parenting that she adopts. My own upbringing has been described in detail on page 12. As I explained there, my parents separated when I was six. From that day onwards I had no further contact with my father. I know he tried to see me because I remember seeing him trying to get in the gate of where I was staying but being turned away. He even came to my school but was told to stay away by the headmaster. I should say here that my mother later told Trish (not me) that he *was* allowed to see me but would often not turn up and I would be left, trussed in my best clothes, in such distress that I would have an asthma attack. I honestly have no recollection of these times. To this day, I still don't really know what happened between my mother and father. All I know is that no-one ever explained anything to me and that one of my few regrets in life is that I didn't try and find out the truth before my mother passed away.

So I spent my early childhood living in council housing with my mother. She even changed my surname to Dean – that of her first husband (and the father of my brother and sister). Eventually she moved in with a man as – I later discovered – his housekeeper, but at the time it was all very confusing. All of a sudden I was living in a nice house with a dog and a very ambiguous relationship with a man called Bill. Was he my step-father? Was he my mother's employer? No-one told me anything. All I knew was that I hated him. When I was ten I had my own room in a small outbuilding next to the house; by the time I was 14, after the inevitable adolescent showdown with Bill, I was living in a caravan in my sister's backyard until I went to university in Melbourne at the age of 17. So, effectively, from the age of ten onwards, I lived semi-independently – or, at least, that's how it felt.

Don't get me wrong – my mother loved me and provided for me, despite the hardship of being a single mum. The independence that characterised my younger years is something that I loved and would probably not change if I had my time again. My time living with my sister had a very positive impact on my life. She was travelled, cultured (for Geelong!) and lived with a fascinating man called Graham who told me all sorts of stories about his life. It was because of my sister and Graham that I wanted to go to university and travel.

In a very different way, I idolised my brother. He wasn't around a lot as I grew up but he was a good local footballer and that gave me some well-needed 'street cred' at school. More importantly though, for me, he married young. Actually, he married the sister of my sister's former husband – brother and sister married brother and sister – unfortunately, the Garrett family did not have a younger female sibling waiting for me. What a missed opportunity. We could've been guests on the *Trisha* show. My brother bought a house and had three sons by the time I was 15. I was envious of the family his children had – he seemed like a great dad to his boys. I knew from an early age that I didn't have a 'normal' family, that there was no dad to teach me to sail or take me camping and I was envious of my friends and nephews in this respect.

By the age of 17, I was living on a university campus in Melbourne, had reclaimed my birth name of Gianfrancesco and had found my father. Unfortunately, he was not interested in me by that stage and had a new daughter from another marriage (it was actually the lady who lived up the street during the time I was with my mother and father all those years ago – hmm!). Over the years I tried intermittently to maintain contact but it never seemed to work. I don't know if my father is alive now but I feel a sadness that he didn't play a greater part in my life. Dad, if you happen to read this book, get in touch.

I can honestly say that my own experience of childhood and being parented played only a small role in determining the sort of parent I am now. It has, however, made me treasure the sense of belonging that a happy family life affords, and enabled me to balance Trish's natural protectiveness of the girls with an approach to parenting that insists on resourcefulness, independence and courage. The latter quality is a definite throwback to my natural father. He would constantly challenge me to overcome my fears, which was a bit ridiculous, considering I was only four years old! Once he made me stand in front of him on the top of a cliff and I was not allowed to step back until I let go of him and stopped crying. This, he said, would make me brave. Recently, I found myself denying Madi the use of her rubber ring in the swimming pool until she had confronted her natural fear of the water. Is this good parenting, or just a repeat of my earlier bad parenting? I'm not sure, but it did lead to a discussion with Trish and I *did* ask Madi how that made her feel, which is something my father never did.

My abilities as a parent are shaped by the experiences of childhood that I bring to this family, but, more importantly, by my observations of Trish, my interactions with the girls and my willingness to learn, particularly from my mistakes. The stuff we bring to a new relationship is like clay and the way we shape and refine that clay is a reflection of the many other factors converging and interacting at that point. I do not feel compelled to repeat the parenting I had or didn't have but I am willing to be shaped and influenced by the constant change and challenge that raising children, within a loving adult relationship, brings.

Conditional Love

Another important value that I have come to embrace as a parent is the idea of conditional love. I used to think that perhaps missing out on the biological experience of parenting (e.g. providing the raw materials, being there at the birth, and the very earliest years) meant that I could only accept and offer conditional love. However, having spoken with Trish and other parents about this, it seems to be more universal and widely held than I had thought.

I love the girls. I would die for them. They truly love me. But...I expect certain things in return for my commitment and love and I want them to expect the same things from me. All satisfying relationships are mutual. That is, each party gets something they need from the relationship. In any relationship that I have I expect to be respected, to be afforded privacy, to be treated fairly and to be allowed to have my influence and aspirations shape the future. I bet many of you are thinking this sounds like rubbish – parenting just isn't like that! Well, maybe it's not and never will be, but it's the goal we work towards as a family.

In practice this means that it's okay to say that you are disappointed with something your children may have done, and that their behaviour might ultimately affect how you feel about them and, of course, vice versa. Once children know it's okay to tell you that *you* have let them down, you can have a truly equal discussion about the effect each person is having on the family. I can tell the girls I am sorry when I make a mistake. I expect to be forgiven and they expect me to get it right next time or, at least, try. How many parents are able to admit to their children that they have got something wrong or are sorry for their behaviour? *We* do, and we do it so that the children know we do not take their love of us for granted.

Many children do not like their parents; perhaps some parents don't like their children but most feel trapped in this cycle of unconditional love, where no matter what we do we will always have the love of our parents. Sadly, I don't think this is true. I know that when Billie or Madi tell me that they love me, they really mean it. I've earned it...and I'll have to keep earning it.

The Future

As we write this book, Billie is plummeting into adolescence and is refining her sneer and attitude to a professional standard. We both know that her talking back really annoys me. Billie has to have the last word in any argument – so do I. Madi is emerging from the sweetness of being six, seven and eight into an articulate and strong-willed young girl with an excellent attitude mentor in her big sister. Where will all this take us? Who knows? All I know is that nothing we have done so far in life will give us the answers.

The Earth has not seen an adolescent Billie Gianfrancesco before. The impact she will have on our family and we on her, for better or for worse, is unknown. But at least we're prepared …we talk openly, we agree on our expectations for one another as family members, we know how to say sorry, we try and learn from our many mistakes and we genuinely like, as well as love, one another. That will be enough to get us through and, along the way, make us all better and more capable people. Earth… get ready!

Billie (Hey, that's me you're talking about!)

The first nanny I can remember was a really nice lady called Maria. We were living in Sydney. I'm not sure how old I was then, but Mum tells me I was about three. Mum was there at the weekends, but Maria looked after me during the week, when Mum was at work. I have no memories of Mark, apart from him occasionally taking me to Wonderland or Luna Park. I can only really remember me, Mum and later on, Madi.

After the divorce I remember actually enjoying life with just the three of us. We went to New Zealand skiing (where Mum, thanks to me and his daughter, met a boyfriend), to Denver, USA, and some more really cool trips. When Mum looked after us then, she was fun and quite relaxed about what we did. I can't remember her shouting at me and Madi that much, for doing stuff wrong, but Madi and I sort of sensed she was still getting over the divorce thing, and tried to be as good as we could.

Back then, Mum would sit down and talk to us about what was okay to do and what wasn't. When Pappy came along life totally changed. When he moved in he sat down, and gave me a chart saying what jobs I had to do, and when (I more or less still have that chart now). I remember looking up to him. It had been a while since we had a man in the house, let alone one who was so involved. There was a downside though. Rules. With Pappy came rules. He obviously likes to run an organised household. Whichever child sets the table, the other one clears it. You make the mess, you tidy it up; no veggies no pudding. I could go on for ever. Mum is probably the most chilled-out person when it comes to rules, but I've gotta have someone on my side.

If Pappy tells me what to do and I don't want to do it, I argue, of course. Mum and Pappy tell me if someone does something I don't like, I should say. So I use that advice back on them. I don't usually argue with Mum, but I will argue with Pappy. With Mum, it's usually a one-way argument, where Mum just nags and I don't really listen. It's far more of a challenge to argue with Pappy, and it's so funny (apart from the bit when I lose my pocket money or get sent to my room).

He thinks that because he's a grown-up, he's more clever and is always right. I can tell when I say something which is more witty and true than what Pappy says – he usually gets so mad he sends me to my room because he can't handle it. I don't think it's usual for a parent to come and apologise. But Pappy does.

When he does apologise, it makes me feel a bit guilty and embarrassed about whatever I've done, but I'm glad he does apologise because otherwise we'd always be holding grudges against each other. And when me or Pappy's holding a grudge, you've gotta take cover, 'cos it ain't pretty! But seriously, Pappy's cool.

Mum's a totally different story. She won't apologise for anything, mainly because she's nearly always right. It's so frustrating the way she is right. It could be about wearing sun cream, what I eat, or things at school. I suppose she's right about exam results and my grades too. All my other mates get money for good grades from their relatives or parents. The most I get is a 'Well done' or, if I get 60 per cent or lower in something, an 'If you don't do better next time I'll see if I can arrange some extra tuition for you.' I was pretty peeved that I didn't get any cash rewards, but Mum and Pappy sat me down and told me: 'If you go round in life expecting money to be handed to you on a silver plate for every little good thing you do, you're not gonna get very far,' which I suppose is true… Still, I could do with some extra money.

So far as a member of this family, I feel part of a team. We have some laughs together and we go through some bad times, but we go through them as a team.

Dr Terri's thoughts…

Trisha, Peter and Billie have all given you a lot to think about. But before examining the issues they have highlighted, I'd like to draw your attention to the huge changes in popular attitudes that have occurred in our everyday lives during the last 50 years. This is particularly important because it will help you to make sense of Trisha's and Peter's comments about their own childhood experiences, and perhaps some of your own too. There is also the sharp contrast of Billie being brought up in the here and now. The saying 'children should be seen and not heard' was not unfamiliar to British culture during the last century, and framed the way many children were brought up.

Some people might think there is nothing wrong with that approach, but research has shown that a more favourable parenting style, with children growing up to respect and maintain social boundaries, is one that places children in a learning partnership with their parent. Think about how different it is for Billie, as she is certainly consulted about many of the decisions that are made for her by Trisha and Peter. I'll go on to discuss parenting styles in detail shortly. Fundamentally, however, the point I want to convey is that we do not own our children – and this is the key change in attitude. A child is an individual in their own right, and the task you take on when becoming a parent is to strike a balance between disciplining your child effectively so they learn right from wrong, and doing so in a loving, supportive way.

Power Over Children

The chapter title is significant here, in that unconditional love can often seem an unquestionable fantasy/reality in terms of both parent–child love and child–parent love. Yet this is not always the case. Many adults can find fault with certain aspects of their childhood, and, as Trisha said in her story, there are some adults who don't respect or like their parents because of childhood experiences, and I believe that is fair. Some parents abuse the power they hold over their children. I am not talking here about the extreme cases of abuse that gain national press coverage. What I am talking about is parenting in a pure or extreme authoritarian style in which the parent dictates to the child, or where the parent is always physical toward the child, by hitting and smacking in a way that breeds fear rather than respect. By 'authoritarian' I mean a black and white, non-explanatory way of interacting with a child that is always strict and without much/any love, manifesting as a 'You will do as I tell you, without question because I am your mum/dad'. In this situation a child may end up doing as they are told, but out of fear of their parent rather than respect (or learning to understand that sometimes parents know best). In a similar vein, if a parent does not take proper responsibility for their child by trying to enforce boundaries such as regular bedtimes and routines, then the child may experience difficulty managing his life within normal social environments (such as school).

Trisha talked about smacking in her account, and I am all too aware that the smacking debate continues in many societies. Some parents want to maintain the right to smack a child as a form of discipline/maintaining boundaries as a final strategy, often explaining their position by stating that a simple tap on the leg, hand or bottom is not harmful to a child. This debate is also made more difficult by parents' own past experiences, with the 'It never did me any harm' line of argument. We couldn't possibly hope to examine all the arguments on this issue within this chapter. I would encourage you, though, to think carefully about how you would define a smack, how often and when you think such an act should be used on a child, and ultimately what you think it will achieve. Research on smacking to date concludes that it has a negative outcome in the longer term, and my own position here is that there are other ways of letting a child know they have overstepped the mark (such as 'time out'). As Trisha pointed out, smacking is often used when a parent has lost control of their emotions in a situation. If you have smacked your child, think about how it makes you feel immediately afterwards.

Tips on Effective Parenting

Research suggests there is a particular style of parenting that may be the most effective way of bringing up a child to be disciplined, while at the same time happy and well-adjusted. That may sound like music to your ears if you are a parent, but it does involve a constant effort on your part, which is not easy. This is because, as I said at the outset of this chapter, parenting is really about the way *you interact* with your child on an everyday, 365-day-a-year basis. A parent is the most important role model for a child, so everything the parent does will have some effect on him. I am not suggesting that if a child grows up with problems in certain aspects of their life, it's all down to their parents, because children are also exposed to a huge number of other variables such as school, peers, television, traumatic life events and so on. What I *am* saying, though, is that if you bring up your child to learn how to solve problems effectively, cope at school, do homework, and feel good about themselves when they have done what you have asked of them, you are equipping them to become independent young adults, and that is the ultimate goal of any parent. But how do you do it?

The Doing Part

The balance you need to aim for to achieve effective parenting is to maintain a *high level of control* over your child, *and* at the same time, a *high level of affection/love*. So the message you want to convey to your child is that you love her so much that you are telling her what to do in order to help her stay safe and learn what life is all about. For example, a three-year-old throws a tantrum when you go out to the shop because he wants a toy. First, your response is to say no and tell him that he can't have a toy every time he wants one (the explanation), and then to stick to the boundary you have just set. Don't change your mind halfway through the tantrum, as you will be conveying the message 'If you keep having the tantrum then you get what you want'. This would not be a good rule for a child to learn and internalise into his developing belief system, because if that is the way he thinks he should try and secure what he wants he will have serious problems as he grows up. Imagine just how much this belief could impede his progress when he starts school. If he wanted to play all of the time, how would he behave in the classroom?

Secondly, and most importantly, you need to look at how you interact with the child when he starts having his tantrum. It's important to keep your cool (remain consistent) and not lose your temper with him (you don't want him to have negative behaviour as a role model), and remain quiet, yet attentive, while he is having the tantrum. I know just how hard this can be for parents, especially when they are out somewhere and their child is really kicking off. But if you remain calm, stick to your guns and try as hard as possible not to engage with the behaviour, then eventually the tantrum will peak (he will run out of emotional energy). Once the tantrum has run its course and blown itself out (a bit like a rainstorm) you can continue to talk to the child and engage his attention in something else. You also need to be interacting with him in a positive way (conveying the message of love), talking about something else, and praising him wherever and whenever appropriate. The message you are now conveying is that you love him and he is a good boy. Basically, you are responding to him positively and sensitively when he engages in behaviour that is desirable. If you always respond to your child in this consistent manner, over time he will learn that you do not always let him have or do everything he wants, because you love him and your decisions are usually for a good reason. Also, you are modelling pro-social behaviour to the child.

Put in plain English, the child is watching you all the time, and is both experiencing and observing that you always treat him with respect, even when you are not prepared to give in to him. This will help him as he grows older, when he is faced with situations in which he needs to contain his emotions and desires.

Now let's consider an older child example by referring to Trisha's story. Think about how she responds to Billie and Madi when they don't want to do certain jobs around the house, or spend pocket money and then want something else. There is a lot of explanation in there from Trisha as to why she thinks they should do certain things. She encourages them to think about the consequences of their behaviour. Madi is a good example. She has pocket money and spends it on the first thing she sees, only to see something better that she really wants later. Rather than giving in to her by simply buying the additional item, Trisha and Peter explain that she had the *choice* of what she wanted to buy. This is helping Madi to develop her own decision-making processes that she will take in to adulthood. If she chooses to spend her money on the first thing she sees, then she has to learn that with choice comes consequence. At the same time the way Trisha and Peter convey this message to her is pro-social and loving. And, remember, Madi may have to go over the same lesson many times before she becomes an expert at it because of her stage of emotional development. She is still a child and will not be able to get everything first time round because her desire to want things may often still outweigh her ability to stop and think first. Your child, too, may need to go over the same lesson a great many times before she becomes expert at it, so don't get frustrated – just remain consistent and be supportive.

In summary, then, you want to strive to be consistent in the way you parent/interact with your child. It's vital to set boundaries so that he can learn how he's expected to behave. When letting your child know he cannot have or do something, you should always provide an explanation, and never go back on the limit you have just set. Once you have set the boundary/limit with him, try not to get involved in any negotiation about it as this will only serve to maintain his frustration and sense of indignation (possibly in the form of a tantrum). Finally, move your child on from the frustration/tantrum as soon as possible, focusing his attention on something else that he can do. Be positive and loving at this stage. Sometimes with older children you may need to revisit a situation some time later to check that they understand why you made a particular decision. I do this a lot with my son, often having time with him before he goes to sleep when we talk about the day and what he is looking forward to tomorrow. Always try to keep the lines of communication with your child open.

Things to Avoid

The *high control-high love* parenting style sounds wonderful in theory, but in practice I know it is very difficult to achieve all of the time. Parents are not super-beings. Trisha is no exception, sometimes, according to Billie, having a quiet or manic time when she seems preoccupied and disinterested in her. However, there are ways of interacting with children that you may want to try and avoid, based on research that shows less favourable outcomes for child development in the longer term.

Firstly, try to avoid giving in to your child all or most of the time. Remember, you are responsible for your child, so he should not be expected to conduct himself in a way he chooses right from Day One without your guidance. Remember, too, that *you* make the decisions on how you raise your child. If you send him the message that it is okay for him to do what he wants and have what he wants, when he wants it, then he may find it difficult to fit in and conform to certain social rules when he gets older. Giving in can often seem the easier option to take, as enforcing boundaries can demand a high degree of engagement and self-control from the parent. Some parents literally allow their child to do what they want out of love, not wanting to say no. Other parents may be very pre-occupied with other pressures, giving the message to a child that they are not interested in the child and so the child is left to 'get on with it'. Whatever the circumstances, in cases like this it is highly likely there will be less favourable long-term consequences for the child–parent relationship. Finally, as I mentioned earlier, avoid simply being focused on enforcing boundaries, without giving explanations (communicating fairly) and expressing love and affection toward a child.

Overall, the aim of this chapter is not to make you feel that you are being told how to bring up your children, but rather to encourage you to start thinking about how you relate to your child, and to give you some tips that you may find it useful to reflect on. The one clear message that Trisha, Peter and I do want to convey is that if you are a parent, then you do have a responsibility to treat children with warmth and respect, even if you don't necessarily always feel like it!

Parenting Support

I believe from personal experience that becoming a parent is the most difficult and important job you will ever take on in your lifetime, and you have usually had little or no training for it. Trisha has pointed this out several times. If you experience difficulties with parenting at times, never feel guilty – just seek the help you need. I have done this in the past, and it has helped me tremendously with my son. If you need to ask for some advice, or simply a shoulder to cry on, there are a variety of services available.

Some of you may have friends who are more experienced parents, for example, or a family that is very supportive. It may be that you have been going through a difficult period in your life and just need to have some space to yourself, in which case letting other family members baby-sit for a night or a weekend is all you need. Or you may be someone who wants to attend a parenting programme to help you refine your skills at boundary setting. There are many national parenting support groups and parenting advice/family consultation centres that are there to support parents and children in working together. Your family GP or health visitor will be able to point you in the right direction.

Another good source of information is the social services, because there are social workers who are specifically assigned to work with children and families. They will know of any good parenting programmes that may be available to you in your area (see also Chapter 10, page 332).

Quiz

Now it's *your* turn to have some input into this chapter. First, I want you to think about your own experiences of being parented – how it was for you when you were a child. Write down who the main parental figure(s) in your life were. Then divide a page into two columns, and on the left-hand side identify and write down (one word only if you like) some of the qualities that you can recall about your parent(s), and some of the ways you remember them relating to you. For example, what kinds of messages did they convey to you and how? These can be positive and negative. Then put a star next to those words/characteristics that you think are valuable. Take a good five minutes to think about this.

Now on the right-hand side of the page, write down those characteristics and ways that you think you use as you inter-act/parent your child. For example, how do you say no to your child? If you are not yet a parent, think about the kinds of char-acteristics that you would like to have to become a parent. As a role model, what kinds of messages do you want to convey – jot them down. Again take some time on this.

Next

1) Try to identify any particular things or characteristics that you do or use, that your parent(s) used.
2) Think about the relationship you have with your child. Are there any characteristics or ways of interacting with them that you would like to pursue?
3) Identify one thing that you might like to change about the way you interact with your child.

Top Tips

1) Decide what sort of parent/s you want to be, and discuss with your partner.

2) Not each child will respond to the same methods of parenting, so work out different approaches for different kids, even though the rules may be the same.

3) Make rules and stick to them. Being consistent makes kids feel safe.

4) Hitting or smacking a child is like Russian roulette – what may not affect one child too badly could (literally) end up destroying another. Is that a game worth playing?

5) If you don't keep up with changes at work, you're likely to lose your job. If you don't keep your parenting style up-to-date with changes in your children, you're likely to lose out there too.

6) Label the child's behaviour, *not* the child (i.e. 'You're acting in a spiteful way,' *not* 'You're a spiteful child').

7) Don't be afraid to ask for (parenting) help from friends, relatives or parenting agencies if things seem to be getting out of hand.

8) Repeat after me: TVs and computers are for relaxation, social awareness, education and discussion – not convenient baby-sitters.

9) Make life real for kids – we don't need to shield them from the bad stuff or our failings as parents and likewise we should not exclude them from seeing our efforts to get things right!

Case Study

Cath (38 years old)
Mark (17 years old) – Cath's son
Julie (17 years old) – Mark's girlfriend

The story so far...

Cath's son, Mark, has been seeing his girlfriend, Julie, for some time. However, the relationship has been rather turbulent, with Cath not approving of Julie at all on the grounds that she is scruffy, undisciplined and therefore a bad influence on her son. Julie on the other hand can't understand why Cath is so unkind to her; she feels she's done nothing wrong and wants Cath to stop hassling and verbally threatening her. Julie says she can't take anymore – it's affecting her relationship with Mark and she fears it won't last if things continue as they are.

Cath has thrown Mark out of the house because of the way he has been behaving. She says he hasn't been prepared to conform to her house rules, such as curfews - she blames Julie for this. She feels Julie is a bad influence, and unless Mark dumps her she won't allow him to move back home. Mark, though, refuses to choose between his mum and his girlfriend – he wants his mum to give Julie a chance and support their relationship. He doesn't want to move back home – he just wants his mum to be there for him. He feels that his mother doesn't really love him.

At one point Mark did go home for a while, but though his mum at that time promised to let him have some personal space, she actually was again trying to tell him how to live his life. During the time that Mark was at home, he and Julie split up and he went out with another girl: devastating for Julie, but great news for Cath. Julie blames Cath for splitting them up. They are now back together and Cath feels cheated by her son; she says her door is now closed and he can't keep running back. Julie says since she and Mark got back together she finds it hard to trust him and it's affected her self-esteem and confidence.

Help!

This is a difficult situation for all three people involved here. We have a mother, quite young, who has obviously brought her son up in the best way she saw fit. She wants what is best for him. However, Cath is facing a difficult time both as a parent and as an individual woman because her son is entering adulthood. He is at a stage of life where he is now actively making decisions for himself, and that means *he chooses* who he wants as a girlfriend. In his mother's eyes this girl may not be suitable, and this is certainly not uncommon. Cath may be feeling very protective over Mark, and may genuinely believe that she knows what's best for him – namely, that Julie isn't right for him (for whatever reason).

In the past Cath has been able to make decisions on Mark's behalf because it has been part of her job as a parent. However, now that aspect of her parenting role is changing, and so it will take some time for her to adjust emotionally. This is very difficult for many mothers. It can be a real challenge to start holding back and allowing your child to make their own decisions, and indeed their own mistakes! So often we think we can save them from the mistakes that we've made, and somehow transfer our own acquired wisdom to them. This is not so, and young people must learn through their own experiences.

Mark, meanwhile, is a young person who is learning how to

become a responsible adult. It is not easy for him, and he seems torn between what he thinks he wants (a relationship with Julie) and his mother. Certainly it seems that he doesn't want to lose her respect, yet at the same time he still feels the need to assert himself in this decision. And to be given an ultimatum by one's mum is extremely difficult – it can often mean that someone will always come off worse. A suggested way forward would be to look for a compromise. For example, maybe if Mark agreed to certain conditions around the home, Cath could respect his choice of girlfriend. In any event, Cath must learn to start letting go: her son will do whatever he wants, despite what she thinks or feels.

The most difficult position to be in is Julie. She is a young woman who is disliked by Mark's mother, and she can't understand why. She is trying to maintain her relationship with Mark, who is simultaneously trying to maintain a relationship with his mother. Mark leaves home, and then returns, only to leave home again. Meanwhile he has a short relationship with another young woman, before finally returning to Julie. Julie openly acknowledges that events have affected her self-esteem, and that she feels a lack of trust in her relationship with Mark. This can destroy relationships, and is something that Mark should really seek to rebuild with Julie if they are going to stand a chance of success together.

In summary, this is a good illustration of how the parenting role changes over time, particularly at the crucial developmental stage which demands that parents begin to let their children go. Much of this chapter has been directed toward parenting younger children, as in Trisha's situation. This case has enabled us to think about the challenges we constantly face in our parenting roles; roles that change as our children grow.

Chapter Four

Is *The Brady Bunch* Just a Bunch of Lies?

Blended families and how to manage them

A Note from Dr Terri

In this chapter we'd like to continue the theme of parenting and interpersonal relationships between adults and children. This time, however, the focus will be on blended families and step-parenting – both increasingly common in today's society. Over the years, the concept of what makes a family has changed a great deal, and people can find themselves in any one of a number of possible situations: now that divorce is socially acceptable and not stigmatised, for example, more and more people with children are choosing to divorce and stay single. There are also ever-rising numbers of single parents who have never been married, and step-parents who may find themselves suddenly having to cope with a new family with no previous experience of parenting at all.

Some of the issues we'll be looking at include the way children react to divorce/separation, the stresses of being a single parent, the excitement and difficulties of becoming involved with a new partner and their children (blending), and living with the knowledge that as a step-parent you will never be the real mum/dad.

Whichever position you find yourself in – single, step-parent, or someone who is recently divorced or separated – you will find there is a fine balance between your own needs as an adult who is under considerable emotional pressure, and those of your children, who may be feeling confused, distressed – or even angry. The goal here should be to strive toward achieving this balance. You may find it useful to think about parenting styles and the various suggestions on how to interact with your children given in the previous chapter. As far as children are concerned, these rules still apply, especially when their parents separate. Let's hear Trisha's take on this subject.

Trisha

If there's one thing that's guaranteed to make me rear up on my hind legs, it's the countless women who appear on my show up to their necks with parenting problems who rush through explanations about their family circumstances with an obvious sense of irritation and frustration – as if these circumstances were completely irrelevant. What's the point in talking about this? seems to be the implication. They can't see that what they're casually telling me about their love lives might just have something to do with the fact that their kids are acting like monsters. These women sit there and reel off the names of the boyfriends they've had, then they angrily tell me how their ungrateful kids wouldn't or couldn't be nice enough to get on with these numerous blokes. So they appear on the show with their children and the current boyfriend who's been around for a few weeks. Junior is acting up, even though boyfriend is happy to be called 'Dad'. Meanwhile, this month's man is indignantly telling the audience that, even though he's been 'good enough' to take on this woman and her kids, the brats won't show him any respect. Excuse me? Where do I start? Whatever coping mechanism I have in place for that particular show has to come into play to keep my rising anger in check.

As an experiment, I recently asked my girls what they remembered about the men I dated when I was a single mum. They looked at me as if I was a nun describing her experiences as a lap dancer in a nightclub right after Evening Prayer. 'You? Boyfriends?' they laughed. Then Billie remembered John – the single dad she and his daughter had schemed at getting me together with. Her memories of the year John and I *dated* were full of the fun she had hanging out with John's gorgeous kids, and what a great bunch of friends they were to have around.

I stress the word 'dated' because it seems to be a concept on the way to extinction where a lot of single mums are concerned. As a result, their poor kids get told to call a different guy 'Dad' every other month of the year. Like I said, these women then scratch their heads, totally bewildered at their children's anger and bad behaviour. Truth is, I had lots of boyfriends while I was a single mum, as the chapter on relationships (page 23) will have told you. However, the men I chose to date had absolutely sod all to do with my kids. To put it bluntly, I don't see any correlation between choosing a potential step-parent and a pec-bound play-thing to put between my bed sheets. I made sure dating was confined to the times when the girls were with their natural father or the few evenings I could afford a baby-sitter. There were *either* children in my house *or* there was a man in my bed. Never both at the same time. Most likely I'd go to my boyfriends' houses. That's how separately I liked to keep kids and crumpet!

I don't think it was any coincidence that I went out with two guys who were passionate single dads. They were the only ones who had any contact with my girls, usually when their children were with them. John I've mentioned. The other one was Steve, and to this day the girls don't recall anything other than that he was Monty's dad and came over when young Monty came to play. Steve and I kept things strictly parent-to-parent on those occasions. Everything other than a friendly wave goodbye was left to when the two of us were kid-free.

People tell me I'm lucky not to have had any serious problems as far as Peter joining our family is concerned. Luck? It's had precious little to do with luck and a hell of a lot to do with common sense. Peter wasn't 'dad' number five or 25. Neither was John – and I went out with him for a year. The girls and I, he and his son and daughter even went on holiday together. The kids had the big adventure of all sleeping in one room and it was a case of 'Oh, what a pain! The grown-ups will have to share a room.' Again, as far as open displays of affection were concerned, when little eyes could see, both John and I decided that Not in Front of the Children was the best policy. Even then, we had discussions about what his kids were and weren't allowed to do and ditto with regards to mine. If John wasn't around and his six-year-old daughter Alice asked me if she was allowed to do something, I'd say to her, 'Now, Alice, you could trick me because I know no better, but what would your dad say if you asked him the same question?' I learned how honest kids could be given half the chance. She'd say, 'Well…he'd probably say no, but I was hoping you'd let me do it anyway.' My response was, 'Seeing as I'm just a stand-in for your dad, I'm going to have to say no as well. Sorry. But, hey, thanks for being so honest. I'll be sure to tell him how impressed I am with you.' It worked a treat. Even though permission had been denied, the chest was puffed out with pride and any disappointment was quickly forgotten.

I never even pretended to be a step-anything. I certainly didn't assume that just because I was a female, I knew better than John when it came to parenting. If asked, I'd say, 'Look, I'm just the lady who goes out with your dad. You're his children, you come way ahead of me.' They weren't just words either. When making plans, John would take my children and their feelings into account and vice versa. If John was at my place when the children's natural father rang up, he was always polite to him. 'Hey, kids, it's your dad on the phone!' he'd shout. Whenever we went on holiday together, I'd remind James (his son) and Alice to send their mother a postcard at the same time as I'd remind my girls to drop their natural father a line.

John and I dated for about a year and he was a totally lovely guy. The reality, as I've said, was it was never going to work. When we finished, I told the girls that even though we wouldn't be dating, they could write, phone or e-mail John's children whenever they liked.

As I said, there's a hell of a lot to be said for dating a hands-on, passionately involved single dad. A word of warning, however: beware of dating the 'absent dad' who either lavishes your kids with gifts and suggests they call him 'Daddy' on your second date, or is obviously uncomfortable around your children because it's like salt in the wound of missing his own children.

Of course, many of the multi-dad finding mothers who appear on my show give the excuse that if they don't hitch up with a bloke quickly, they'll be down the drain financially. They need to put food into their children's mouths, they say. These mums feel the prospect of 'taking on' a woman and her kids is so unattractive that they'll take the first guy who doesn't run a mile in the other direction.

Funny how most of them quickly forget that emotional hunger will harm their kids a hell of a lot quicker than any other type of going without. Plus, I've never yet met a kid used to seeing their mum with a different man on the go every few months – and the continual rewriting of rules at home that goes with it – who hasn't been emotionally screwed-up in some way.

Deciding to Introduce Peter

So what made me decide it was okay for the girls to get to know Peter? He wasn't even a dad, passionate or otherwise. Without being a Jack-the-Lad, in fact he was one of the most blatantly single guys I'd ever come across. I think it was because we spent our first date talking all night without a drop of alcohol involved. He immediately struck me as someone who was a great listener and was really into learning about new stuff. Also, he had been left in no doubt that given even the remotest choice about what was more important – a date with him or spending time with my kids, he didn't stand a chance! The first night he spent at my place I pointed out that he was only doing so because the children were with their natural father for that particular weekend.

Again, a lot of the women I meet on my show go on about how their kids come first, but that argument falls down in seconds. They get angry if their kids tell them to make a choice and they don't even begin to explore *why* their kids feel so anti the new guy.

Telling the Kids About Someone Special

That's exactly what I did. Even though the girls were only six and two years old, I told them over the course of about a week that I'd met someone special to me who I wanted them to meet. A boyfriend. End of story. 'What if they didn't like him?' they wanted to know. I explained that however they felt about him was okay. Just because I really liked him didn't mean they had to too. I assured them that I would never love anyone as much as I loved them and that if they really hated this guy, I'd still see him, but not when the girls were around. Hey, I'm no martyr. I was praying they would like him for the same reasons I did, but I was together enough to realise it was important to let them know that their opinion counted up front.

I decided to 'arrange' the meeting to happen on home turf, where the kids knew they ruled. I introduced Peter as my friend and then spent a hell of a lot of time just carefully watching how they all interacted. Billie was stand-offish, but then Billie always is with new people. She's like me; she tends to circle like a shark and watch with beady eyes. Madi being a toddler, was more curious. I went about doing boring house-hold stuff while observing them. I remember Peter getting into a conversation about cartoons that apparently both he and Billie liked and I didn't. To this day *The Simpsons* is hallowed ground and must-see television for Peter and the girls and I'm out of the picture when it's on the box.

The next time I 'allowed Peter the treat of being with me and the girls' (that's how I saw it in those days – not as *me* being lucky that he wanted to be with me and the kids) was at the beach. I remember being impressed by the fact that Peter asked Madi if he could play football with her, and then played it on her level. He praised her when she scored a goal, let her boss him about and didn't talk down to her. To this day, even though she was only two at the time, Madi can remember that football game 'with the nice guy who needed a haircut!' Again, I spent a lot of time just watching what was going on.

Because the girls and I were a family, I was adamant that Peter was not going to move into our house. And that's the way it stayed for the year we dated. Gradually he started sleeping over occasionally when the girls were there, but, again, there were no 'in your face' displays of affection in front of the girls and he would be up and out of bed before they got up.

Then, as in all relationships, came *the* defining moment between Peter and the girls. Madi started nursery school in Australia at the age of three and I was mortified to realise that there was no way I could be at her first school concert. I was tied into doing a mental health conference in another Australian state. The night before the concert, the girls were staying with Mark, their natural father, so I had carefully ironed a beautiful dress for Madi and sent it over on a hanger.

Mark had made it clear he wouldn't be able to go to the concert, as he'd be at work. But before I could even get upset at the fact that poor Madi would be the only kid at school who wouldn't have a parent there to see her perform for the first time, Peter volunteered. This was ludicrous because he was going to be lecturing in Perth, a five-and-a-half hour flight away on the western coast of Australia. But no, he was adamant. He would fly to

Perth, go straight to the conference venue, give his hour-long lecture, take questions, and then rush straight back to the airport and fly another five-and-a-half hours back to Sydney and race to the school in time for the concert.

If spending all day and night on a plane (bearing in mind that he has a phobia about flying) wasn't enough to prove that Peter was pretty special parent-material, his and Madi's description of what happened when he got to school were enough to melt my heart. Apparently, when he arrived, Madi was standing on stage, tearful and tired. Suddenly, she saw Peter come into the hall and her little face lit up. With a bright smile, she nudged a classmate to point out that, yes, a grown-up had come to see her after all. We still have Peter's photos of that day: Madi absolutely beaming.

I know it's not the grand gestures that make a parent, but little did I realise then, that when it comes to being a parent (and I don't think of Peter being a step-parent), that's him all over. He would 'kill' to protect his girls.

Despite appearances to the contrary, I was pretty broke while Peter and I were dating. I was determined to keep the girls in the same private school where (in Billie's case) all her friends were. She didn't need any more upheaval than that she'd gone through already. I owed the school a fortune. Because of Billie's childhood asthma and Madi's early extreme illness, I was also way behind in paying my private health insurance. I'd re-mortgaged the house, eventually downsized the car and sold off designer clothes left over from the height of my television days, but even so was staring bankruptcy in the face. Then, one day, Peter picked up the phone and told Mark that since he'd decided to marry me, he would like to be responsible for the financial upkeep of the girls. At first Mark was wary. Would this mean he would lose his rights when it came to seeing the girls? Peter assured him that the two things had nothing to do with each other. Mark would get to see the girls as much as he always had. To cut a long story short, Peter sold his house and paid the outstanding school and medical fees.

Marrying Peter

The first time Peter asked me to marry him I took a rain check. One of the reasons for doing that was to put the whole concept to the girls. Trust me, we had long talks about it and what it would mean. I assured them that Peter would continue to be, well, Peter, just that he would live with us full-time.

A few months later, Peter did his typical romantic thing and checked us into a hotel on Sydney Harbour while the girls were spending the weekend with Mark. That balmy Australian evening he suggested we go for a jog through the Botanical Gardens. Picture it: the city skyline, twinkling lights reflected in the gently lapping waters on the harbour. Peter stops me mid-jog and asks me to marry him – again. Eat your heart out, Mills and Boon! How's a girl to say no a second time? Jokes aside, by that time I'd had ample opportunity to be impressed with Peter's willingness to learn all he could from both the girls and me when it came to parenting. This was a man in search of a family if ever I saw one and I had the added bonus of him obviously being so gently, but passionately, in love with me, the mummy, the woman, the friend.

About six months later, in January 1998, we were married. We chose not to get married in Australia because we knew that thanks to my media profile, the day would be anything but private. Even though we'd planned to visit England at Christmas so my parents could meet Peter and see the girls, we decided not to get married there either. In fact we kept the fact that we were getting married secret from our families. We didn't have the money to fly people over and I guess having had my parents see me get married twice, already, I felt a bit uncomfortable about having them see me go through it all again. Neither of us wanted to go through the family politics of which relatives should and shouldn't come either, so we arranged things on the quiet (over the Internet, would you believe?) and chose Italy, where we could combine Peter's heritage with Billie's and my passion for skiing and, hopefully, be away from prying press eyes.

Our wedding day was fabulous. We got married in Cortina, and the girls were very much part of the ceremony. The mayor conducted a civil service which was all about the importance of family and included Peter pledging to be the best parent he could. The girls held the rings and talked about us *all* getting married. You only have to look at our wedding photos for proof that this is how we all felt.

It was in Italy that I suggested the girls might like to call Peter something other than by his Christian name, which had always been a bit too avant-garde for me to cope with. I remember our being on a train journey and looking through an Italian dictionary. It made sense to look for a word that described an Italian father, what with Peter's heritage and all. The girls and I settled on the European 'Papa', which quickly became 'Pappy' – and so it's been ever since.

I'm not going to pretend it's all been plain sailing with regard to the children, Peter and the ex. I learned very early on about not running down my ex-partner. I'm no angel and in the acrimonious early days of our separation and divorce, there were times when the venom just slipped out of my mouth. On these occasions I felt triumphant – for a millisecond. Then I would see the look on my little ones' faces and realise that slagging him off wouldn't do him any harm – he wasn't there to hear it, after all. It *would*, however, mean my having to deal with the distress it caused the kids.

On the other hand, I could never do what Peter's dear mother Joan once admitted to me she'd done with Peter's father. She presented Peter with such a glowing picture of this man that when I first met Peter and he told me about his dad, I found it totally unbelievable that the Pope hadn't got round to hearing about him. Seriously, Peter being bundled into a car and away from home in the middle of the night did not sit well with a portrait of a demi-god, so, I knew that however well-intentioned, someone, somewhere, was telling porkie-pies. Over the years I've known Peter, I've seen the damage that seeing an absent parent in such an unrealistic light can do. Especially when you finally track them down and they spurn you.

Without going into details here, when it comes to the girls and their natural father, I give them cold, hard facts. If I don't approve of anyone's behaviour, I explain why I believe it's wrong, but I also explain that everyone, when they reach adulthood, is free to live their life however they want.

Children make up their own minds about absent parents. If you try to 'steer' them one way or another it will only blow up in your face, if not immediately, then when they're much older and even more damage has been done. You don't want them turning around after ten years, angry that you painted a parent in a bad light for your own selfish reasons.

Billie accuses us of being hung up about her relationship with Mark. We've since learned, though, to give her some breathing space and allow her to make decisions for herself. She knows we're there for her if she wants to discuss it.

Madi, on the other hand, has a very different relationship with 'Mac', as she calls her natural father. Whereas Billie can only vaguely remember the four years Mark was around, Madi was only a few weeks old when he left and has never experienced him as anything other than an every-other-weekend-parent for a couple of years. She regards him, rather, as a 'grown-up friend' and simply doesn't have any of the issues Billie does at this stage.

I think it's important to point out that not all your children will be at the same stage of emotional development at the same time – either with the absent parent or the step-parent. Age and memories are a big factor here. I have to make sure Billie is sensitive about how she talks about Mark to Madi. I strive to make both of them know they can talk to me about their natural father in any way they want and by now they know that I won't betray their feelings or even comment on them. Both girls, however, are deeply suspicious when my parents start talking about Mark. Because of past events they worry confidences may be broken. I tell the girls that they're clever to be working out who they feel they can and can't trust on certain issues. They needn't invest everything in any one adult, *including* me.

And that's where Peter has been brilliant. He's discussed with them what it's like not having a natural father around, painful though that must be for him to do. At times, he has acted as a go-between for Billie and Mark – Peter has even offered Mark advice on parenting and relating to the girls. After all, Peter has had far more hands-on and day-to-day experience with them.

So when did this man I love change from being Peter to Pappy? Very gradually – the process is still going on some six years later. Peter and I spend a lot of time discussing parenting and our individual philosophies and how they have an impact on what we pass on to the girls.

As far as I'm concerned, Peter might not be the girls' natural father, but he's 100 per cent their dad – and not just because he has joint legal guardianship and the girls legally have his surname, as well as their father's. Peter is their dad because over the past six years he's earned his stripes to be and has gone at the girls' pace. Neither Peter nor I tried to engineer them towards seeing him as anything other than their mother's partner for quite a while. If the girls had called him anything like 'Dad' before the first year and we were married, I would have reminded them that he isn't their dad. It's still like that. At home, he's Pappy. I understand, and I'm proud that they describe him as their dad at school.

Okay, now maybe you understand why I get so cross when female guests on the show start this 'Daddy' nonsense in anything under a few years!

Peter

Before I got involved with Trisha, I didn't like kids. I had never even held a baby and I felt really awkward around children. I always had this impression that they were waiting for me to be funny or to do something silly – and that they always left disappointed. Whenever I spoke to a child it always seemed to be about ridiculously adult things: 'So, what do you think of the new motorway? Fast, isn't it!' To a four-year-old, this was absurd.

I had been in several long-term relationships and children had never been something that I or my partners had wanted. It was always spoken about as something for the future: 'We'll know when we're ready'. But we never were, and I certainly never was. When I met Trish, I knew very little about her, although I was vaguely aware that she had children. The children were simply not part of the initial attraction, in either a negative or a positive sense. I was nothing more than a new boyfriend and I never expected to meet the children, let alone become important in their lives. Neither Trisha nor I set out to create a family through our relationship. We both knew that it was an inevitable consequence if the relationship was going to flourish, but our dating was completely about us and our value to each other as lovers, as friends and as partners. The concept of being a step-parent was hiding in some dark recess at the back of my brain but as our relationship became increasingly meaningful it had to be confronted. My way of considering the prospect was consistent with the way I had thought about many important things in my life – just deal with it if it comes up, it'll be cool. Ultimately, it *was* cool but it required some serious thought and discussion as the significance of this merger between myself and Trish's family commenced. Along the way, I have changed and grown as a person; I've had to face many difficult and painful issues and, hopefully, learnt a few good lessons which I share with you below.

Making My Parenting Debut

Before I tell you about this you need to know that the life Trisha and the girls had was almost the direct opposite from mine. They were living in a conservative, affluent and suburban part of Sydney. I was living in the grunge 'inner city' in a poor, undesirable area.

The children were in a private school; I was a product of the state schooling system and despised privilege and élitism. Trish was a vegetarian and the children ate very healthy food. I was happy to eat three-day-old (un-refrigerated) Irish stew prepared by my flat-mate John. Trish drove a cool Land Rover Discovery; I drove a banger that had recently caught fire. I was also overweight, shy and a little uncomfortable in Trish's world. To put it bluntly, I was potential fodder for these cool kids with their roots firmly in the 'north side of the harbour' (called the North Shore) and the thought of meeting them filled me with terror.

Meeting the girls for the first time: My first meeting with Billie and Madi occurred one evening at Trish's home. I was waiting there when she returned with the girls. They had been told about it in advance and it was a brief and relaxed meeting that focused on our shared interest in cartoons and computer games. Billie (six at the time) was the most suspicious of me; she wore a leather jacket (I couldn't get over that!) and already had 'junior attitude'. However, we got on well and before I knew it the girls were asleep. The really important thing from that meeting is that it was low key. Trish had told them well in advance and sought their permission – after all, it was their house too. I think that all too often parents fail to adequately consider the wishes of children at this early stage and just 'spring' the new man, or, worse, the 'new dad', on them without much discussion.

Our next meeting occurred a week later. Trish phoned me and invited me to go to the beach with her and the girls. I remember being surprised that this 'formal' introduction to the children was happening so fast. However, I later learned that she had given this a great deal of thought. We had a great day at the local beach. Madi and I got on really well playing football though Billie was still a bit stand-offish. To any outside observer, we were a happy family unit. To me, it was a date with my new girl-friend *and* her children. Nevertheless, it was a great day because I felt relaxed with the girls and I had come to realise that children could actually be fun!

Once again, I think the key to our first meeting was that Trish had told the girls all about me, I was relaxed and it was just good fun being in each other's company. No one was looking beyond that. I gradually spent more and more time with the girls (with Trisha) and we had soon become friends.

Falling in love with a woman (and her kids): Our relationship was blossoming and I was spending more and more time at Trish's house and, inevitably, with Billie and Madi. It was absolutely clear to me that my relationship was with three people and, although I tried, I could never completely separate Trish from the girls.

There are several critical factors that, from my experience, determine how successful the introduction of another adult into a single parent family will be. The first is dialogue. There has to be a dialogue between the parent and the children that seeks to explain any possible change, listens to fears and concerns, and establishes what the children want or don't want. It is also really important to be truly aware of why you are introducing another adult into the family: is it for adult company, an additional parental figure, or just convenience – or perhaps all three? There are no rights or wrongs in my view but it is unforgivable not to be honest and insightful on the issue.

Secondly, timing and pace are critical. Our first real meeting (the day at the beach) was timed by Trish to be at a time when there were few pressures, when she would be with the girls anyway and doing something that they were familiar with. In any first meeting, all the convenience and comfort must be prioritised for the children – we adults can look after ourselves. The pace at which future contact unfolds should be determined through discussion and intuition. Again, there is no magic formula, but if you are in touch with your children you'll know if it's too fast.

I guess this also raises another important principle. Clearly, the relationship a mother has with her children is going to be far more important than any relationship with a new boyfriend, no matter how great he is. Unfortunately, in the excitement of romance, this is often forgotten and the children become the 'side act' in the new life. This was *never* going to happen with Trish. As I have said earlier, I was low down in the pecking order and I wasn't about to argue with that spear she was carrying!

Finally, it is essential that everyone is honest and that the adults are open to accepting change. Being introduced to children is one thing – we can all walk away from that. However, developing a relationship with a family, earning the trust of children and, ultimately, having them depend on you, is a serious commitment. It is true that I fell in love with Trisha from inside her family. My love for her as a person has never been separated from my love of her as a mother and, eventually, from my love of Billie and Madi. Too often, these bits are kept separate and the new adult loves the other adult but not necessarily the children or the total package. I am fortunate that I had to embrace all of these elements in my relationship with Trish.

Being trusted to be alone with the girls: Okay, so you are in a relationship and your new partner has children. You have met the children and are getting on really well. Everything seems fine, until you realise that your taste of parenthood has been under the watchful eye of a real parent. It's like having driving lessons – after the sixth lesson you feel you have it mastered but the first time you drive solo it's a totally new and scary experience. So it is with being introduced to parenting, and I will never forget the first time Trish left me alone with Billie and Madi. I must say that, despite my anxiety, it marked a very important milestone for us. It meant that I was considered reliable enough and/or skilled enough to be trusted with the most important thing in Trish's life – her beautiful girls. There had been a few times when I was asked to baby-sit for a few hours when Trish had to be somewhere but these occasions were rare. Now, I learnt that Trish had to go somewhere for five days (the UK, actually) and I was being asked whether I would like to stay with the girls. Naturally, I didn't hesitate to say yes but I was terrified at the thought of all that responsibility.

Before continuing, it's important to say that the normal arrangement in such circumstances would be that the girls would stay with Mark, their biological father. Billie and Madi were asked what they wanted and, much to my delight, they said they would rather stay at home with me – after all, all their stuff was there. To his credit, Mark did not make this difficult for us although it must have been really hard for him to accept.

Not just 'doing' but 'feeling': It was a really challenging few days for me. Getting up in the night for Madi (who was two at the time), getting breakfasts, getting them to school and back again, cooking dinner ('But I don't like Irish stew!'), baths, bedtime stories, washing and a full-time job on top of all that. This is, of course, no different to what thousands of other parents do, but I was, and felt like, an absolute beginner. I constantly felt that I had tasks to do. All of a sudden, the relative luxury of just hanging out with, and enjoying, the girls, was replaced with tons of work and I became pretty obsessed with 'doing' and not 'feeling'. There was one moment when I was snapped out of this.

It was three o'clock in the morning and Madi had woken up in a terrified state after one of her many nightmares. I went in to her and calmed her down (thinking, 'job done') when she asked me to stay with her because she was still scared. She pleaded with me not to leave her alone, so I curled up on her floor until she fell asleep. Lying there in the light of the night-light I asked her why she wanted me to stay and she sobbed, 'because I love you and you're nice'. From that moment onward, I worked out that parenting is not just about doing but also about feeling and that nothing in my life had rewarded me in the way those few words did.

Oh, and a plug for Billie here, without her help (and advice!) I might not have survived those five days. She was my little advisor on their routines, likes and dislikes, and their legitimate right to treats whenever requested (never was sure about that one). She was very grown-up. At last, I had met a child who I didn't have to try and talk down to – I could be myself *and* she found me funny!

Feeling a Fraud

One of the most difficult things for me was the distinction between who I thought I was and how I was perceived by the outside world. I am sure that this is the case for many step-parents and, perhaps, it is even worse for stepmothers.

When people assume the children are yours: After the glorious success of my five-day parenting survival camp I felt like a fully-fledged, accredited step-parent. I had a unique and genuine bond with the girls that involved mutual respect, love and a developing recognition of me as a father figure. I believed that I had a legitimacy to my role in this family that extended beyond my relationship with Trish. At least, that's how it seemed to me.

At this stage the girls were calling me Peter. That was fine because lots of children call their fathers by their first name (just look at *The Simpsons*). I desperately wanted my perceived legitimacy as a parent to be recognised, or at least, blindly accepted, by the outside world. Unfortunately, the reality was very different and the following is a typical conversation that occurred every-where we went together, from hardware stores to school, from bus stops to toy shops…

PUBLIC: *My, aren't they pretty girls!*
ME (*trying to move away because I know what's coming*):
                    Yes…they're gorgeous aren't they.
PUBLIC: *Where do they get their lovely curly hair from?*
ME: *Their mother.*
PUBLIC: *Ah…but they have your eyes/nose/mouth.*
ME: *Ah…yes, I guess…*
PUBLIC: *Yes…definitely, a resemblance.*
ME (*by now I am feeling like a liar; girls are looking
                    confused*): *Actually, I'm their stepfather.*
PUBLIC: *Oh, I see, you're not their real father? I'm sorry…*
PUBLIC/ME:*(awkward pause) Anyway, best get moving…*

This exchange, which still happens, though to a far lesser extent, used to leave me feeling totally deflated. You think…no matter how much I love, influence, care for, commit to these children, I will *never* be their real dad. The real dad can provide the raw materials, have limited contact, make a new life, move on, etc… but will *always* be their 'real dad'. Part of being a step-parent is accepting that this is inevitable and just the way it is, and that you can only do the best you can. Having said this, it doesn't get much easier to deal with it.

From Peter to Pappy: One of the very specific things that I did as a new person in the children's life was to let them decide what to call me. Trish supported this and, in her own way, encouraged the children to make sense of my role through their naming of me. At first I was 'Peter', but then gradually it became clear to all of us that there needed to be a word that described a closer family connection. The girls agreed that they would call me 'Papa' (which later became 'Pappy') and still reserve 'Dad' for Mark. Again, this was great from my point of view but there is something special about being 'Dad'. I know there are many men who enter families as step-dads and insist on being called 'Dad'. I can understand why they do this, because it establishes their role and status within the family but means little in reality. The term 'Dad' is a special one; it has to be earned and the children, in my view, have to bestow it.

Since we have been in the UK the children have had much less contact with Mark. It's interesting that in private (at school, or with other kids), the girls call me 'Dad' but to my face it's still Pappy. That's fine but there is a gradual and consistent change that reflects my place in their life. I am, in every sense of the word, their father – I love them, care for them, share with them, and shape them, I will be there for them no matter what happens between Trish and myself. After six years, my relationship with the girls has its own independent value and I am happy to be a big part of their lives and to be called whatever makes sense to them. One day, I hope it will be 'Dad'.

Dealing With the 'Other Dad'

One of the hardest parts of becoming a stepfather has been dealing sensitively with the 'other dad', the 'real dad', Mark. Inevitably, you enter a family with its own recollections, its own stories and its own way of understanding loss or change. Far too often, that understanding is based on vilification and/or distrust of one party. In this case, Trish had forced Mark to leave her and the girls a little over two years earlier, after their marriage broke down.

As a newcomer, it's really important not to get too involved in family beliefs or recollections. There are always two sides to every story, as Trish acknowledges elsewhere in this book, and I wasn't going to try and take sides. The reality was that if I was going to be an effective parent I needed to have a relationship with Mark that was productive and congenial. I have always tried to achieve this and, for his part, I think Mark has as well. I think I have learned some useful lessons along the way that have helped keep this relationship viable.

Acknowledgement and respect: I was taken from my father when I was six (see page 12) and have always wished he had played a greater part in my life. So it should come as no surprise that, in my role as parent, I have always stressed the importance of the children maintaining contact with Mark. This has been very difficult for me at times, particularly when it's clear that the situation is causing a certain amount of distress for one or more of the children.

My mother had many reasons, and ample opportunity, to run my father down in my eyes but she never did. I'm glad she didn't, because it made me value that part of me which is attributable to him. I think Trish could run down Mark in front of the girls, but she never does, and I respect her greatly for it.

Trish and I have always agreed that we would encourage and facilitate contact between the girls and Mark whenever *they* want it. The problem with many contact arrangements is that they reflect the wishes of the adult and not the child. Our position is to help Billie have her wishes respected, to try and facilitate communication between our daughter and Mark and to be there to build bridges. Despite all the ups and downs, all the resentment I may feel in trying to secure a role for the 'other dad', we try very hard to recognise Mark's role and to encourage respect for him in all our dealings.

Jealousy: Jealousy, I suspect, plays a big role in the relationship between many stepfathers and 'real dads'. I used to get very jealous when, after a week of getting up early, cooking breakfasts, dealing with tantrums, sickness and whatever, the children would return for a weekend with Mark besotted because it seemed that they had been showered with gifts, stayed up late and done whatever they wanted. I thought…'This guy has it all – the single life, the love of two beautiful children, none of the work and never has to feel awkward in the hardware queue!' Every time they came back I felt I had to rebuild my relationship with the girls.

I suspect that if Mark were writing this he might describe many of the same feelings because I *do* think it's a mutual experience. What I didn't know, however, was how resilient my relationship with the girls actually was and how much of the time they spent talking about me when they were with him – which must have really been hard for him. As the years have passed, I feel much less jealousy as my role, and his, have become consolidated. There are things Mark has that I will never have, like seeing the children when they were newly born, being there for their first steps and (in Billie's case) words and, never having to justify being 'the dad'. I can't change any of this, but I *can* remind myself that I have seen the girls grow up, and that to a large extent they are a reflection of me. People are constantly saying that Madi is just like me… Do people still say that to Mark…I wonder?

Competition and influence: Another common feature of the relationship between 'dads' is the desire to compete for the affection and loyalty of their children. I never felt I was guilty of this, largely because I never had a sense of being entitled to it. However, a common scenario involves both dads playing one-up-manship in terms of the car they drive, where they take the children on a day out, how much they spend on them and what they let them get away with. This has got to be very bad for the children because they learn to manipulate this competition and ultimately get rewarded for it. I think Mark and I have handled this side of it very well...but influence, now that's another matter.

I am a strong believer that parents have a great responsibility to influence the development of character in their children and Trish and I take our role very seriously in terms of helping the girls to determine right from wrong, develop a social conscience *and* learn to deal with life's knock-backs.

Contact with the 'other dad' is a good thing but it requires communication and teamwork to ensure that children are not being given conflicting messages or that one approach to parenting is not being undermined by another. Over the years, Mark and I (and Trish) have spoken about this many times. It has often been heated, with many other issues being drawn in along the way. However, to some extent we have collectively been successful because the dialogue is still present, there is an acceptance of changing roles and, above all, it is the children who determine the direction and parameters of the relationships.

Billie

In my year at school, quite a few of my friends' parents have split up, so it's no big deal. Some of the boys find it quite hard living with their mums and only seeing their dads on weekends because they feel they need another man around and it feels strange living with just females. Actually, hardly any of my girl mates have parents who have split up. I think I'm the only person out of my friends who has a step-parent.

I don't really think of Pappy as a step-parent because he's really the only dad I can remember having. I don't think it makes a difference that I'm not genetically his, because he's been around from when I was little and he doesn't act any differently from the way a real dad would. When my friends are talking about their dads, I'll talk about Pappy just like them. I think any girl my age could never really just live with her dad and see her mum occasionally. The things I talk about with my mum, I could never talk about them just with my dad. So I can understand how the boys at school living just with their mums must feel.

It's hard to write this 'cos I never really think about Pappy being anything but Pappy until I've been asked to sit down and put my feelings into words!

If Pappy had come along and I just didn't like him, boy, would I have made everyone's life a misery! Even if Mum and Pappy had a baby, I know it wouldn't get treated any differently from us, unless it was a boy. Mum doesn't have any boys in her family and Pappy has always wanted a little boy.

If I was meeting someone for the first time and they asked who my father was, I wouldn't have to think about it. I'd say Pappy.

Dr Terri's thoughts…

These accounts certainly make for interesting reading. Peter's dialogue provides a fascinating insight into what it can be like as an individual with no experience of children, who then meets up and falls in love with someone who already has two.

Parental Separation

First, let's consider the impact of parental separation on children. I think this is important before we go any further because there are many conflicting opinions on separation, divorce and single parenting in society today, and we don't want to get bogged down into moral debate.

Separation is about change: When parents separate, it signifies great emotional and practical changes for children in everything from their daily home life and routines to the way they will spend their time in future at weekends. There are different points of view on separation/divorce and single parenting, which range from advocating that adults should stay together, no matter what, for the sake of the children, to religious beliefs about the sanctity of marriage. But, whichever side of the debate you're on, research suggests that in terms of healthy psychological development, it is the *quality* of a child's family life that matters, rather than the family *structure* itself. That's the good news. Divorce and single parenting is not in itself detrimental to children – it is more important that a child grows up in a happy, balanced environment where parents are not always verbally or physically in confrontation with one another. Rather, it seems to be the poverty that often accompanies divorce, in terms of loss of income to the parent who is left with the main childcaring responsibilities, and the emotional difficulties that this parent can subsequently experience, that can sometimes affect the quality of parenting post-divorce.

There is also the matter of how the two separated parents resolve conflict with regard to their children, concerning issues such as access visits, financial matters such as maintenance payments, the way the children are educated, etc. This may be problematic, given that the two people involved may have often found it difficult to talk through problems, and that one of the reasons why they decided to separate may have been precisely *because* of their lack of communication and understanding and inability to resolve conflict. In cases like this, decision-making over the children could be particularly difficult for adults involved in the early stages of separation.

The early stages: Trisha faced immense emotional trauma as a result of the separation from her ex-husband, which we shall be hearing more about in Chapter 7 (page 200) when she talks of her depression. It must have been very distressing for Billie and Madi at times, particularly at first. However, children can be very resilient, and if some *consistency* and *structure* is maintained in their life at this time of change, it can help them to adapt. Despite her trauma, Trisha's love and commitment toward her girls never wavered, and she was able to redress the balance in terms of her own emotional needs by getting the help she needed in the immediate aftermath of the separation. This is not easy for everyone, however, and many people can become preoccupied with their own emotional needs for a very long time, making it more difficult for them to parent their children effectively. Research indicates that it's often women who bear the brunt in terms of the demands placed on their emotional resources. When parents separate, it's usually the mother who takes on the main role of child-rearing. In addition to the emotional trauma she may have suffered, she will often be faced with having to adjust to a significant loss of income, which may mean she has to go out to work, or work longer hours than before. This may be compounded by the fact that she will also take over all responsibilities that she may have previously been shared with a partner/husband. Women (and men) who have to go through this will be left emotionally depleted for a while, and so are less able to focus on their children and maintain the correct boundaries at a time when the children need the extra security.

The effect of all this on children can be significant. Again, research indicates that where both parents remain involved in their children's lives, the outcome for the children is likely to be more favourable in the long term (particularly, it seems, for boys with behavioural problems). This is a very simplistic interpretation of the research, however, and some situations between parents can become so acrimonious that a cooling-off period may be required. Ultimately, though, parents should always put the needs of their children first, and not use them to score points against each other. This might sound absolutely fine in theory, but in practice it's not always that easy when emotions are running high.

The overall message, then, is that the outcomes for children are better in cases where parents have maintained 'reasonable' contact. So what are we saying here? Well, just that if you do find yourself getting divorced, the sooner you can get a regular routine of access established, the better it will be in terms of helping your child(ren) to adjust.

Children and their reactions: When parents separate, children can sometimes react with difficult behaviour. It can take time for them to adjust to the new situation they find themselves in – all at a time when Mum and Dad are fairly emotional themselves. Just think about it from a child's perspective. Your whole life is constructed through your parents, whom you believe know everything and are always in control, so if they then begin to waver a little, and you see that they're stressed out, it can be quite frightening. This sense of unease is compounded by the fact that as a child you are not yet fully able to understand and control all your own emotional processes. It can all seem like too much.

Thus, as (a) parent(s), it is important that you strive to maintain your child's sense of security by reassuring them and maintaining a routine that is as near to normal as possible. The message to be conveyed is that life goes on and it *will* be okay. You also need to allow them time to talk about how they feel when they want to. This will vary with individual children, and some may not want to talk for quite a while. You should also be prepared for a number of other reactions, such as anger, distress, or attention-seeking behaviour that is challenging and difficult for you to deal with. But, remember, children do not have the emotional repertoire that you do – hence their alternative outlets for venting unhappiness.

In addition to the message that everything will be okay, you should never hide the reality of the situation from your children. It's much better that you support them in coming to terms with the fact that Mum and Dad are never going to get back together, even if this is what they really want to hear. Also, when parents separate children sometimes blame themselves, thinking that if they had been better children their parents would not have split up. Again, it's important to keep reassuring them that this is not the case. They may not internalise this message for a long time. Just be supportive and persistent. It can take years.

One final note on the 'separating' aspect of family life. Be careful not to place too much of a burden on your children by confiding in them about your own emotional difficulties. Many adults do this with expressions such as 'I am so depressed now that I am alone', or 'I am so unhappy that I can't see any future', or 'It's all Daddy's/Mummy's fault'. This may cause your child to adopt a parental role over *you* in order to try and rescue you emotionally. Children in this situation may become a good listening ear, and appear to be coping really well. The parent may even think they are being very responsible and mature about things. But this will be to the children's own emotional detriment, and later on, when they reach adulthood, they may experience emotional difficulties themselves as a result, such as not being able to say no at work, or to keep personal boundaries and take care of themselves. This is because their own emotional needs ceased to be met during this crucial developmental stage due to concentrating on their parents' needs at a time when they have not yet fully developed their own emotional repertoire. Thus, even though they may appear okay on the outside, the internal picture may be completely different. Trisha pointed this out when she commented that people who said 'My daughter is my best friend' made her feel very uneasy. Your daughter or son should always be just that – your child, whom you support and love, not your mate whom you confide in.

To summarise, then, when children experience separation/ divorce, it can be an upsetting and emotionally challenging time. As a parent, be open and supportive at all times, conveying the message that although it hurts, things will be okay again one day. Children do not have the same emotional resources as we adults, so don't expect miracles. Instead, maintain the firm and loving parenting style described in Chapter 3 (page 55). This basically means being understanding when they display difficult behaviour, and trying to get them to talk about why they are upset, while also letting them know that they still have to keep within the normal limits they have always been used to. Don't be angry if they are difficult for a while – they need time to adjust to change. Finally, help them to come to terms with the new reality they are faced with, in a calm and loving way.

Now – On To Blending

When it comes to blending, or getting it together with someone else you have met, all the issues just mentioned should feature heavily in helping your children to move forward and cope with the new people coming in to their lives. It goes without saying that once you are separated/divorced and begin the dating game again, it should be different this time round because of the children. Trisha's account of her own situation is very passionate – she firmly believed that her children always came first in any equation. She doesn't suggest for one minute that divorced people should not indulge in the dating game, but, rather, that they should most definitely protect their children from a barrage of different men/women while Mummy or Daddy is trying to find a new partner. This I fully endorse, because if we are in the business of putting children first, then we want to maintain a stable, consistent environment. Environment also means people. Thus, you may find yourself dating more than one person before you find that special person whom you might just want to consider introducing to your children.

Blending means forming real relationships with children at their own pace: As you've seen from Trisha's and Peter's accounts, when you decide to get together with a new partner, the children have got to be involved. For Trisha and Peter, Peter's meeting the two girls was a good, albeit nerve-racking process. They took things one step at a time. When Trisha thought the girls were ready for the introduction, it was planned carefully *with* Peter and it was a success. Peter was involved with the girls even before he met them. Also, the girls were informed about Peter too. However, quite often the first meeting and early stages of new relationships with children can be difficult. The child(ren) may reject the new adult by being angry, upset or unhappy. They may feel the new person is going to try and take the place of their absent parent (absent, as in on a daily basis), or, worse still, take their mum or dad's affection away from them (a mixture of fear and jealousy).

My advice is stick with it, and talk to the child. Be patient, never forcing him to feel he has to like the new person. Also, convey to him that his feelings are being taken into account. This could be expressed as, say, 'I understand that you may not be feeling very happy at the moment', or 'What is it about X that makes you feel unhappy?' By doing this you can pin down the specifics and have something to start working with. That way you will have a dialogue with your child. Remember, it is the interaction between you and your child that counts, and the more you can both talk to each other, the more understanding will come over time. Finally, the potential new partner must be working just as hard at forming a new relationship with your child to ultimately make your relationship work. If they can't show a commitment to this, then they are neglecting a fundamental part of you.

The good news: As we know from Trisha's and Peters' experience, many thousands of families blend together successfully. (This is backed up not just by research, but by my own personal experience.) Even in the greatest success stories, however, there will be ongoing issues to face, such as the one that Peter pointed out about not being the 'real dad'. His account of step-parenting was very personal and thought-provoking and doesn't require any further explanation from me. Overall, though, he knows that he, Trisha and the girls are leading a fulfilled and happy family life. And the girls know they have two special people whom they can always count on: Mummy and Pappy.

Quiz

Trisha's and Peter's experience of blending as a family with Billie and Madi was very well planned and they still have many challenges that lie ahead as the girls grow and mature. Now, take some time to think about your own experience. It may be that you are someone who is forming a newly-blended family, or that you yourself have originally come from a blended family.

1) Identify your own current position. Are you:

- A natural parent?
- A step-parent?
- An adult with experience of a step-parent?
- A single person with no children?
- In a relationship with someone who has children?

2) Write down ten factors that you believe you can bring to a relationship in your identified role (e.g. trustworthiness, determination, sense of perspective).

3) Put a number from one to 10 against the factors you have identified in order of importance. For example, put number one against the most important factor, right through to a number 10 next to the least important factor.

4) For *each* of your 10 factors think of one positive and one negative aspect of how that factor might impact on a relationship you are having with a significant other and possibly their child(ren).

Once you have taken time to complete this exercise, is there anything that you have thought about that surprises you? Can you do anything in your current position to enhance some of those most important factors that you have identified?

Top Tips

1) Keep the children informed about any new relationship that might impact upon them.

2) Consult the children over the timing and place for any introduction to the new adult.

3) Don't assume that you know how to be a dad just because you are a man or (for women) assume a mothering role just because you're married to the children's father. Actually seek advice from the children about which role they would feel more comfortable with: parent's partner, friend, step-parent etc.

4) Don't forget to *feel* amidst all the doing of parenthood.

5) It's okay to be scared by your new role and responsibilities.

6) Don't be afraid to ask the kids what to do or how to do it.

7) Don't disrespect the parent who has left, and accept that you may never be 'real dad' or 'another mummy'.

8) Let the kids work out what to call you.

9) Don't allow anyone else to remotely parent for you – if you are there every day you have earned the right.

10) Take it slow – *The Brady Bunch* wasn't built in a day!

Case Study

The Cast
Sally (40 years old)
Trevor (58 years old)
Justine (17 years old)

The story so far...

This case study is about the issues that can arise when children are approaching young adulthood, in a blended family with younger siblings around them as well. The background is that Trevor, 58 years old, and Sally, 40 years old, have been married for about 13 years. Sally has been married before, having had two children with her previous husband, who died when the children were fairly young. Then, some time later, she met and married Trevor who has taken on Sally's first two children (Justine, now 17 years old, and John who is now 20 years of age), having been their stepfather since they were five and eight years of age. He and Sally also had two more children together, who are now nine and ten years of age respectively.

In the earlier days of married life family time was generally very good. Trevor can recall how he really loved being a father figure to Justine and Mark, and how he and Justine got on really well. However, now that Justine is 17 years old, both Trevor, Sally and Justine are experiencing some difficulties. Justine now believes that she is grown up, can make her own decisions and choices, and can look after herself. However, she seems to be getting into muddy water. She decided to pack her college course in, has tried a few different jobs that have not amounted to anything, and is now dating an older, married man. She says that all her parents do is pick on her, and her stepfather in particular just argues and finds fault with everything that she does. Sally is going out of her mind with worry and finding it really difficult to cope with the constant arguments between Trevor and Justine. Also, Sally is genuinely concerned for her daughter's safety and overall wellbeing, because Justine stays out all night, and is seeing this older married man.

Trevor says that he believes Justine is at risk of getting hurt, and has come home before having been beaten up. He is genuinely worried about her, but she will just not listen to anything that he has to say. She tells him to **** off in front of her younger brother and sister, which he finds particularly difficult to deal with. Sally feels torn between her husband and her daughter and doesn't know what to do.

Help!

This is a particularly difficult time for this family. Sally and Trevor are trying to manage a difficult teenager, whilst at the same time juggling two younger children as well. The history would indicate that this family used to feel relatively satisfied with the status quo, and that John (now 20) is getting on okay. However, there seems to be a sticking point for Justine, who says she is currently feeling picked on by everyone around her, including college. She says that she can not understand at all why her mum and step-dad are being the way they are because she is doing nothing wrong. What she is doing here is externalising all blame for the current situation on to her stepfather, and to a much lesser extent, her mum, and failing to take into consideration the potential consequences of her own actions. She is also not acknowledging any aspect of the caring element from her parents. It is fairly normal to clash with parents over sensitive issues, and despite what Justine might want to think to make herself feel blameless, to expect them not to react to her throwing college in, seeing a married man and leaving all the jobs she has tried is somewhat naïve – even for a self-confessed mature 17-year-old!

The way forward could be for Trevor and Sally to get some outside help for the benefit of all the family, including the younger children who are probably finding it very tense at home at the current time. It would help Justine to get some independent counselling to help her explore why she is feeling picked on by everybody (the reason she gave up school, college and her jobs). Secondly, Trevor and Sally need to work together as a team, rather than feel split by the situation (Sally isn't helping this at all). Trevor has been a stable figure in Justine's life for some years, and he and Sally could be supported to respond to and try out some more potentially effective ways of negotiating a way forward with Justine. Family therapy could be one possibility, and can be a wonderfully effective way of helping families who are struggling to be able to find a way forward in a fair and balanced way. The bottom line is that Justine probably needs a lot of support, although she is not feeling very receptive to anything at the moment. Although she is saying that she is now old enough to make her own decisions, she also needs to consider that part of being 'grown up' means that one also has to consider the needs of others around you – such as your younger brother and sister, mum and step-dad. Finally, if Justine feels that she can choose what she wants to do, she also has to be prepared to accept the consequences that come with it. I wonder whether she has thought about some of the very real potential negative consequences that her parents are trying to save her from?

Chapter Five

The Power Game: Bullies and How to Detect Them

A Note from Dr Terri

In this chapter we're going to explore the subject of bullying, a topic we definitely need to be aware of as parents. Trisha herself has had first-hand experience of bullying. She is also a parent with two children at school, and has to maintain a good awareness of bullying and the way it can affect children, so that she can be vigilant as a parent. Both she and Peter had to deal with a situation that affected one of the girls, which they will share with you shortly. I hope that their experience will bolster any sense of despondency you may feel if you yourself are facing such an issue, and give some useful tips on how to move forward, rather than simply feeling powerless.

Bullying in itself is a harsh term to use, and there are several definitions of what it means. We are not going to favour any particular one here, but rather, will focus on the types of behaviour and underlying principles to look out for, so that you can start thinking about the wider implications that bullying can have. Also, what most people forget is that bullying doesn't just occur in school settings, but is very common in the workplace, home environment and anywhere else you care to think about. It is a serious problem, and don't underestimate where it might occur.

Generally speaking, bullying can be viewed as any form of physical and/or emotional/psychological negative action(s) directed toward an individual. Fundamentally, there will be some kind of *abuse of power* (even if this is only perceived) by the perpetrator against the intended target victim. This can be directly applied by the perpetrator, and/or by others who are manipulated by the perpetrator. It's worth saying here that the threat of an act, causing fear, even if it is never actually carried out, is also construed as negative and detrimental. In serious cases, such acts and abuses against the target victim are prolonged and persistent, which can be extremely wearing on the victim's ability to remain resilient against such negative attention. Finally, there are instances where a negative act may occur only once, but its severity and impact is so intense that it constitutes bullying because of the deeply lasting impact it has on the victim, as well as fear of further action.

So what does all this actually mean? Put simply, bullying is about the way people (children included) socially interact in an abusive way. Sometimes one individual can feel the need to assert themselves over another, for a variety of reasons, and will abuse their position in any way they believe gains them some social, emotional/psychological advantage (and possibly status) at the victim's expense. In terms of school bullying, some years ago it was believed that the bully was socially ill-equipped and unable to make any kind of mark with their peers, which is why they resorted to bullying. However, recent research has altered this perception, and it has been found that the bully can often be a very intelligent individual, possessing great social skills and qualities that enable them to be more adept at manipulating those around them to their advantage. This is particularly true for the business world, where highly successful people have been found to possess more ruthless qualities than their colleagues (some would even go as far as to say they were psychopathic, but that's a subject for another debate). Let's now hear about Trisha's experience of being bullied, and her own perspective of the subject from a parent's point of view.

Trisha

This chapter has a flash title, but a simple meaning: in a word, it's about bullies. I have this saying that I often trot out on the show: 'We all do what we think we need to do to survive.' I believe that's what being a bully is all about.

When the word 'bully' comes up, people immediately think of the school playground type. Having experienced a few months of pure hell at the hands of this kind of bully as a child when I first returned from East Africa – and, without even realising it, being very affected by it, right up until the point where my breakdown and subsequent therapy forced me to face it – I don't take school-yard bullying lightly. But if I were to just concentrate on that in this chapter, I'd be doing a great disservice to reality. Because bullying occurs in families, at work and in relationships. And it's not always about raised fists and voices. In fact, some of the most damaging types of bullying are carried out with saccharine-sweet smiles and the ability to make others feel guilty. That sort of bullying can shred self-esteem even more than the 'upfront' aggro type because it causes the bullied person to doubt themselves in a far more subtle way. If you're on the wrong end of this bullying, you end up thinking you're very flawed because you feel so vile about yourself when this other person is being so sweet/helpless/trusting/needy. At least when faced with a bunch of fives, it's easier to work out who's right and who's wrong, even though you're the victim. Don't get me wrong. I don't condone or write off bruises as being nothing, but they heal a hell of a lot more quickly than psychological damage does.

It amuses me the way we kid ourselves that the Big Bad Bullies are 'out there'. *Them*. Sorry, but they're *us* too. Someone has to create the bullies. Be honest here. Your kids may well run home to you with tales of being bullied or you may stumble across the awful realisation that it's happening and feel the seething anger of the wronged. But how many kids run home with tales that *they* are the bullies? And even if you *did* stumble across information that made it look as if your child was a bully, would you be equally as indignant? If you've ever been in the situation where you have (rightly) gone to a school head to discuss your child being bullied, the chances are that, if the teacher is honest, they'll admit how hard it is to bring the subject up with the parents of the offending child. Why? Because, by extension, the parents of such children are seen as bullies themselves. Easy answer? You can shriek on all you like about how the school system is flawed and the teachers don't know what they're on about, but the reality is that those teachers are usually right. All kids have a go at asserting their dominance over someone they see as a weaker member of the species, but those who adopt bullying as a way of life are very often victims of bullying at home, either overt or covert. If you feel powerless, put down or brutalised in the very environment you expect will make you feel otherwise, it's obvious that you're going to try to find another forum to exert your power.

So how do you spot if there's a bully in your family? (We'll deal with school later, because, quite frankly that's the easiest part of this subject and less damaging than if you have bullying in what should be a family's sanctuary.)

Terri will give you an exercise at the end of this chapter to help you think about what sort of behaviour threatens or makes you feel uncomfortable in some way, but let me give you an idea of the kind of behaviour I'm talking about here:

1) **Constantly putting down** your partner or one of your children – even as a 'joke': 'Hey, fatty!' 'Oi butt-face!' 'Look at the state of your mother!' 'Your father's a waste of space', and so on. Either done at home or in public.

2) **Picking on the child** you feel has 'let you down' or 'failed you'. (Chances are that that child reminds you of yourself when you were younger and you don't want them 'making the same mistakes as you did'.)

3) **Hitting** your kids or partner.

4) **Emotional blackmail** – manipulating others, however 'sweetly', to make them feel guilty.

5) **Always dictating** to a partner or child how they should dress/wear make-up, etc and belittling them should they 'disobey'.

6) **Checking on a partner** by constantly phoning them, text

messaging them, etc. The message here is that they're not to be trusted. See what that does for their self-esteem, not to mention your sowing the seeds of your relationship's destruction.

7) **Refusing to discuss** anything and using the 'silent treatment'. It's like school kids 'sending someone to Coventry'. In other words, emotionally excluding someone. Being deliberately isolated is damaging.

8) **Deliberately teasing** and tempting a partner with sex but denying them at crunch time.

9) **Treating a partner like a child-slave**. Talking down to them and demanding that they see to your every need without your giving anything emotional in return. Take note: 'I bring in the money, so you owe me my every whim.' This is deciding to have a relationship with someone for just about every reason – except love.

10) **Taking total control** of the purse-strings (except where one partner is a chronic gambler/addict, etc.).

11) **Racial bullying** in a mixed heritage family, where children have different hair types or skin colours.

12) **Constant jokes** or teasing about a family member's disability, e.g. an inability to read or write, a physical impediment, or their being taller or shorter than the rest of the family.

13) **Always criticising** and concentrating on someone's perceived faults. Or constant referrals to past mistakes. Very destructive and controlling.

I think that gives you an idea. Note: violence was only one of the behaviours listed as bullying in my list.

My Own History

As the only 'coloured' (that was what we were called then) four-year-old in a school in Brentwood, Essex in 1961, I got teased about my skin, but I certainly wouldn't call it bullying. Besides, the teasing only ever cropped up after we'd had Enid Blyton stories read to us. The stories in question featured 'bad, wicked gollies' and I still don't like the horrid things. Many people called the black community's reaction to those Enid Blyton tales an over-reaction, but I can totally understand it. No teacher back then ever had what it took to explain that not everything black with 'woolly' hair was evil. They all seemed to think that a four-year-old branded thus by the rest of the class should just shrug it off.

I was lucky when it came to racism, in that my (white) father did a brilliant job of going through different kinds of possible scenarios with me and coming up with a range of responses I could give – all of them hilarious and designed to turn would-be-aggression into laughter. I remember one ridiculous story he told me about God calling people together and having the best ones stand at the front. Then He'd have an upset stomach (we're talking the squits, here). The results were, well, explosive, and, naturally, the closer to God you were, the browner you got! Oh, sure, cue indignant letters about blasphemy and totally ignore how the hell you deal with a little kid's anguish in a country where the only other 'coloured' people were half your family. My sisters had to endure being labelled 'pakis' because of their skin colour and, at one time or another, people doubted out loud that we four sisters really were related to one another, because of our range of skin and hair colours.

At expatriate school in East Africa, no one racial type dominated, but, kids being what they were, they still found other ways of excluding each other. I never really thought I fitted in, but then looking back, I was an awkward kid who seemed to be too mature to mix with the little ones and too childish to hang out with the big ones. I was long, thin and very unattractive and I don't care what you say, not being blessed on the looks side can end up making you marginalised. But, hey, it did me the world of good. I developed a sense of humour to endear me to my peers.

But it was on our family's return to England when I was about nine years old that I was really introduced to all-out pack bullying. Again, my sister and I were the only black children in the little Norfolk village school. As we walked there every day we used to hear chants of 'Blackie, blackie' before we could even see the building. Forget about 'good mornings' to greet us. We would walk through those school gates straight into a sea of insults and fists, and there were so many children involved that it seemed as if the whole school was against us. I will never forget, however, this girl called Julie. She was originally from London, as Cockney as they come. Long blonde hair scraped back in a ponytail. 'I'll fight wiv yer! I'll fight wiv yer!' she used to say, day in, day out. I could never understand why a blonde-haired, blue-eyed beauty would want to join two weedy black girls to get involved in a fight that was unwinnable. But she did. And she taught me an invaluable lesson – that of sticking your neck out and lending any strengths you have to the underdog, because, boy, could Julie fight. I've often wondered what happened to her because I'd love to thank her personally for helping to plant those seeds of moralistic strength within me.

The teachers were not only no help, but my overwhelming impression was that they saw my sister and I as an unwelcome disruption. After one occasion when some boys had tripped me up in the school canteen and my tray had clattered to the floor, a dinner lady barked at me to stop snivelling and pick it up, adding that I wasn't getting any more food. When I ran out crying, a teacher followed me, sat me down on a step and, albeit as gently as he could, explained that I had to expect this sort of thing as I wasn't 'from here' and had to deal with the fact that others wouldn't therefore accept me. I think the term 'toughen up' was used. In hindsight, I can see that, thanks to East Africa's then strict expatriate schooling system, my sister and I were educationally way ahead of our UK peer groups and were probably additionally disliked as 'know-it-alls'.

Why didn't we tell our parents the whole story about what was going on? I can only go from a kid's eye viewpoint, but at the time my father was looking for permanent work back in the UK, and after the wildness, freedom and adventure of East Africa, it seemed to us kids that there was already a lot of tension in our small rented cottage and we didn't want to make things worse.

Not that I knew it back then, but neither of my parents had really experienced racism as kids. Mum had spent her childhood in her native Dominica, in the West Indies, where the vast majority of people were the same colour as her, and Dad (who was white anyway) was brought up in snow-white 1940s Norfolk! Apparently, Mum did come up to the school and ask me to point out the bullies, but I don't recall it – probably because unfortunately it had little or no lasting effect.

Although we were only in that school a few months, that feeling of what a therapist friend of mine later labelled as 'racial guilt' stuck with me for many years. I never saw myself in terms of colour until then. Like all kids, I thought my family was how it was: one brown mummy, one pink daddy and sisters of every hue in between. But, again, I think, this was a good thing. I still refuse to see myself as a 'black sister'. Despite outward appearances, I am the sum total of a mixed heritage and I'm a Trisha, so there! No amount of bullying, racial or otherwise, will force me to see myself as others want me to be.

Mind you, when I got to my posh grammar school in Surrey, there was a time when I turned into a bully too. I only got (racially) teased once because, as a rarity in the school, I was rather in the category of one-off exotica to be cherished and promoted. Dad taught me a useful way of dealing with these insults on one occasion. He told me to ask 'Why?' at least three times. (Look behind the name-calling for the cause, was his theory.) Aha! I'd 'nicked' this girl's best friend and the way she dealt with her anger was to go for my Achilles' heel – my colour. Once I realised that, I included her in our second-year games and we ended up fairly friendly.

But I could be a right little bitch too. Three of us girls used to go around together and when one of the other two decided she wanted me exclusively as her buddy, she would tease the other girl mercilessly. Actually, I didn't join in the nasty remarks about how fat her legs were, but to my shame I'd go along with it, by laughing at the bullying girl's comments. I didn't comfort the hurt girl. In other words, I bullied by default and in so doing, encouraged it. But – and I believe this is crucial – like most kids, I didn't see this as bullying. It was far simpler than that. I wanted to align myself to someone who I saw as hipper and smarter and didn't have the guts to go up and admit it to this poor girl. Instead I just let the bullying girl do it for me. I say this because I do believe that we've generally ended up misusing and there-fore devaluing the term 'bullying'. Peter has a great theory about this, in which he compares it to the way animals behave when a strange-looking member of the species wants to join the herd. There'll be more about this later (see page 158) but, basically, that's what humans do. And don't give me any of that 'It didn't happen in my day' tosh. Sure it did – it's just that the label 'bully' wasn't so readily applied. We need to be very clear with our children about the difference between teasing that's normal (even if not nice) and bullying. We also need to use practical examples of our children's behaviour to make them realise the difference.

Coping With Bullying as a Parent

I remember Billie at school in Australia getting together with a bunch of girls and deciding not to speak to one of their gang. In their mind, they had perfectly justifiable reasons not to and it would 'teach her a lesson'. It was only when the poor girl's mother came and asked me what was going on between Billie and her daughter when they'd been such good and close friends that I worked out what was going on. When I pointed out to Billie that, as far as I was concerned, what she was doing was 'bullying', she was absolutely shocked and appalled. I simply asked her to imagine herself in this girl's place and that did the trick. What I'm saying is that adults think children can automatically differentiate between justice, teasing and bullying and I don't believe that's always the case. Children often think that if they're not thumping seven shades of you-know-what out of a kid, then whatever they're doing is okay.

When we came to England, Billie – an outsider with a 'funny' accent – was bullied. She was seen as a threat by one girl in particular. My initial reaction? To march up to the school and put an end to this 'monster' once and for all. This was my baby, all teary-eyed and with badly bruised knuckles from fighting! But Peter got me to see reason with his 'herd theory' and together we sat down with Billie and talked it through. She didn't want us to tell the headmaster, or anyone else for that matter. The shame element, I think. But Peter and I *did* go and see the headmaster and he knew who the bully was before we even got to her name. It helped that I had made a point of canvassing the parents of the other girls Billie told me this vixen was also bullying, and they backed me up and gave me some insight as to what might be happening in this kid's private life.

It ended with both the 'Bully' and Billie being given a teacher to whom they could talk in times of trouble. It fortified Billie and, for a while, calmed the 'Bully', although she didn't really change 100% till she got to high school and became a little fish in a big pond instead of the other way round. But even Billie ended up feeling sorry for her and this in itself made her stronger. More recently, little Madi has gone through feelings of being picked on to the point of having to be taken to the doctor with physical symptoms of stress. I thoroughly recommend getting involved with other parents right from the word go, although it has to be said that the parents of many tormentors would probably be pretty fierce if approached on that score – which is exactly why their kids are displaying the sort of behaviour they are. In the end, by talking to other mums and supporting Madi, everyone seems to have worked out a class 'pecking order' and things are okay. In general, being pally with parents is a way of dealing with little skirmishes before they become big ones.

There's a downside to this, however – namely, you must be prepared to listen and take action if your child is the one who is labelled a trouble-maker. In other words, don't go into the 'my kid's an angel' act. Similarly, don't take it as read that they are the devil of the piece. Coming on heavy with your child in a bullying 'If you're bullying, I'll have you' style won't get you very far. It's better to start by asking what's happening between them and X, and how they are feeling about school in general. If you're going through a divorce, there's a lot of arguing in the family, or someone close has died, you need to be aware that these are vulnerable times for your child, whether as bully or victim. If you send your child to school unclean, or even smelly, know that you are setting them up to be bullied by kids who come anywhere near them or have to sit next to them. It's how children voice disgust at enforced discomfort. At the same time, by not keeping a child clean, you're sending out a clear message that he or she is not worth it. (Mum always says soap and water washes away everything except sin!)

At Work: The hotbed of bullying, however, is the workplace. If you find dealing with a bullied child wearying and frustrating, trying to have a relationship with a partner who is being bullied while earning a wage is every bit as bad. In the male-dominated macho production offices and newsrooms of 1980s Australian television, you could have shut the whole shop down by simply banning the use of four-letter words and venom. I remember right up to the night before Billie was born, I'd stay standing in meetings because taking a chair would have meant being loudly and viciously labelled a 'wuss' by a few of the more scary male staff. I coped as I always have – with sarcasm and humour; things I'd learned from being put through the wringer years ago.

Although I could cope with the constant banter, I saw many people start to go under. Poor managers usually bully because they don't have the skills to motivate and lead their staff in any other way. I've run seminars and workshops on workplace culture and stress, and bullying comes up time and time again. And it's not always the stereotypically brash male manager who's the culprit either. I once had a female boss who did a pretty good job of intimidating people with mood swings. One minute she was ranging from hysterics and tears to sudden displays of shouting; the next she was everybody's buddy. It nearly drove *me* mad and I saw it demolish her subordinates. A typical scenario was that she would, say, sing an employee's praises until it seemed they'd become too popular. The minute that started happening she'd begin to run them down. The next thing I'd hear was that 'unfortunately she'd had to let them go'. It wasn't until a number of them pointed out the blindingly obvious to me that I realised what was happening: to become too popular was to dance with the devil. In the end I summoned up the courage to take it up with her superiors who'd started noticing all was not well among the staff anyway and she was moved sideways and, eventuallly, out.

But the fact remains that this woman 'controlled' the staff by using a mixture of unpredictability and threats, and in my book that's a covert type of bullying. It has to be said here, that it was her reputation of being brilliant in her job that was allowed to take precedence over the fact she basically had poor people-skills and was floundering. So companies can't walk away scot-free either – after all, they are responsible for employing people who can manage people correctly, as well as having specific skills.

At Home: So let's get on to the homefront. Is there any bullying in our household? Well, I know he doesn't mean it, but I have occasionally felt on the receiving end of a few bullying tactics from Peter. I think it's because he's so intellectual and has always had jobs where he's in charge of loads of people. I'm rubbish at time-keeping (my little bit of rebellion) and can be disorganised in Peter's eyes. He can get a bit stroppy if he feels I'm not being time-efficient, and starts what I call 'barking' at me – you know, all knitted eyebrows and short terse commands. Early on in our relationship, I took loud and vocal exception to this and we ended up having a serious chat about it. To his credit, Peter owned up that he could be a bit of a bully sometimes and we agreed that if he started doing it, I could, in a voice as calm as possible, point it out to him and refer to the conversation we had had. And that's what happens. It's then that he realises what he may have slipped into, and it immediately heads off any friction.

We can all become bullying in our behaviour, but when it becomes someone's major way of getting their needs met, that's when it starts to be truly destructive. As I said, if only we debated the damage bullying in the *home* does with the same intensity and passion we focus upon bullying at *school*. Because doing the former would be the fastest way to stamp out the latter. Intimidating households (either physically or emotionally or through emotional neglect) create all those little monsters who make other kids' lives hell at school.

Peter

My first recollection of being bullied was as an eight-year-old living in Australia. I used to practise cricket for hours in the local cricket nets, often by myself (don't ask how). There was a gang of local kids who never liked me – I was a little overweight, I didn't have a dad around and lived next to a cemetery. That was enough to mark me out as different and a suitable subject for their intimidation. They were always calling me names and letting down the tyres on my bike. I would just accept it and they just kept doing it.

One day, I was in the cricket net with my batting gloves and pads on. In those days, batting gloves were covered in short rubber spikes. These boys turned up and started to let my tyres down. But this time, for some reason, I went over to them and told them to stop. I can't tell you why I did this, other than that I was so sick of lugging my bike back home and having to tell my mum that they'd done it to me again. As I approached, one of the kids went to punch me and I got in first. The thing is, I had my batting gloves on, so what was usually a pretty feeble right cross turned into a lethal blow that made his mouth and nose bleed. When I saw his blood I felt empowered, his friends felt scared and he started to cry. I told him he would have to carry my bike to the nearest petrol station and pump my tyres up. As I marched through the council estate with the local thug carrying my bike and bleeding from my blow, I felt like a liberating army. He pumped up my tyres and promised never to do it again. We actually became friends after that and I realised that he wasn't a bad kid – just bored, like me. My reputation flourished and I was never bullied again. I owe it all to the fact that I made a stand – and, of course, those spiky batting gloves!

Bullying is also about cultural context – something I have learnt since moving to England from Australia. Before we start punishing the identified bully we need to make sure that we really understand the personal and cultural factors that may be underpinning their behaviour. Take my experience, for example. In Australia, I was considered a softly spoken, gentle(ish) and un-blokey sort of guy – certainly not intimidating or aggressive. Never in my entire career had anyone suggested that I was a bully. Yet within a few months of working in England I had a reputation for being a bully. Why? Firstly, it was because, as an Australian, I was naturally direct and opinionated when it came to my views. We Australians say what we think, we debate assertively and we don't care too much about offending people if our view is different from theirs – and we are like this so that we can get things done. All of a sudden I found my confidence and directness being interpreted as aggression and intimidation and, believe it or not, was actually reprimanded by my employers for being too confident. In my eyes I certainly wasn't a bully.

Here's another (delicious) example. I used to play a fair bit of cricket in Australia and, as with most of the sport we play, it was played aggressively and to win. Recently, I was playing competitive cricket here in the UK, with a local team, and I was bowling (pretty well, I might add). I felt that there was a real chance of a catch close to the batsmen so I asked the captain to put a fielder very near to the bat. The captain refused on the grounds that (a) no one was willing to do it and (b) someone might get hurt. I couldn't believe this and let the captain know how I felt. The team perceived me negatively as being aggressive and willing to win at all costs, whereas in Australia this would have been the minimum expected of me as a bowler playing competitive cricket. I'm sure the Australian cricket team are considered to be bullies by most English cricket fans and players, whereas the reality is that they are competitive and aggressive in a culturally appropriate way.

So, the first thing to say about bullying is that we need to understand a little bit about its context and, just as importantly, why it is happening. What is the purpose of the bullying? You will nearly always find that bullies feel threatened, want to dominate or take revenge, or lack the skills to negotiate and discover compromise.

In Billie's case it was crystal-clear to me that the bullying she was getting was about the threat she posed to the established pecking order. This is where the 'herd theory' comes in...bullying is a natural response to a change or threat where established power and/or relationships are challenged. A herd of wild animals will often establish an identified leader, usually the strongest, who will make decisions for the herd such as where to set territorial boundaries, and determining social roles and pecking order. The herd likes this because they know what to do and when – it simplifies an otherwise complex social structure. In a way the class system is like this, too, but that's another story... don't get me started!

The other thing a herd will do is to abandon and/or damage the weakest members. Once again, this is done because that weakness is a threat to the group, making it vulnerable in some way. In animals, this vulnerability is often associated with the group becoming slower and more open to attack, or feeling that its ability to work as a team or to reproduce is in some way threatened. In humans, the weaker members are most likely to be identified as those who are the most different – it might be the fattest, shortest, smartest or slowest. In each case the presence of this member might represent a risk to the group's status as a whole in some way. The bully seeks to counter this by distancing the group from the weaker person, or by establishing control over the person through physical intimidation.

When Billie arrived at her new school she was immediately identified as a threat because she possessed some of the qualities that had been used to determine the existing leader of the herd. She was good at sport, attractive, confident and articulate. In the animal world, when a new member seeks to join a herd they are assessed for their abilities to assume leadership – if they are a threat then there will be a fight to establish the order, which is then usually respected. In humans, it's not quite so simple because we may also aspire to lead the group, even if we lose the fight, so we continue to challenge for the top job – animals generally don't do this once the pecking order is established.

In Billie's case she was immediately targeted. She found herself socially excluded and devalued by a rather elaborate process of propaganda. These are the basic tools of the bully – attacks that are focused on you physically, on your emotions and on your social standing within the group. It was clear to me that Billie was having this conflict because she wasn't willing to just accept her place in the group – she wanted to be top dog! I understood why she was being bullied and I also knew that Billie was probably resilient enough to see it through physically. However, it was the process of social exclusion that was most damaging to her and the most difficult thing for her to counter, as she simply didn't have any other relationships at the school to draw on for support. In some respects, many groups within our society are subject to the same forces because of skin colour, illness, ethnicity – such people are subject to bullying on a grand scale while society seeks to preserve the status quo. The same things happen in the workplace. Bullying, or harassment, is one of the top causes of work-related stress in the UK.

The answer is to try and make the playing field a little more equal by balancing the bully's natural advantage with outside intervention that will enable the bullied person to make a legitimate challenge and/or resolve the conflict in other ways. We did this by getting the school to intervene a little so that Billie could tackle the bully on a more equal footing, which she eventually did. In the workplace, we try and even things up by ensuring that there are systems in place to protect people's rights, to assist in promoting equal opportunities, to build skills that help people to be assertive rather than aggressive and to enable potential to be fulfilled without being perceived as a threat.

In all the various situations where bullying can arise, there are several key principles for dealing with it effectively:

1) **Understand the bullying** – what is it's purpose? Are you sure it *is* bullying? Ask yourself what is the nature of the threat that *you* represent?
2) **Tell someone** – you can't deal with bullies by yourself.
3) **Accept outside intervention** to level the playing field.
4) **Find support** in others with similar experience.
5) **Be prepared to fight** (physically and/or psychologically) if you aspire to leading the group or want to make a stand.

One final thing to say about bullies is that in some cases they are just malevolent people who are motivated simply by the pain or discomfort they cause to others. I am of the firm view that most bullies are motivated by far more complex factors related to fear but there is no escaping the fact that, when all is said and done, there are some cruel and evil people in the world and it's best to just avoid them if you can.

Billie

(*Trisha's note:* Billie doesn't seem to want to discuss what happened when she first arrived at her UK prep school from Australia, but has this to say about when she was involved in what we [parents] classed as bullying in her Australian school.)

When I was about seven or eight, four other girls asked me to be part of a group called The Spice Kids (pretty sad, I know, but it was quite cool at the time!). The five of us used to go around with each other at break times singing Spice Girls' songs. This one girl who had been my best mate since pre-school wasn't invited to be in our group. When she asked if she could be in the group with us, the other girls told her there was no room for another member. I decided that instead of sticking with my best mate, I would hang out with this 'cooler' crowd. I kind of like forgot about her, although I didn't mean to.

Apparently this girl started getting upset at home, and told her mum, who, in turn, told my mum. One day, Mum sat me down and told me that by leaving my best friend out all the time, I was actually involved in what she called bullying. When Mum used that word, I was shocked! I didn't know what to do. I didn't want to be bullying my best mate, but I wanted to hang out with my 'cooler' friends as well. Then one morning on the way to school, Mum told me that there was this newer and better all girl-band, which was better than The Spice Girls. They were called All Saints. So I let the other Spice Kids know that they were out of date, and left them to start hanging out with my best friend again. The whole experience taught me that sometimes we don't realise that what we're doing is basically a type of bullying, until someone points it out to us.

Mind you, sometimes I know what I'm up to. Especially when it comes to my younger sister. Sometimes I wind her up because seeing her reaction is funny. (Don't think I'm evil because I know all big brothers and sisters do this!) Of course, when Mum gets involved, I get into trouble.

Dr Terri's thoughts…

There are several important points to make from Trisha, Peter and Billie's accounts of bullying. First of all, the reasons why someone is bullying are likely to be fairly complicated, and this individual may actually require some support to help them change the way they are behaving. Also, context and cultural variations in behaviour and mannerisms (sometimes misinterpreted) can play a part. Furthermore, we *all* have the potential to bully others, whether it be as children in a school environment or the workplace. Maybe you have been on the receiving end of bullying in the past but haven't given so much thought to how you have treated others (intentionally or otherwise) in the past.

Finally, if you are experiencing bullying, or you believe that your child is at school, *always* get outside help. This will enable you to cope in the first instance, and resolve the situation in the second instance. Schools should have a bullying policy that will set out exactly what steps they will take if you even suspect that your child is being subjected to bullying behaviour. It should be included as part of any school prospectus, so ask to see it. Go and speak to the head teacher and make your concerns known straight away, and request their support for your child and yourself. If a school cannot resolve the problem, then they should request some external help from local child agency services to further advise them, and support your child and the perpetrator. The best way to resolve such situations is to work together with the school, which, in turn, should be doing everything in its power to ensure that your child is safe.

Quiz

I want you to think of a time when you have felt really uncomfortable and threatened by someone, whether physically, emotionally or both. Once you can identify this, take some time to think about the following:

Ask Yourself
- Who was it?
- What was the situation, time and place?
- What types of words and actions were being used against you?
- Were you physically afraid?
- Were you emotionally afraid?
- What sort of sensations were going through your body (e.g. racing heartbeat, feeling physically sick)?
- What kinds of thoughts were you having at the time?
- How did you respond at the time?
- For how long did this incident affect you, and in what ways?

- From your answers can you identify what you would consider to be some bullying/intimidating actions and behaviour?
- Can you now identify what it feels like to feel bullied, threatened, forced or intimidated? Have you felt like this since the above incident?
- Thirdly, and this is a tough question to ask yourself and give a considered answer, do you think that you have ever made someone else feel like this (intentionally or otherwise)?

Top Tips

1) Put your own house in order first! Identify the power-hungry in your family and deal with them. Those who feel bullied at home will either become bullies or the bullied at school.

2) Right from the first day at school, get involved and keep involved with as many other parents as possible and discuss bullying with them before it even comes up.

3) This is controversial, but I firmly believe that 99 per cent of teachers are *not* equipped to deal with bullying. (Would you be if you'd gone from school to college and then back to school?) Encourage your school to forge ties with police youth groups or charities like Parentline, MIND, etc who can educate and support teachers when it comes to bullying.

4) Have you tried to understand the context or meaning of the bullying behaviour? Make sure you do.

5) Be clear from the start where your current place is in the pecking order. If you want to change that then expect some fireworks.

6) Don't ever accept less than the standards you set for yourself in terms of someone else's behaviour and language.

7) Don't *ever* accept violence or the many excuses that are likely to accompany it as justification.

Case Study

The Cast

Ann (37 years old)

Tim (29 years old) – her husband

Susan (15 years old) – her daughter

The story so far...

Ann and Tim have been together for five years and are now married. Ann has three children from her previous marriage: Susan is the eldest. When Ann met Tim she asked her children if they were happy for her to continue seeing him. All three children accepted Tim, call him Dad, and seem to have settled down well as a family. However, during the last 18 months the family situation has really suffered. They moved to another area, and Susan began to be bullied at her new school. The first problems started with a change in her behaviour. She became moody, difficult and would not go to school. She argued a lot with her younger brother and sister. Then Ann and Tim noticed that she was losing weight and unhappy with her clothes. As things progressed Susan would not go to school at all, and was actually making herself sick to the extent that she was taken to hospital after vomiting blood. At first Ann thought that Susan might have met a boy and was having under-age sex. Eventually it came out that Susan was being bullied at school, and was afraid to go.

Ann went to the school to complain. She was told that Susan could be just as bad as those bullying her, and Ann felt very confused and angry with Susan. Tim's response was to be more authoritarian with Susan by grounding her if she would not attend school. This caused even more arguments and tension within the home, and made life for the whole family very difficult. Tim eventually warned Susan that if she did not go to school he would throw her out of the house. Ann again approached the school, but received no support. The situation has reached the point where Ann is desperate to support her daughter but doesn't know which way to turn because she knows how extremely distressed Susan is by the bullying, but Tim believes they should be tougher with her, and Susan is feeling completely alone and isolated. She is also very worried that her education has suffered, and would do anything to either go back to her old school, which she knows isn't possible, or have a home tutor. The school has written to Ann and warned her that if Susan does not start attending school, Ann is in danger of being prosecuted as a parent. This really frightened Susan and she did try to go, but stopped again when the bullying persisted. So the situation remains, with Tim feeling that Susan should stop taking things out on the family because it is affecting his and Ann's relationship.

Help!

This is a really sad situation. Susan is a young person who has had to move school. Prior to that time everything was okay for her generally, and family life was fine too. She has always been fully accepting of her stepfather. Susan's behaviour and mood changed significantly (Tim believes that she is now a hypochondriac) which is a clear sign that things are not right for this girl. Not only is she making herself physically sick and not eating (potential for an eating disorder), but she is refusing to attend school, which she has never done in the past. Parents are advised to look out for signs such as when a child or teenager keeps complaining of general illness to avoid school. In this case, Susan is actually making herself ill, which is a clear sign of distress. So nobody is disputing that Susan isn't suffering emotionally for some reason.

Response

First, it is important to say that when a young person experiences problems it always puts a strain on the family. The age of the child doesn't matter: for example, if your child is having problems managing him or herself in primary school and is exhibiting behavioural problems, it can be stressful for you as a parent to know how to cope effectively with it. In addition, as a parent you want to support your child, and help them to overcome the problem, which sometimes is not straightforward. The situation here is not unusual in that if one of their children is unhappy, it's bound to affect the whole family. Susan should be praised for actually telling her parents that she is being bullied, because children and young people often feel too distressed and helpless to actually tell anyone.

I would suggest to Tim that he and Ann should be there to support Susan. Ann has been to the school a couple of times and has not received a satisfactory response, so they should both go together to see the school's policy regarding bullying, and request that an attendance officer visit their home. The school has a duty to investigate the situation thoroughly, and put measures in place to help Susan attend school. The bottom line is that some schools are much better at this than others, and it's the parents' responsibility to really push a school that may be dragging its feet. The school should be listening to parents who are expressing genuine concern for their child's welfare. In this case Susan's distress is being manifested in her weight loss. She needs professional support at this time, and either the school can request specialist child/young person services to become involved, or Ann and Tim could go to their GP and ask for Susan to be referred for specialist support. This would also help the family, as many services of this nature also work with the family when a young person is distressed. Tim has found it really difficult to cope with the situation, which is completely understandable. He phoned his mother to ask her if he is doing the right thing by being strict with Susan, as that is how he was brought up – with strict boundaries. However, I would say that merely grounding Susan or threatening to throw her out of the house is not going to resolve her problems, and may ultimately increase her anxiety and make matters worse. Rather than seeing a situation in black and white terms, that is, that she has to go to school or else, it is more productive to ask the question: 'how can we tackle the situation in school, despite there being minimal response, so that Susan can feel that she can return?' The answer to this is that it may take a few months, and much work on both Susan's and the family's part, with some professional guidance.

A *final note*

I am fully aware that in the past there was a stigma attached to services – that if you needed help or support, then there must be something wrong with you. Let me assure you that people who are professionally trained to help you deal with difficult times in your child's development are there for your benefit. There are some very dedicated people who will help you in any way they can, even if it's just to listen. But these services can also help you to change practical situations, as well as relieve emotional distress, so don't be proud – you'd be amazed at how many people and families need a little helping hand once in a while. Think about it: is it better to struggle on and bury your head in the sand so that problems become worse, or to get support and actually resolve the issue?

Chapter Six

Fighting Fair: Conflicts and Discipline

A Note from Dr Terri

Much of this book has been about the way people relate to one another, so it seems reasonable to now turn our attention to the fact that we don't always get along. There are many times when we don't see eye to eye, and may even argue and disagree. This is all perfectly natural. It can be a healthy way of progressing in any given relationship, and a way of growing and evolving together, particularly within a family dynamic. Problems can arise, however, when disagreements become long-standing quarrels that do not get resolved, giving way, instead, to resentment and unhappiness. Also, depending on your own natural disposition, you may be someone who, when angry, blows up and can become very scary, and this can cause problems too. So we now want to turn your attention to thinking about turning conflict into something positive, by trying out some conflict resolution techniques, as advocated by Trisha.

Trisha

I'm trying to think back to how I came across the whole idea of conflict resolution. I'm pretty sure it was in the days when I was an Australian television reporter and I was drawn to the subject like a moth to a flame. Easy to understand why. When growing up, I slowly but surely became petrified of conflict. When my father lost his temper, he terrified me and, like so many teenagers, I tried to act as if I didn't care by using the foulest language or simply running away. I remember us kids leaning out of the bedroom window, screaming at one of my sisters to run while Dad chased her through the allotments. We all knew what would happen if/when he caught her. I've described elsewhere how what my parents call smacking affected us all.

Conflict with my mother, although it sometimes involved 'smacking' (on a far lesser scale than that meted out by my father) was more likely to come in the form of angry words. Sure, it was distressing, but at least with my mother you could tell when a verbal storm was brewing. There were definite flashpoints of conflict. One was the weekend washing-up. As soon as lunch was finished, I'd disappear upstairs to brush my teeth. My parents saw this as my way of doing anything to get out of doing set chores.

But actually, at the time, I didn't know why I felt this sudden and desperate urge to start teeth-brushing. Nor did I understand why I had to touch each tap four times, hot first. Then I had to brush my teeth four times in each direction, rinse my mouth out four times and then touch the taps again. Then I had to wash my hands four times and pat them on a towel first one way, then another. I now know I was going through the early stages of using rituals to control anxiety. It was probably a mild form of obsessive compulsive disorder, which stress can still trigger in me today. Back then, if I didn't do my rituals I genuinely believed I would die. Again, I know this was a form of expressing an inner panic. Ironically, one of the triggers for it all was the conflict I knew would start brewing towards the end of the meal. No way was I going to explain what was going on inside me to my parents. I couldn't explain it to myself and, besides, it would only have been seen as some bizarre excuse given to get me out of doing the washing or drying up. Even after leaving home, at the first signs of conflict, I would either run and hide (i.e. lock myself in the loo, deep breathing and trying not to cry or panic) or I would just stand rooted to the spot, willing myself not to throw up.

One of my sisters loses her temper like my father, and I used to find there was no way I could have an argument with her without bursting into tears almost straight away. My frustration at the seemingly inexplicable way I responded to conflict with her made me cry even harder, so it simply became easier to avoid her. So I started getting into tight spots, because, basically, I went out of my way to avoid conflict. I'd say yes to everyone and everything, rather than have to argue my point. Don't get me wrong, I was a great debater, providing the subject had absolutely nothing to do with me or my personal life. But when it came to things that directly affected me, assertiveness was almost impossible, and, believe it or not, I still have an ongoing struggle with being assertive.

The flip side of the way I approached conflict was that once I'd allowed people to walk all over me for a certain amount of time, I'd lose my temper in such an aggressive, incoherent and destructive way that it literally put my life at risk. I know that sounds melodramatic, but it's true. I've only truly lost my temper twice in my life and both times I've landed up in hospital. I turn my anger in on myself because I get so enraged that I've yet again allowed myself to fall into situations I've seen coming a mile off but have been too scared to confront and avoid. And, surprise, surprise, I just happen to end up reporting on Sydney's Conflict Resolution Network and the work of one inspiring lady called Helena Cornelius. No coincidence at all! I ended up doing their course in Conflict Resolution (1989-1990) and it had a huge impact on me.

Conflict Resolution on the Trisha Show

When I tell people that conflict resolution is at the core of my show, they often get confused because they think it should be all about avoiding conflict in the first place. But conflict is natural. In fact, it's often essential. It only becomes destructive when people get into the habit of using it as an everyday form of communication with the rest of the world. We've all met people who seem to be permanently angry with just about everyone, and I don't think you'd use the word 'happy' to describe them. Besides, their anger usually ends up making them physically sick. There's medical proof that these kind of people are more likely to suffer from high blood pressure and heart problems. On the other hand, there are people who spend a hell of a lot of energy suppressing their anger, and they end up every bit as sick as our overtly angry friends.

It's important to realise that sometimes we feel there's some-thing to gain by hanging on to conflict – a sense of righteous indignation and superiority, maybe. Feeling hurt and being angry go hand in hand and sulking, or being spiteful or resentful are ways of hanging on to anger. I've had guests on the show who have refused to speak to a family member for years, or held grudges for generations. They're deeply unhappy about it, but being right seems to have become more important to them than being happy. I guess that when it comes to seeing a way out of conflict, that's the precise question you have to ask yourself: What's more important? Being right, or being happy? And forget labels like 'goodies' and 'baddies'. Look closely and *honestly* at any arguments you've ever had, and, go on, admit it. Did you add fuel to the flames? If you really believe you've never done anything to fan the fire of conflict, then you have a serious prob-lem of self-delusion.

A willingness to work things out is at the heart of conflict reso-lution. You know the saying: 'Where there's a will, there's a way.' Letting go of conflict frees you. Okay, you may have to go through a period of intense conflict for a while, thanks to your ego scream-ing for you to be the righteous one whatever the outcome, but ultimately, once that conflict has lifted, illnesses can disappear, stress diminish and you will literally lose that pain in the neck.

One important flashpoint for conflict can be the matter of disciplining children. What's the real purpose behind discipline and rules? Let's face it, we're trying to educate our kids in the way of the world; to have a moral approach to things, to not have a screaming row filled with swearwords and tears every time they do something we feel is out of order. So how do you *not* fan the flames of conflict? I learned there are certain ways of talking to people that are guaranteed to annoy them.

In her book, *Everyone Can Win: How to Resolve Conflict* (Simon & Schuster, 1989) Helena Cornelius gives some examples of real communication-killers. These include:

- *threatening*
- *overpowering*
- *criticising*
- *name-calling*
- *interrogating*
- *refusing to address the issue and constantly changing the subject*
- *poo-pooing someone's feelings or problems*
- *giving untimely advice*
- *using logic to put down someone's emotions*

No one confides in someone who uses these kinds of conversational tools. The result is usually anger, either simmering or overt. So what kind of language can you use to get people to meet you halfway rather than feel they have to fight you?

I'm a big believer in using 'I' statements. Basically, you start with a non-emotive, factual statement of what's happened. Next, you state how this has affected you, and, finally, what you would like to see happen as a result.

Example: A family member starts swearing at you – something you absolutely hate. You start shouting at them. The tension goes up and the chances are they'll deliberately swear even more because it becomes impossible for them to back down.

Here's an alternative way of dealing with this. After the stream of expletives, you say, 'When you start swearing at me like that *(statement of fact)* I feel scared and helpless' *(emotion)* OR 'I shut down' *(effect)* OR 'I want to walk out' *(an impulse you resist).* 'I'd like it if we could talk without the need to use that sort of language' *(a statement of what you'd prefer to happen).*

As I said, that's the direction in which I steer guests on the show. First, we 'map' the conflict – jargon for 'Okay everyone, let's all put our emotional cards on the table.' Everyone then gets to tell their story and be heard, however angry they may feel. I'm looking not just for the areas where the most conflict lies, but also where two opposing parties actually agree on things, even though they may not realise it. The important thing I want guests on the show to realise is that in order for a situation to change, *they* have to change in some way. There are always areas in which people can compromise, it's just that sometimes we get so entrenched into being sure that we're right, that we become blind to everything but the other person's wrongs. We forget that people aren't all bad or all good. Most of us are made up of shades of grey!

I bet you've looked at the 'I' statement example I've given and are thinking 'Oh, sure. I can't see that ever happening.' But it's worth trying if conflict is becoming a way of life for you and you're heartily sick of it.

Going back to the show, there are several reasons why, even though, yes, all this takes place in a television studio in front of an audience, nine out of ten times people resolve their conflict there. Obviously a major reason is that they feel they have no place left to go and they desperately want to sort things out. But in front of cameras? Well, here's where the next important factors come into play. I call these things 'time, territory and a clear and uninterrupted opportunity to talk'.

Before every show, I go round and talk to all the very nervous guests who are about to appear and I tell them that I realise their arguments probably follow a similar trigger and pattern. The person they are in conflict with may filter out much of what is said because for them, the time for all this to come up is wrong: it's the kids' tea-time, their favourite soap is about to start on television, they're just about to go shopping and might miss the bus, there's a car alarm going off outside – whatever. But you can be sure their minds will take the opportunity to focus on these other distractions rather than deal with the painful subject ahead.

Then there's the question of territory, or where the conflict takes place, because this can make one person feel very powerful and the other feel that they don't have a right to voice their feelings. You have a row in *his* house, or in *his* shed. You take issue with her in *her* front room, *her* car, or in *her* family's place. Without a word being mentioned, the power-balance is all off. If things come to a head in someone else's place or somewhere public, forget any idea of ever getting a true picture of how anyone feels. They'll just go for the jugular to shut you up as quickly as possible and to hell with sorting things out. Then there are all those interruptions – the phone, the children, the postman, the dog barking – all things that'll take at least one person's mind off what is being said. Chances are they'll feel they've heard it all a million times before anyway, so they'll start shutting down the minute they hear the words they know will lead to an altercation.

So what I'm saying is this: where and when you choose to bring up a touchy subject is very important. Deciding to bring up the fact that your child has scribbled on the wall yet again while your're in the middle of cooking the family tea, just before their favourite television show, while the dog's barking and the phone's ringing, is a dead cert for conflict. The thing is, the conflict won't be about the scribbles on the wall so much as about your frustration that your child's attention is everywhere, except where you want it to be – on you and your message. Likewise, choosing to discuss the issue of your other half not pulling his weight five minutes before the Man. United v. Arsenal game will guarantee a vicious verbal assault about 30 seconds before kick-off!

No, conditions can't always be perfect, but you can set up discussion times like this: 'Okay, when would be a good time for us to sit down and discuss such and such?' What's so wrong with making appointments to talk about things that are bugging you if the alternative is an argument that is heightened because of time restrictions? Similarly, if a touchy subject comes up when, say, you're visiting your parents, how about simply saying, 'I'd prefer to discuss this when we get home this afternoon'? Oh, and don't be swayed or tempted to do otherwise and start a family melee! When the time comes to talk seriously, agree to stick to the subject and don't go off on tangents. If the other person starts to 'wander', keep your cool and simply say, 'I'd find it easier if we just talked about XYZ right now. If ABC is worrying you, let's talk about it as soon as we've dealt with this issue.' Again, stick to your deal.

The minute someone resorts to violence, know that there is no way the argument can be resolved there or then. If you feel threatened by someone's behaviour in an argument, try saying, 'I feel intimidated by you when you act like this. I'm prepared to talk this issue through with you when you have calmed down/when I feel less threatened by your behaviour.' Words often aren't enough in a case like this – you need to remove yourself from the situation as soon as possible. Unfortunately, like many sorts of behaviour that surface during conflict, being on the receiving end of violence or continuous verbal aggression is something you can end up getting used to. Know this – it'll be something your children will eventually get used to, too. They in

turn will be more likely to find themselves in violent relationships, either on the giving or the receiving end.

When guests come on the show, it's no one's territory.
People are kept to the subject by yours truly, and since everyone will have spent a long time talking to our researchers
before they even get to the studios, people at least feel they've
been listened to by an unbiased person. Many of them will feel
it's the first time their feelings have been heard and that in itself
makes them feel their views are relevant and important, even if
only to them. All parties involved in the dispute, even if they're
only the purveyors of (damaging) gossip or views that will
affect the arguers, are listened to.

The other thing I tell guests is to get all their emotional cards
on the table: get it all off their chests, so that their feelings and
issues can be dealt with. Secrets and suppressed feelings are the
things that can rear their ugly heads if not dealt with during
conflict. Some people say, 'How can you deal with conflict so
publicly?' It's certainly not a new idea. Back in Roman times,
people brought their problems and arguments and conflicts to
their peers and elders. They still do that in many developing
countries. All television does is simply to open up an age-old
tradition. I'm not going to play Miss Angel here. Sure, we get a
television show out of it, but because we follow up on our guests'
stories and refer them on to counsellors, organisations and
mental health services in their areas, we'd know pretty quickly if
what we were doing wasn't having a positive impact. Many
guests appear with their social workers' or medical professionals'
blessings. See the irony, though? Me, hater of conflict – and what
kind of show am I involved in?

Let me beat you to the next obvious question. If I follow the
rules of dealing with conflict positively, does that mean Peter and I

never argue? Ha! Sure we do, and I'll probably spend the rest of my life trying to perfect conflict resolution basics. Peter is well versed in the same stuff and sometimes we get sick of doing the 'reflective listening' bit and just want a good old ding-dong. But it's a bit like dodgem cars. Once you know the basics of driving, at least you have the skills to steer straight and avoid major collisions when you get fed up of bumping into each other all the time. If you didn't know how to drive, your whole experience of cars would be crashing, whiplash, jolting and very little sense of progress.

Peter

When Trish does something to annoy or aggravate me, the first thing I do is to seek to understand where she is coming from and we have a dialogue together to identify the common ground, the win:win scenario. Then we each make a peaceful compromise, embrace and move on with our lives. There is usually a harp playing in the background and it's not unusual for us to be showered with rose petals as we stroll towards the sunset hand in hand with all our disagreements solved. Yeah, right!

Trish and I argue, just like everyone else. In some ways, because we know what we need to do to resolve conflict effectively, we are worse than everyone else. Sometimes when we argue it actually feels like we are at work and often we don't have the energy to be constructive. Anyway, being constructive and positive all the time is boring, predictable and certainly not the real world. After all, we are two complicated and unique human beings, not diplomats!

In many ways, we are complete opposites in our response to conflict. When I am angry or frustrated I want a response. I want to deal with it, get it over with and move on. I can't stand it when the other person doesn't want to engage with this, or, worse, actively withdraws from a discussion. Of course, I understand why they do this. It's because I can be pretty intimidating and aggressive when I'm riled, and this is often fuelled by a powerful sense that I am right. Trish, on the other hand, withdraws from conflict. She evades the contest and, in her view, protects herself from the distress she feels when I get angry. Probably a wise thing to do, but it drives me crazy. Typically, she will leave me alone or bury her head in a newspaper while I bounce around, insisting that we talk about it. So, we end up with two very different types of behaviour:

> *TRISH:*   *withdrawn, rational and right*
> *PETER:*   *dramatic, explosive and right*

So, how does this resolve itself? Well, inevitably I give up and withdraw too. The temperature drops and at some point someone will make a gesture such as a cup of tea (cue the Nescafé ad), a cuddle or even just a conversation. This symbolises that the resolution can begin and at this point we start to do all the things we should have done from the start, such as listening, clarifying, understanding and, importantly, compromising. Trish and I are pretty good at learning from our stupid behaviour and we rarely argue over something more than once – that's because we can usually find something else to disagree on! Generally, though, our arguing and resolution of conflict brings us closer together and, if I am completely honest, I do enjoy the intellectual contest, but this is no comparison to the making up.

Another area where we disagree is in terms of losing our tempers in front of the kids. Trish very rarely does this and feels that it's wrong and potentially damaging. I think it's okay. We are all living in the real world and with each other and frustration and anger are a normal part of human relationships. Of course, there is a line we do not cross. Our anger as parents should never be out of control, should never involve aggression and should not continue to be unresolved. I always make a point of explaining my anger and try to help the kids understand what has provoked this response, and, importantly for them, how to avoid it in future. I am very interested to see what Billie says about all this, but in my view there is a certain honesty involved in being a parent and it's about both being fallible and recognising where you have been unreasonable and making amends. It is also about making sure that, as a parent, you don't rely on anger or intimidation to get your needs met. That's the lazy way...talking and working together is a lot harder, but ultimately more sustaining.

Billie

I think Pappy can sometimes be a bit scary when he loses his temper at me. I see it coming because I kinda ask for it anyway. I'm into horoscopes and me being a Sagittarius and Pappy being a Leo means we both have to get the last word in, which can make things difficult. I always know when I should stop in an argument, but, the way I look at it, you might as well fight to the end rather than making up halfway through. After the argument I obviously feel upset, and I will probably apologise if I feel I've done something wrong. It's not as much 'fun' arguing with Mum because she doesn't let me go as far. She just says, 'You make the choice you want. It's your decision, but you have to face the consequences.' And walks off! If someone gets into a big argument, I feel I have to win and if I back down during it, I've lost. But with Mum, I feel like I can make a decision, but I've still got my pride as well. If I make the wrong decision, Mum leaves me to face the consequences and, chances are it's a punishment I agreed to in the first place!

When Madi and I argue, and she goes squealing to 'Mummy', Mum often says, 'Kill each other quietly!' There was this one time when Madi and I had been at each other's throats all day. We were in Tesco's and were fighting over who should push the trolley. Madi kept ramming the trolley into my feet, and I kept pushing her out of the way. Suddenly Mum turned round and started yelling, 'Go on! If you wanna fight, do it properly. Go on, Madi, give her a good punch. C'mon, Billie, you can get a good kick in there. Come on! Really go for it!' Everyone was staring at her. After a couple of swipes, Madi and I just stood there speechless while Mum was still whooping and shrieking in the middle of the confectionery aisle. We thought she'd gone mad. But, hey, it stopped us fighting and we didn't fight for the rest of the day. I know that's called reverse psychology. It was just Mum acting so differently that made us stop in our tracks.

I hardly ever see Mummy and Pappy argue or lose their tempers at each other. I can tell when they're cross with each other because Pappy goes and sulks and goes and plays on the computer or PlayStation™ and Mum starts cleaning everything. It doesn't really last that long though. But when they're like that I don't really care because everyone's like that sometimes.

Dr Terri's thoughts…

I don't need to say too much here because I believe that Trisha and Peter have given you a good idea of what fighting fair is all about. Instead, I will summarise the main points, which you may find helpful when starting to think about how you can turn conflict into something productive. First, conflict is natural, so don't feel bad if and when it happens in relation to you. Think about it this way – if you never disagreed with your partner, family or friends, would you be getting your own needs met, or would you be repressing your feelings for much of the time? Conflict can be a good way of clearing the air, getting things off your chest, and actually being able to grow and move forward emotionally. However, it is *the way* you deal with conflict that makes it productive as opposed to destructive.

Change Again!

When dealing with conflict, the tip is to *change* the language or *words* you use. Try to be less confrontational, and more assertive. Now this isn't easy and can take some time to get the hang of because, again, it is about changing the way you respond in difficult situations. What I mean is, rather than saying 'You make me feel really angry', say 'I am feeling really upset'. Trisha called it using the 'I' word, and this can make such a difference if you keep applying it. The meaning that is conveyed from this is that you are talking about your own feelings, rather than accusing or verbally attacking the other party. Consequently, you have some ownership of what you are saying, because it is about how you are feeling. That way it becomes more difficult for the other party to contradict you. If, instead, you had used the 'You make me feel angry' approach, the other party would almost certainly have to immediately begin defending themselves against you because of the position these words would put them in. I hope this is making sense. Using 'you' instead of 'I feel' is more threatening. The 'I' word really does work, so try it.

Options and Compromise

When dealing with conflict, be it with your partner or your child, start by thinking about what it is that you are trying to achieve. With this you *must* also consider the other party's needs and feelings as part of the equation. If you don't, then you are not fighting fair. Once you have identified what your main goal is, if you like, you can then generate a whole host of options or possibilities around this. The purpose of this is to make you now look for some point at which you can both agree or feel relatively satisfied so that *both* of you are okay. If you simply say 'This is what I want', you will run the risk of the other party saying 'Well, I don't' and all that will be achieved is a stalemate whereby you are both completely opposed to one another. The purpose of resolution is to get the two parties to come closer together. Once you have identified your goal, you can then say 'Well, how do we get there?', which then allows the other party to be involved in coming up with options, as well as making them take some responsibility for the agreed outcome. That way they are more likely to subscribe to it! And remember, if you are taking account of another individual's feelings, then you may have to compromise. Compromising doesn't mean you have lost, but, rather, that you are ultimately able to go forward together and develop. The whole basis of this is the way you socially interact and communicate with those around you.

Let's consider an example as part of this chapter's quiz. Outlined below is a scenario. Your task is to read the scenario and then think about, and write down, what you would do differently if you were fighting fair.

Quiz

The Issue: Samuel is being resistant to spending some time with his dad.

Samuel is 13 years old and his mum and dad are divorced. He lives with his mum and sees his dad every so often. Over time there have been a number of difficulties between Samuel's mum and dad (which is not uncommon), and naturally this has affected Samuel from time to time. The current situation is that Samuel's dad wants him to join him for a week at half-term, and Samuel doesn't want to go for so long. He would rather go for three days because he really misses his mum and gets very home-sick/insecure due to past tensions. Also, his dad now lives a long way from his mum.

Although Samuel wants to go and stay with his dad for three days, his dad wants him to stay for a week. Dad becomes upset by Samuel because, understandably he thinks that Samuel should want to spend as much time as possible with him, and he has got lots of fun activities planned. However, Samuel, for his own reasons which are important to him, wants to stay for three days only.

Samuel tells his dad this on the phone, and a disagreement ensues = *conflict.* Dad tells Samuel that he has to do as he is told and will spend the week with him, that he should consider his dad's feelings and not be selfish. Dad tells Samuel that he is making Dad feel sad and unwanted. Samuel becomes distressed, feels guilty and responds by saying that he will not go at all then, and refuses to speak further with his dad for a while.

Outcome = *stalemate*. Both Samuel and his dad are now occupying completely opposing places. Nobody is happy.

Your Task

I will give you a head start by outlining the goal in this case:
For Samuel to spend some time with his dad.

- What has Samuel's dad failed to acknowledge?
- Is there an imbalance of power, and if so how (see Chapter 3, page 88)?
- Can you generate some possible options to this situation? Brainstorm and write them down.
- What would you do differently, bearing in mind that you are not allowed to dictate, or use 'You make me feel' language! If you are looking for some compromise, who do you think should be doing most of it and why?

Top Tips

1) Don't get used to arguing as a way of life. It's a hard habit to break.

2) Be aware of flashpoints such as tiredness, alcohol, work stress brought home, financial worries, etc., and agree that once someone flags up one of those conditions, you will postpone discussions/chats, etc., until later.

3) Don't bring conflict into the bedroom. Full stop!

4) There are no second chances for violent behaviour until *after* the violent person has had help to deal with his or her problem. Every time you 'put up' with violence, know your children will do the same in their future relationships.

5) Big ask – but try to 'hear' the other person's feelings rather than simply focusing on the horrible words they may be using.

6) On the other hand, try and take the emotion out of the other person's expression. Imagine that you are reading what they say on a sheet of paper – react to the content, *not* the emotion surrounding it.

Case Study

The Cast

Louise (35 years old)
Fred (22 years old) – her husband
Jodie (34 years old) – his lover

The story so far...

Fred has been married to Louise for four years, and throughout that time has left her on a number of occasions. Louise was previously married with children, and left her first husband for Fred. She subsequently lost the custody of her children and had a daughter with Fred. Fred met Louise when he was just 17 years old, and admits that he didn't really know whether he loved her, and has been unfaithful to her several times. Even when Louise was pregnant with Fred's child, he left her for a few weeks at a time because he said that he couldn't cope with her moods and possessiveness. The relationship has been a turbulent one.

Fred finally left Louise when he met Jodie. They began a relationship, which Jodie thought was going really well. However, Louise wanted Fred back, and over a period of time she would phone Jodie up to tell her that she and Fred had been seeing each other and having sex. This, understandably, has caused much friction between Jodie and Fred. Fred, however, denies that he has been seeing his wife behind Jodie's back.

Help!

There seems to be a lot of confusion surrounding Fred. The first issue he needs to address is to determine what he really wants. Is he ready for a monogamous relationship, or is he fooling the women in his life? His past behaviour and affairs and his uncertainty over whether he really loves Louise suggest that he has not yet reached a position of wanting firm, long-term commitment. After all, he is only 22 years old, and met Louise when he was just 17.

With regard to Louise and Jodie, perhaps they could each try being assertive with Fred and telling him how they're feeling, rather than fighting with each other. Fred is the common denominator in their dispute, and so should take some responsibility for helping to resolve it fairly.

Chapter Seven

Down or Depressed?

A Note from Dr Terri

Life is full of ups and downs and you can't predict what will happen from one day to the next. So the way you deal with the downs is extremely important in terms of your own mental health and that of your family. There are many situations that can push us to our emotional limits, including loss of work, a death in the family, loss of a relationship, and even loss of money. But, amazingly, for most of the time we're equipped with the most fantastic coping mechanisms. It's when those coping skills let us down, or, literally, break down, that there can be serious consequences. This chapter will help you recognise the early and more advanced signs of depression, in yourself and those close to you, and will show you the various steps you can take to move onwards and upwards. You'll learn how to know when you or a family member is not coping – for example, is your teenager typical or is he/she trying to escape through drink or drugs? How do you tell if you or they are just a bit down, or really depressed and straying into a danger zone?

Trisha really seemed to have it all. She was Superwoman. After having both babies, she was back at work within days. She had a great career and at one stage co-ran her own television production company and gave the impression of having a good relationship. Always, from outward appearances, the life and soul of the party. But there were many occasions when, standing by a busy road, she would be overwhelmed with the desire to just step into the traffic to escape the indescribable and terrifying emptiness she felt. Keeping ridiculously busy was her way of avoiding being still for long enough for the blackness of depression to creep in. It was only during the period of hospitalisation following her breakdown that professionals realised she'd been having these feelings on and off since she was about 14 years old. After her breakdown, cognitive behavioural therapy and other ways of being helped to recognise the triggers of her illness became her salvation, helping her to change the way she lived her life, to become the person she is now. Exercise was, and remains, an extremely important way for her to manage her moods. Let's hear Trisha's first-hand account of what depression was like for her.

Trisha

Tuesday 1 August 1972

…Last night J. told me she thought I'd changed recently – become more detached from everyone else, even [my best friend] Sue. She

said she thought I was deep and hard. S'pose that's true. I keep switching off – not hearing wot [sic] people are saying. It aggravates Sue – well, it annoys me too. When I stop hearing wot [sic] people are saying, I stop seeing as well. Wot's [sic] happening to me?

I wrote this when I was fourteen-and-a-half years old. A few pages on from this entry, I'd stapled in a thank you letter from BBC Radio's Alan ('Fluff') Freeman's Show. He used to have a 15-minute segment called Poet's Corner and I'd sent in some poems that I'd written about death. They were so deep and profound that the BBC sent me letters from recently bereaved people saying my poetry accurately summed up the hell they were going through. The thing is, I know (and my diaries back this up) that nobody I knew had died. I'd actually been writing about the death of my inner self and the terrifying emptiness I felt.

I kept diaries from about the age of nine till I was 17, and then on and off right up until I was in my early thirties. Some of the entries are still almost too painful to read – and way too personal and raw about myself and my perception of life to reveal. Flicking through them now, though, I can see troughs of despair that often seemed to come out of the blue without any obvious trigger. So, the question is, was I going through good ole teenage angst…or bouts of depression?

I reckon just about every family tree has at least one illness, which keeps cropping up amongst its branches: high cholesterol or heart disease, breast cancer, asthma, osteoporosis, problems with drink or drug-taking… In our family, one of those blights has got to be mental health problems and mental illness. And not just in my immediate family either.

How come admitting you and some of your relatives have lousy mental health is still shrouded in shame? I mean, there are regular magazine and newspaper features about the awful, but valiant struggle several generations of one family have had with, say, heart disease, always accompanied by a photo of said family. But imagine a photo accompanied by this caption: *This is me with three generations of our family, many of whom have had psychiatric help at one time or another.* I don't think so!

I was once invited on a fund-raising 'Fun Run' for a breast cancer charity, and every runner had the name of a loved one they'd lost through the disease prominently and proudly pinned to their T-shirt. Imagine if there were a similar awareness-raising event for mental health? Can you see people daring to wear the name of loved ones who have had a spell in a psychiatric ward, are on medication, or are grappling with suicidal tendencies? Even if the runner *were* brave enough to do this, in most cases the rest of the family would be outraged, claiming they didn't want anyone 'to know their business'. Oh, but they'll give you all the details of Dad's heart attack or Auntie's broken leg.

These days, more and more people with mental health problems are coming to realise that the added burdens of secrecy and shame make their illness so much worse to live with. However, they're often pushed into staying 'underground' because their families just can't cope with that person 'going public'. I live in hope. Cancer had the same stigma once.

When I was growing up, I had no idea what mental illness was really all about. You might think that strange, what with my father working as a psychiatric nurse in large institutions and my mother spending some of her working life nursing in them too. Throughout my childhood I vaguely remember both parents discussing 'the patients'.

For many years we lived in a 'hospital house' that came with my father's job at Holloway Sanatorium in Surrey. This old-fashioned mental institution was a fabulously grand building and I loved it. I'd go 'up the sani' with Dad and he'd leave me to play the organ in this cavernous hall decorated with 18th-century portraits of solemn, spectacled gentlemen. Now and again, a 'patient' would shuffle in, stare and listen to me playing. Occasionally I'd try to talk to 'them', trying to mimic the way I thought my father spoke; a sort of mixture of care and authority – but they'd usually just shuffle off again. I knew some of them rambled about stuff they saw or sounds they heard that weren't there, but I had no idea what was happening to them or why. I was never scared of them. They all seemed so benign. Looking back, it was probably because of the psychiatric regime that was used in those days – mainly medication. (There's an argument that it's still that way in some hospitals.) Never in my wildest dreams did I think that any of 'us', in our family, could become one of 'them'.

My First Experience of Depression

The diary entry I started with begs the question, 'when did I have my first bout of depression?' It was written in the days when we lived down the hill from the sanatorium and my parents worked there. I remember this coinciding with a build-up to one particularly bleak time; at a guess, I'd say I was about 15 years old. It was a descent into the pit that happened slowly but surely over the course of a year to 18 months – again, feelings, situations and incidents that are even now almost too painful to read in the diaries I religiously kept.

Somewhere along the line I looked at a photo of myself in a burgundy boat-neck sweater and Oxford bag jeans and decided I was way too fat. I prided myself on getting to the stage where breakfast was a biscuit and (climbing up to the top pantry shelf to steal it) a swig of sherry. At school I shoved the food around my plate and even though I was really hungry, I got a high from not really eating anything.

There was a girl at school with this amazing waist-long blonde hair who was a few years older than me and I thought she was stunning. She had the same approach to food as me. If I remember rightly, she eventually ended up as one of 'them' in the sani. (In the early 1970s, as far as the general public were concerned, eating disorders were unheard of.)

Somehow I managed to practically avoid eating anything at tea time. Then, at some point, my father suddenly noticed my dramatic weight loss and threatened to drive me to and from school (to conserve my energy, I think) if I didn't start eating. At least, that's the only threat I remember, because the thought of losing the independence of going to school by train was a shock. Round about the same time, I started hearing how my heroine of self-denial at school had started losing her long blonde hair in handfuls. To cut a long story short, my obsession with food and sherry went as suddenly as it began.

Then, I can still relive the day I was having a furious row with a classmate I didn't get on with. There were hordes of us from the same school all waiting for the train. This girl's hat blew off and she jumped down off the platform to get it from near the rails. I can still see the train coming in; me shouting at her to get back up on the platform. We tried to help pull her up and in her panic she started flailing her arms, and we let go. I'll never forget the train hitting her and being the first to the edge of the platform to see what had happened to her. Incredibly, she survived, but it was all so traumatic that on the Friends Reunited website, two other women who witnessed the same scene all those years ago, referred to the accident under their Memories section. The guilt of letting go of her, and disliking her, kept my mind churning over for quite a few nights. That was until I visited her in hospital. I was one of the last to do so and it was a very awkward and uncomfortable visit for both of us. But I left that hospital room realising that if you didn't like someone and something bad happened to them, it wasn't your fault. I also learned that it was okay to not like someone but still care about his or her welfare. Guilt – nil. Flashbacks to the accident – lots.

Last, but, horribly, not least, I was sexually assaulted one night by a man with a knife. My parents, sisters and I took a rare trip into London to visit an old friend of Mum's from the West Indies, who was having a party. I was allowed to bring a school friend. It was round about Christmas time, and therefore my birthday. The party was in full swing, the guests mainly adult. There I was with my woman-body, but the brain of a child, when a drink-fuelled bloke with a piece of mistletoe started trying to slobber me. I freaked.

In those days, I was a fledgling smoker who indulged more for the show-off factor than out of any necessity or desire. I grabbed my girlfriend, Evelyn (already an accomplished smoker), and together we went outside 'for a fag'. It's too painful to go into all the details, but, in short, here's what happened.

As we strolled up the road, we saw two guys get off a bus and come towards us. We did the 'I like yours' joke to each other, but as we passed them, the good-looking one suddenly grabbed Evelyn's arm. She immediately aimed a kick at him. With that, he started chatting me up while his friend started chatting with Evelyn. I remember feeling smug that I'd got the 'hunk'. Somehow, Evelyn and I got separated, and I was suddenly being dragged up an alley. He pinned me against a wall and told me what he wanted me to do. Bear in mind that, not only was I a virgin, but I had absolutely no sexual knowledge other than 'snogging'. I tried to get away three times – once by appealing to an elderly man who came out of his house in response to my screaming. When he told the bloke to let me go, my attacker responded by telling him that my name was Janey and we'd simply had a lovers' tiff. I kept repeating my real name and address to the old man to get him to believe me. He did, and, bless him, kept on at this bloke, giving me time to run away. But the guy came after me. He soon caught up with me and tripped me up. In the next alley my screaming brought two couples to their back doors. I'll never forget how they decided to go back inside, leaving this guy (his name was Paul, it later turned out) holding me up against the wall by my throat. It was then that he told me to do as he ordered, or he was going to cut me. I prayed out loud to the night stars and just kept on praying. Those prayers were answered – by Evelyn. She and the other guy had come looking for me and had heard me screaming. While the guy with Evelyn told Paul to leave me alone in no uncertain terms, Evelyn, apparently ran up to the nearest house, where there was a party going on, banged on the door and said, 'Help, my mate's being attacked!' The minute Paul saw all these burly blokes in party hats charging up the alley, he was off. The nice guy walked Evelyn and I back to my mum's friend's house and no one had even noticed that we'd gone. We just went upstairs and sat in the dark in some room and smoked and smoked. But *this* time I really inhaled.

I can remember exactly what I was wearing that night: my orange midi coat with a black smock top underneath and black flared trousers. My top was ripped and the zip in my flares was busted. Inside, a big bit of my soul was broken and the seeds of years of sexual hang-ups were sown. On the show, if I ask a guest to briefly tell me about a particular traumatic event and they end up living it blow by blow as I've just done, I instinctively know they're reliving it; they're back there in the alley or running faster than they ever did in a school race and *still* getting nowhere.

I poured my feelings into my diary and I started writing bleak poetry about death again in intimate detail. The only person who knew exactly what happened that night was Evelyn and she saw it more as an adventure, because after all, she *had* been the hero. I wrote a song called 'Don't Look Back, You're Doing Fine Now' about it, but I wasn't. I didn't tell anyone else the whole truth – not even my parents – because I felt guilty and that it was somehow my fault.

Not long after, Mum and I were standing by a busy road, waiting to cross over to where I had a Saturday evening job washing up in a pub kitchen. I used to get terrible period pains in those days and would sneak extra distalgesic tablets to cope with almost crippling cramps. I don't know how many I used to take, but this particular time I was pretty off my face. I remember a huge wave of terror sweeping over me, but at the same time feeling quite cold and raw. I remember looking into the roaring traffic and all the headlights, and calmly working out when would be a good time to step out into the cars. What stopped me? The mere fact that my mother was there and I decided I didn't want her around when I did it.

Breakdown and Hospitalisation

My life has been 'decorated' by patterns of swinging between obsessions and depression. I've either practised the family trait of head-in-the-sand syndrome of reality-avoidance or swung over to the other extreme with bouts of destructive impulsiveness. (Hindsight is a wonderful thing, especially when aided by almost two years of twice-weekly psychotherapy!) After my total breakdown in 1994, I also acquired the added ingredient of panic attacks, but more of that later.

Somewhere along the line, you may have read about my spell in an Australian psychiatric hospital. You may have even thought how enlightening it was of me to spill the beans about it. Sorry to disappoint you, but if I'd had my way when I was wheeled into that hospital – apparently with a towel over my head to hide my identity (I was told this later as I was well and truly out of it after taking an overdose at the time) – no one would have ever found out. So what that I was then an Australian Government Advisor and high-profile campaigner for the rights of people with mental illness, or that I championed people to stand up and talk about their mental health problems as one would about any other health difficulty? That was 'them'. This was crushed, broken, suicidal 'me'.

How did I end up being rushed into a psychiatric hospital in the first place? Actually, I now know it was a culmination of …well, my life up until that point. When I read press articles that cram together the things they know have happened to me, I feel a mixture of shame and incredulity. And yet, until I went into therapy I sort of assumed all those sorts of things happened to most people – that was what life was all about.

My breakdown and *second* suicide attempt were the result of many things: lousy relationship choices based on a warped idea of what the love of a man was about; the sort of things I talked about in Chapter 2 (see page 25). As I explained there, I'd drifted into a relationship with Mark, on the rebound from my first marriage and after dating one of Mark's best friends. I was a television current affairs reporter in those days and he was a video-tape editor. Like the rest of the television network staff we were young, brash and driven. Basically, all we did was work the most stupefying hours on earth, then get together, smoke dope and get stoned, crash out for a few hours and then back to pressure-cooker work chasing stories, door-stopping politicians and busting a gut to make deadlines.

Also, in those days, and for years after, I was still hung up on showing my father that I could be so good at something that one day he might even praise me. Somewhere along the line it turned into an obsession with work and my career, and showing people (and myself) that I could do it all. It was also a result of being so afraid of conflict that I preferred to bury my head in the sand and smile on the outside, while internally getting really, really angry with myself to the point of explosive danger. Again, diary entries from my childhood chart how my fear of conflict and anger started and gradually grew.

In the months leading up to my breakdown, I was heavily pregnant and presenting and co-producing a daily television health chat show. But I was also one of three owners of the production company that was commissioned by Australia's Channel Ten television to make the series. I gave birth to Madi on a Thursday after a two-and-a-half hour labour, took the Friday off, left her in the hospital crèche on the Saturday and went for an hour's power walk. On the Sunday I went for a light jog. After all I'd been working out in the gym with my personal trainer up to the day before I had Madi. Having seen me go through the same sort of fitness-fuelled pregnancy with Billie almost five years before, my obstetrician just rolled his eyes and shrugged.

Immediately after Billie's birth, I had rung the Executive Producer of *7.30 Report*, the live prime time current affairs show I was then fronting and explained why I was late in. She suggested she send a television crew over and I could explain the 'funny thing that happened on the way to the studios' to our ratings-winning audience myself. (I'd been on air the night before, so they'd wonder where I was.)

Two-and-a-half hours later, there I was, sitting in a business-like chair, fully dressed and made-up, cameras rolling and chatting away; a picture of perfect television professionalism. I did a piece to camera explaining to my viewers that I'd be handing back to a colleague in the studio to front the rest of the show as I had been 'otherwise detained'. At this point the camera shot panned down to reveal baby Billie in my arms. If it had panned down further the viewers would have also noted that I was sitting on a rubber ring – thanks to still being sore!

Five years on: Seven weeks after her birth, Madi stopped breathing and we had to rush her to our nearest general hospital. I spent three nights and four days sleeping on a mattress on the floor of her isolation room. She had a severe infection in her lungs and the doctors were having a hell of a time treating it because the tests they ran couldn't pinpoint what type of infection it was.

My darling little Madz was hooked up to an alarm that was meant to go off when her breathing was failing. One night it went off roughly every two hours. A team of nurses or doctors would rush in and start working on her. I did every deal with God I could. I lived in my nightie, because I once started walking towards the shower and no sooner had I left the room when the alarm went off. No way was I going to leave my little round-faced one. I talked and talked to her. I told her to be strong. I sang to her. It was important for me to breast-feed her to keep her fluids up, even though she was on a drip and surrounded by tubes and machines. Luckily she had started off a robust baby. While I breast-fed her, the nurses would leave the door open in case of an emergency, and I'd sit there, haggard, in my scruffy nightie, willing her better, and singing to her while she weakly sucked away. Suddenly I'd be aware of someone standing in the doorway and I'd look up to see people who were visiting another child on the ward. 'Hey, look! Look! It's that woman on the telly, isn't it?' If I could have screamed without frightening Madi, I would have. In those moments of utter despair, I felt like an animal in a zoo.

The whole time I felt totally wired and on edge and, as I explained in the chapter dealing with relationships, shortly after-wards, what passed as mine totally unravelled. As usual the person I was most angry with was myself. I was angry at ignor-ing all the warning signs about my relationship. There were issues surrounding Madi's illness that I cannot and will not go into, that made me incandescent with rage. Again, I turned that anger inwards. I guess that if you're the sort of control freak I was, when things go hopelessly wrong you get angry with your-self for failing to be as in control as you *should* have been.

My emotional fuel tank was now only running on empty – I'd long ago used up my reserves. I was breast-feeding at night, doing school runs, presenting a television show, writing scripts, still doing work chairing Australia's National Community Advisory Group on Mental Health for the Federal Government, cooking, grocery shopping – you name it, I was doing it. And on top of it all I had a husband embroiled in an affair

I just got to the stage where I was sleeping three hours a night. My brain was skidding like racing car wheels in mud – it would jump from terrifying scenario to 'evil-revenge-on-other-woman-type' fantasies. At first I was scared of a future in which I was alone with two small babies. Then, as things got worse in my head, I started being scared of a future called Daylight and the Next Day. I had still hardly told anyone Mark was having an affair, mainly because he had pressured me not to after I'd phoned my mother over in the UK and she'd given him an earful I'll bet he'll never forget!

My wonderful female GP had managed to work out that my relationship was on the rocks and I was having a tough time coping, and had prescribed anti-depressants for me. Mind you, I'd still done my best putting on my, 'I'm-a-bit-teary-but-I'll-cope' act for her. To put it quite bluntly, in reality I was going crazy and I knew it. I just wanted the pain and exhaustion, the crippling anger and isolation, terror and out-of-control feelings, to all go away for a while.

Then, one evening, I started working my way through the drinks cupboard and bathroom pills cabinet. It's at around this point that people who are hopelessly clueless about the depths of their depression and mental illness start spouting all that 'pulling oneself together' tripe. And, for a good measure of guilt, they trot out the 'How selfish! She should have thought of the poor children' line. I hope and pray that those people never have a bout of mental illness themselves, because if they do, with attitudes like that, their sense of failure will be far more acute than mine could ever be. The shock of losing the very mind they're using to so eloquently formulate their condemnation will send them down the slippery slope a great deal faster. But that's like describing the taste of roast suckling pig to a life-long vegetarian!

When I 'came to' in the psychiatric hospital, I was shocked that I was still around. Ten seconds after that feeling, the black curtain came down again as I realised I hadn't escaped. There are no words to describe the pain and fear I felt and there's no way I particularly want to relive that hell by trying to describe the indescribable. Back then, as I couldn't put what I felt into words, I simply didn't speak at all – for almost three days. I just sat on the end of the bed as still as I could, thinking that if I didn't speak and didn't move then nothing would notice me living and

I'd be safe. People came and sat and talked to me, but I didn't really hear them, and although I could see them, I convinced myself that if I 'tuned them out' they wouldn't be able to see the dirty horrible thing that I knew I was.

If someone was wearing strong perfume and came into my room, it terrified me. I wanted to scream and be sick, but I couldn't move in case they realised I was real. If someone was wearing bright colours, it was totally offensive. It made me deeply angry. I still don't know why.

Eventually, a clever senior nurse called Elaine arranged for me to have a television in my room. By this stage I was saying maybe half a dozen words a day. I remember watching Billy Connolly touring Scotland on television. Elaine would lean in my doorway gently commenting about what was on television. She kept her eyes firmly on the screen instead of staring into my face and look-ing for 'signs' as everyone else seemed to do. She made it 'safe' for me. Talking about Billy Connolly was 'safe'. Directing the conversation to 'the box' was 'safe'.

Other nurses would insist on keeping my door open when the nanny brought Madi in to be breast-fed, 'just in case...' Elaine realised that breast-feeding was one of the few connections I was able to make with another human being, so she plumped up pillows for me, complimented me on what a great mummy I was – and then shut my door and left me in peace. Those were about the only moments I could silently sob my heart out and realise I had to stay around, if only to give this darling little Baba her next feed. Like I said, Elaine was as clever as she was compassionate.

I spent a week in the ward on Suicide Watch, then after another month I was allowed home on condition that I had two sessions of psychotherapy a week. I'd avoided medication all this time because no one had been able to really reassure me that it wouldn't be passed on to Madi via my breast milk. Although I'm sure in one way it made things tougher, in another way I'm glad because it meant that I (and the mental health professionals) had to give far more thought to managing my illness through methods other than pills.

Backed by my psychiatrist I made it a condition that my ex be out of the house before I was discharged, but I was still a mess when I got out. By this stage I was having panic attacks that seemed to come from out of nowhere. It would seem as if someone had suddenly turned the volume up and anything coloured red would suddenly become unbearably loud and angry looking. I'd start panting and trying to make myself go small by backing up against a wall or curling myself into a ball. I learned to sit down quickly or my legs would literally go from underneath me.

Recovery

So how did I make it through all this? Although I had no immediate family with me in Australia, I'd managed to notch up some powerful allies. One was my (then) nanny, Maria. I'd helped her get help when one of her family members had had a mental health problem and now she repaid me in full…and then some! Not only did she look after the children, she looked after me. She'd cook meals for me and leave them in the fridge covered in clingfilm, ready to be stuck in the microwave. She'd run baths for Billie and then say, 'Hey, let's not waste the water! Jump in, Trish.' Without those simple kind acts, I would probably not have really bothered with food or washing. I had friends who'd phone and check up on me, and even though I often gave them the old, 'I'm doing fine now' bullshit, deep down it registered that they cared.

And, life-saver of life-savers, I got out the stroller (I'd invested in a special lightweight jogging job that could take kids up to six years old) and put five-year-old Billie in it, got out the baby back-pack and put Madi in that and walked and walked and walked. I absolutely powered along, to the point where I was panting. I'd make up a little 'breakfast bag' of goodies for Billie: toast and fruit and a little carton of juice and off we'd go. The constant rhythm of my steps, the warmth of Madi against my body, the whirring of the toy windmill Billie and I had stuck on the push-chair... I discovered what zillions of pounds worth of medical research has just backed up: exercise is an absolutely crucial ingredient of coping with, managing and recovering from depression. Any treatment that doesn't include it will never be as successful as regimes that do. Plus, I started making friends with neighbours I hadn't even known existed, and slowly but surely, my feelings of isolation were peeled back. Trotting through the sunshine or squealing and dashing through the pouring rain, dressed top-to-toe in macs, the girls and I battled on.

Cue end of film credits. You can get up from your cinema seat knowing Trisha made it through...

Well, actually, it wasn't that easy. Billie had had problems as a result of all that had happened and I'd decided to enlist the help of a child psychiatrist I knew. It was the best thing I could have done. One of the things this child psychiatrist got both Billie and I to do was to draw up a chart of the days of the week. We had packets of those sticky stars teachers put in children's exercise books to reward good work. When Billie and I had a 'bad' day, we'd put a blue star on our chart. An okay day got a silver star and gold was for the great days.

By looking at the chart we could see that life wasn't all blue stars, it's just that after a rough time, you tend to remember the Blue days and their disasters far better than you do the Golden ones. It was a powerful way of getting us both to discuss the day and our feelings about which colour star the day merited, but in a way a five-year-old was comfortable with.

And all the time I was having painful sessions of psychotherapy, which was all about dealing with my behaviour patterns and my bouts of depression and mood swings into obsessive behaviour, as well as understanding what drove my disastrous choice of partners. Sometimes I'd just sit there staring at my psychiatrist in an echo of what I'd been like in hospital. Other times, he would come right out and ask if I was feeling suicidal – which was great because instead of just grappling with a mess of terrifying thoughts and fears, I actually had to think about whether I was in danger of wanting to run away from things again. If I did, we could start dealing with it.

At first I baulked at the notion that I had ever had depression. 'People with depression just sit about, down-in-the-dumps. They don't laugh or smile – they don't do much of anything I thought. *I* wasn't like that! Just the opposite,' I insisted. And so I was. I had so much energy I was practically jumping out of my skin. My eyes were like saucers. I was buzzing. I was one of those people you read about in the newspapers. 'She had it all. She had everything to live for. New baby, successful career, life and soul of the party, etc. We have absolutely no reason to think she killed herself. It must have been an accident...' I was a so-called 'smiling depressive'. Frantically busy in a world that pats the frantically busy on the back and asks them to be even busier. Super-this, super-that. Different *exterior*. Same *interior*. Fighting the same monsters with different tactics.

Doing it all and being it all to a ridiculous degree can be like a brightly-painted, flimsy piece of balsa wood covering the mouth of a deep, dark, slimy-walled well. I was running just as fast as I could because I was too petrified that if I stopped, that multi-coloured piece of wood would give way.

One thing we did finally unearth during my sessions of psychotherapy was the fact that this had been my *second* suicide attempt. After the first one, I'd simply been patched up and discharged after a short stay on a general hospital ward. Well, I say 'simply'. That's far from the truth really.

My first suicide attempt, in 1986, was even more destructive than the second. Again, it was the result of a hopelessly messy relationship with someone who was ten times more dysfunctional than me. This was my marriage to Robert, which I describe in my chapter on relationships (see page 29).

The night I discovered he'd secretly asked my male friend Noel to take over having a sexual relationship with me, was the final snowflake that caused the avalanche. I had never before, and have never since, experienced the all-encompassing rage I felt that night. And when Robert went into what I called 'politician-speak' to explain why it was necessary that he share intimate details of the sexual practices I liked with a male friend of mine in order that he would know how to 'satisfy' me, the result was something akin to a gun going off in my head. I was screaming with anger and at some point I dashed down to the kitchen and picked up a knife. Let me tell you, at that stage there was no way I wanted to harm myself – rather, I just wanted to keep Robert away. In the end I was so scared of committing murder that I turned my rage, and the knife, on myself.

It took four-and-a-half hours of microsurgery, courtesy of one of Australia's best surgeons, to repair what I had done to my wrist, followed by about a year of intense and painful physiotherapy to fully recover, and at one stage, the surgeons thought I'd probably lose the use of my left hand. (As soon as a doctor told me this I thought, 'Right, you buggers, I'll show you!') In fact, to this day, I only have about 40 per cent feeling in that hand. I always check water temperature with my right hand as if I do it with my left I can easily scald myself and not feel it until real damage is done. I had to learn to type and play the piano all over again and I still get waves of unbearable nagging pain. Sometimes my hand curls into a claw without my even realising it. Gripping the hand microphone on the show is a godsend, because then I don't have to concentrate too much about what my hand's up to. Although I can joke about it, every now again, in the dark days, I look at the long jagged scar on my wrist and wonder how the hell I could have done that to myself.

By the time I was discharged from hospital, I was hopelessly hooked on the drug pethidine, freely prescribed in order to help me cope with the intense pain. My mate Noel took me to an ashram in the Blue Mountains outside Sydney and there, with my arm and hand in a massive baseball mitt of plaster, I stopped taking the pethidine and went through the most evil cold turkey for a few days. I just knew I mustn't have a drug like that around, in case I got angry again...

When I finally did go and see a psychiatrist, she was hopeless. Robert insisted on coming along to the sessions to 'supervise' me and she let it happen. When we had sessions that he didn't attend, I *still* didn't trust her. I thought Robert had managed to 'get to' everyone else I trusted, I thought, so what made her any different? I just kept smiling and telling her I was fine now. It worked.

Off the Rails

So, basically after my second suicide attempt, all those years later, in 1994, I had to rake through all the 'stuff' from back then. My depression came and went over the next three years – years when

I was frequently bailed out by people the rest of the world tends to write off.

I went through a phase of going out clubbing with a vengeance. It was the way I filled every other weekend when the girls stayed with their father. Madi was a year old by this time and I had just finished breast-feeding her, I had my figure back and was ready to party in a way only those who have had a spell on the edge of a precipice can. You name it, I just about did it. I experimented with Ecstasy, although I wouldn't touch marijuana with a bargepole, being well aware by this stage that it was a definite trigger of my depressive bouts (as it is for thousands of users). At the time, not a lot was known about 'E' and when I mentioned to my shrink that I'd tried it, he didn't exactly discourage me from carrying on. He told me it was a drug that had been used in certain forms of therapy years before in Germany.

In case you're scrambling for the name of this 'enlightened' medic, perhaps I ought to tell you that he fled Australia and was subsequently struck off in his absence for misconduct. Not for taking drugs, but having inappropriate relationships with female patients. I 'escaped' his attentions and had to see yet another psychiatrist, this time a female, to get over the confused mixed messages I had got from him. He had done me a lot of good in terms of helping me to cope with my suicidal tendencies and depression, but he did some pretty manipulative stuff as well along the way. But that's another story…

Anyway, armed with what I read as approval from my psychiatrist to explore my 'dark side', I was off! One night, a young gay guy with an amazing amount of insight rescued me from a potentially tricky situation when I was blissed off my face. He sat me down and gave me a good talking-to about looking after myself. He countered my scepticism by revealing that he too lived with a mental illness. It's all very well 'self-medicating' yourself to get the phoney high Ecstasy gives you, he said, but you sure as hell better be ready to struggle through the awful 'downer' you get the morning after. And it was even worse for those prone to depression anyway. Invaluable advice. After taking Ecstasy half a dozen times, I discovered he was right. The 'downs' were more likely to do me in than my good ole straight-forward depression! To this day, Andrew remains one of my dearest friends.

Back in those days, we used to have mini chat shows in the corners of gay clubs discussing everything from sexual abuse to domestic violence and depression. The word got out that I was a mental health campaigner and the gay men and women I mixed with couldn't give a stuff about my celebrity status. They were so protective towards me. They could sniff out a journalist from 100 yards away, come and warn me, and smuggle me out the back door of the nightclub.

They knew all about marginalisation. Feeling mentally unwell locks you out, but so can being gay. And being *driven* to mental ill health because of the issues that surround coming out and acceptance – well, that's a double bummer. It was because of those days that I became involved in working for Sydney's Gay and Lesbian Mardi Gras and The Bobby Goldsmith AIDS Charity.

Then there were the people with mental illness who I worked with while chairing the National Community Advisory Group on Mental Health for the Australian Government. It was made up not only of people who'd experienced mental illness first hand, but others who were carers of those who had. They were the first to send me flowers when I was in hospital. Amazing, because you don't get to see many bunches of blooms on psychiatric wards.

The first meeting I shakily chaired after my breakdown, they were so there for me. 'Welcome to the Club!' was the message. In their company, I could actually laugh at some aspects of my experience. I could talk about what was happening in my head without them labelling me a 'loony'. I remember at one meeting, we were discussing paranoia. 'I thought people were pointing at me and saying my name…' I confided. 'Er…Trish, mate – you are a star on the telly, so they probably were!' they laughed.

It took me a long time to go back to work 'on the telly'. I was approached by quite a few television executives, but turned them down flat. One, however, was more tenacious than the rest. Lena had been a doctor in her native Russia and was now working as a senior television producer. She had been asked to put together a prime time health television show and relentlessly approached me. After about half a dozen phone calls, I got exasperated. 'Look, there's no way I can work in an office or work to deadlines any more!' I snapped. So she arranged for me to be able to work from home, the hours that suited me, and to be supported at all times. And on the days I couldn't get out of bed, well, that was okay, too. The fact that she'd created those conditions for me, and that my illness was out in the open, took most of the pressure off me. Gradually, I was back making programmes part-time.

The fact is, my first full-time job is the one I'm doing now, the *Trisha* show. And again, when the then Anglia Television executive Malcolm Allsop, flew all the way out to Australia to headhunt me for it, I told him exactly what he was taking on. Thanks to his faith in me, we spent time more working out the *conditions* I would be working under, rather than the money I would work for. That's why I base myself near the studios in Norfolk and why I live in the countryside. It's why I often make journalists, photographers and Granada television executives travel here to see me, rather than the other way round. It's why I refuse to have an agent or a manager. I've turned down potentially lucrative ideas and offers of television projects an agent or manager would crawl over broken glass to get, what with the commission to be made and all. I survived being skint and I'm not in a hurry to muck about with my mental health any more – no amount of money's worth that!

Family Support

Keeping me mentally well while living with a predisposition of depression, rather than simply being a victim and 'suffering' from it, takes a team effort. Peter and the girls have a vital role to play in this. I've always been open with the girls about my depression, but I do it in an age-appropriate manner.

The female psychiatrist I went to after my first doctor did a runner was really good at involving the girls, even though they were only six and two. I'd often have to bring them to appointments with me. She explained to me that the worst thing a child could experience was helplessness and confusion over why Mummy was sitting there silently, head hanging, and thoughts such as 'Is it *my* fault Mummy is like this?' She would chat to Billie about why Mummy was coming to see her.

Over the years, Billie has worked out the warning signs of Mummy 'going on one'. Peter's been great in encouraging her and making it okay for her to comment on my behaviour, either privately to him or straight to my face. Defensive as I initially felt, I've come to realise that their field of expertise (as for all of us) is survival. Mummy falling to pieces is a direct threat to that, so anything they can do to draw her attention to the fact that she's risking her mental health has got to be a good thing. Actually, one of the main 'warning signs' is when I start getting busy like a 'mad rabbit'. This usually means doing several things at once. I might start by arranging flowers while trying to feed the dog and load the washing machine at the same time. Then I'll open the mail and unload the dishwasher at the same time. I start snapping at Peter and the girls and start having lots of conversations that are never finished. Well, that's what they tell me anyway. I'm sure they'll tell you a lot more about what they look out for, like how much alcohol I drink... Peter's great at just taking the tea-towel out of my hands and saying, 'Look, you go for a run, darling.' I get the message. And I go for a run.

Exercise, Sleep and Food – Vital for Good Mental Health

Exercise is still crucial to my mood management. And, yes, I'm obsessed with it. I've decided it's a fairly harmless obsession to have, even though the way it often dominates my life annoys Peter at times. Luckily Darrell, my personal trainer, has had some pretty big ups and downs in his own personal life to deal with and therefore has a good grasp of the mental importance I place on working out. He knows I prefer lycra-less gyms where people leave me alone, and he makes sure people keep away from me. He even knows to give me a more aerobic-type work-out immediately after my period, and a strength-based heavy weights programme just before. If he sees I'm wound up, we go and work out in the boxing gym with a punch bag! I train with Darrell three times a week and run 3 to 5 miles at least five days a week. Plus I take hand weights with me when I walk the dog most days. When we pick holidays, there has to be either a gym or a running or rollerblading track wherever we're going. As I said, I'm obsessed, but I've been hooked on worse things.

Sleep is important, too. I have bouts of insomnia, which I don't freak out about because I know now that my body will catch up after a few mega-nights' sleep. The sleepless nights I watch out for are the ones where either a song or a thought goes obsessively round and round in my head, hour after hour. Then I'll tell Peter what's happening and together we'll work out what it is that's getting to me.

We have a huge family calendar on the wall with what everyone is up to marked out on it. That way, I can see at a glance whether I've got too much on my plate. I can either make sure I've got lots of time off before and after something special that I'm doing, or I start clearing my diary. I've got over the guilt of saying 'no can do' to people by fairly recently insisting on having a personal assistant, Gaile – she's a godsend who knows what I'm about.

Food is another important component, and I take what I put in my mouth very seriously. I know I'm prone to what I call 'dysfunctional' eating. Put plain and simply, I'm just as likely to eat for eating's sake as I am to starve myself for weeks. Therefore I'm pretty unadventurous with food, and I kinda always stick to the same daily menu: hot water and lemon, wholemeal/whole-grain toast and marmalade for breakfast; a huge bowl of salad with half a dozen prawns for lunch (sushi when I'm in the studios recording the show); grilled fish and vegetables or a vegetarian meal in the evening, followed by a low-calorie pudding. As I write this I've just forced myself to stop drinking for a week because Peter pointed out I was hitting the bottle pretty hard. Boy, come 6 p.m., it was hard not to reach for the bottle, so I sucked boiled sweets and drank low-cal fizzy drinks instead!

Helping Others with Mental Health Problems

Once you've had a skirmish with depression, you can start to get a bit scared about any major mood changes, and think, Oh-oh! Is it happening again? But I know from experience that I can feel justifiably down or grief-stricken without 'going mad'.

In earlier chapters (see pages 9, 30), I talked about my younger sister, Winnie's, suicide bid, and how she ended up in hospital with horrific burns and on a life support machine. I was in Australia when it happened, and I still remember the morning my mother telephoned to tell me that Winnie had septicaemia and they didn't know how long she could last. The news was like a physical blow to the stomach. I literally keeled over screaming when I got off the phone. A few hours later I was on my way to England, praying all the way – my faith has so often got me through. My Aunt Mary was staying with the family and she was my rock of support during the six weeks we drove up and down to Brighton Hospital. Basically, she helped shore up my faith in God at a time when He was seriously in my bad books. It's often suggested that Winnie's suicide was a factor in my own break-down. But, remember, by the time it happened in 1988, I'd already been in hospital myself and had a pretty good idea how it felt to have your mind trap you in a scary place. I couldn't begin to imagine the tortures of schizophrenia without the vastly improved medication and management that's available these days.

All of us spent hours sitting with Winnie, talking to her while she was in the drug-induced coma she was put into, so painful and severe were her injuries. I told her about my mental health struggles. I told her it wasn't right that we should be crippled with the added burden of shame and embarrassment. I cried and got cross with her for doing it. I got cross with myself. In the end I found acceptance.

When she finally died of kidney failure, my family felt like it was imploding and everyone grieved in different ways. Some got busy, others fell apart. My other sisters and I suddenly spent a lot of time going over and over the past. I took advantage of the excellent grief counsellor at the hospital and urged other family members to do so with varying degrees of success. Between Aunty Mary, the grief counsellor and God, I reached a new level of understanding. I decided not to let Winnie's death destroy me because that's not what it was about, any more than when acting on a suicidal impulse I've thought of anything but the deep personal pain here and now.

My greatest therapy, though, was to stand up and talk about it. I decided to do this as a reaction to the virtual distaste others had about what caused my sister to suffer. It wasn't an easy decision because other family members hated the idea of my talking about it publicly for all sorts of reasons, not least their own painful feelings. In fact, they still do, which I can understand. Winnie herself hadn't been any more comfortable with people knowing about her schizophrenia (when otherwise her life was so fulfilling) than – believe it or not – I am about people knowing about my own mental health problems. But I didn't talk about what happened for the sake of kudos. Instead, I worked tirelessly for ten years to change everything to do with mental illness, from law, rights and treatment to the stigma surrounding it, the rights of carers and the money the health services got, albeit in Australia. And when the then British Home Office Minister Paul Boateng visited Australia and suggested I come back to England and replicate my work there, I declined. I walked away from 'the Fight' on 2 August 1998 – ten years to the day dear Winnie left us.

Talking about mental health issues and making people aware of them is something I'll always do, be it through print, television, politics – whatever. I make sense of Winnie's death by knowing that I have had the opportunity to change the outcomes of thousands of lives, all thanks to her. So, yes, somewhere in there, I've got resilience. Knowing there's a predisposition to mental health problems in our family, I feel resilience is something I need to foster in my girls. Actually, as the T-shirt slogan says, 'Shit happens!' Indeed it does, and it's having the resilience to cope with it that's the key to survival.

If you aren't as receptive to hearing about your children's downs as their ups, you're not encouraging them to share bad news with you. Sometimes they may blame their sadness on you or something that you, as a parent, have done. Peter's taught me loads here. He's taught me to put defensiveness aside; to sit and listen quietly and to ask questions (painful though you fear the answer may be). Then, if need be, to go away and think about it or discuss it with your partner. And finally, to never be afraid of going back to the child and apologising. Peter's so great at that. He'll go into Billie's room, shut the door and start with, 'When I did so and so, I never realised that you'd feel such and such...' I've still got training wheels on in this area!

Over the course of my marriage to Mark collapsing, and becoming a single mother, I had to grapple with a lot of losses, one after the other: first, the loss of what had always been – imperfect though the relationship was, I was used to it being what it was and wasn't convinced it could be any other way. Then I literally lost my sanity for a while, and was faced with the additional burden of the constant drudgery of divorce, lawyers and threats of court appearances... Through illness and because I was a single mum, I lost the ability to work and, to a driven creature like me, shutting down and walking away from my production company was pure agony and defeat. As a result, I lost status, money and lifestyle – having to sell off designer outfits that represented the 'high life' was not a good feeling, I can tell you. I lost all the constant social contacts work brings with it. Finally, after all the therapy, Time The Great Healer and meeting and marrying darling Peter, I thought, 'Yippee! Those days of dealing with the "lows" – so much loss in one go – are well and truly over!' Especially when, out of the magic blue yonder, I got the job offer of all job offers and Peter told me to 'go for it' with his 100 per cent support. Within weeks the whole family was in England… And Peter fell apart…

Peter

The gentle *thwack* of leather on willow on a quaint little village cricket green. Me, the ferocious Aussie pace bowler, saviour of the local cricket team, newly arrived and fully accepted into village life. Perhaps a few ducks watching patiently from the boundary while this idyllic weekend scene unfolded…

This was one of the many images I had about life in England before we left Australia. Other images and ideals that comforted me during the countdown to my departure included being a fulfilled 'house-husband' (yes! no more going to work for me), finally learning to speak Italian and being able to flit off to Italy on a regular basis.

As everyone does, I compiled a mental picture of how great all this would be in terms of helping me deal with the anxiety of giving up my career, leaving friends and family and moving to a country I had never particularly wanted to spend a great deal of time in. I was to quickly discover that the reality would be very different.

The possibility of us moving to England had been on the cards for most of the previous year and, although Trish and I had talked about it a lot, when it happened it still came as a bit of a surprise. In fact, I was in my car when she rang to say the opportunity was now real and 'Did I want to go?' She made it clear that if I didn't want to then she would respect my views and turn the offer down. Without reservation I said 'Let's do it' and it remains one of the easiest 'big life decisions' I've ever had to make.

At the time, we had been together for about two years and I had seen Trish's career wind down, her depression become more prominent and her sense of satisfaction with life dwindle. I don't know if the depression was responsible for her discontent or whether it was the other way around. It's like that with depression – the 'chicken or egg' analogy: does depression make us discontented, directionless and unfulfilled, or does it occur in response to these feelings? Either way, it's a vicious circle and Trish was caught in it. My life, in contrast, was complete; I was at the top of my career, fulfilled in love and enjoying my new role as a parent and provider (I was the main breadwinner back then).

Trish was on medication for depression during this period and it had a marked effect on her (and me). The medication was necessary because at this stage her depression was having an increasingly negative effect on her day-to-day life. With her depression and no medication, Trish was preoccupied and isolated, but there would be good and bad days. With medication, she was less troubled, but there was almost none of her bubbly and confident self. She would lose herself in mindless computer games and was always tired. As for most people with depression there was a major slump in her libido, so sex was virtually non-existent. The medication just made things go from bad to worse in that respect.

During the six months or so that Trish was really depressed and on medication I felt so lonely. I really wanted to feel close to her both emotionally and physically. Trish thought this meant that because there was no sex, I would run off, and that this was only fair because she didn't deserve me. She was really down on herself and the harder I tried to be patient and understanding, the guiltier she felt. It was a no-win situation for me. I guess I learnt that you can't *do* anything to fix it; you just have to be around and perhaps not even try too hard. I know now that if I wait she'll come out of those periods when she sort of disappears emotionally. It's more annoying than anything now because it always happens when things are going well between us. Either way, the person you loved isn't always there and you feel a real sense of anger that something is taking her away from you.

I've worked in mental health services all my life, and I have recommended anti-depressant medication to hundreds of people but, until I had first-hand experience of loving someone who was taking it, I never questioned whether the 'cure was worse than the disease'. When Trish gets depressed I guess I am the carer, but what does that actually mean? I think it's easier to define relationships involving someone with a mental health problem as having a carer and a person who is 'cared for', but in our case it has always been mutual.

Caring for someone you love is an instinctive thing; it does not deserve special recognition or a label. Caring is a normal part of a loving or supportive relationship and there should be no distinction between caring for someone because they are depressed (Trish) and because they have a personal crisis arising from moving to a new country (me). We all express caring in different ways, use particular techniques that may or may not be useful, and expect different things in return. I have never wanted to be identified as a 'carer' just because my wife has depression – in our relationship, being the carer or the 'cared for' are roles that we constantly swap.

I knew that Trish had lingering doubts about her talent. In Australia, there are very few black faces on television (Trish was the first!) and there were many people, including, to some extent, Trish herself, who thought that the success of her career hinged on the fact that she was 'exotic' (in the sense that she wasn't the blonde, blue-eyed stereotype of Australian woman-hood). The move to England represented a chance for her to test her talent in a country where there are many talented and prominent black people, many of whom are on television. I knew that if Trish succeeded here then it would be very re-affirming to herself in terms of her talent and value in a career sense. I also knew that the move would be risky for me, as I had to give up my hard-earned job for Trish's three-month 'test' with Anglia Television. However, I also knew that it was one of the most important things I could do for her and, at the time, it was an easy decision. Besides, I had a magical village cricket career awaiting me!

It wasn't long before I came to question my decision. I arrived in England on a spousal visa, which meant that I had few 'citizen' entitlements, no job, no friends, a famous wife and no sense of who I was. I couldn't hire a video, get a driver's licence, contribute financially or even enrol in a language course without proof of identity and residency. I didn't have any of these things and, oh, there was no village cricket team. My role in the family suddenly seemed greatly diminished to me. I took the children to and from school and waited uncomfortably with the 'other' mums. The most distressing day of all was when Billie started crying after school because the boys had been teasing her that I was weird. Why? Because I didn't go to work like the other dads.

I felt lost. Until then, my identity, as for lots of men, had been strongly defined by my work. It is very important to most men to be able to define themselves by what they do rather than who they are. I felt worthless and this was compounded by the rapidly emerging success of my wife. For the first time in my life I began to get a taste of what depression was like. I was sad, put on weight, had trouble sleeping and was grumpy most of the time. I have a bit of a problem with stress at the best of times, but during our first few months in England, I was just constantly pissed off. Little things seemed like big things and minor problems seemed like the end of the world. I felt constant desperation; that if I didn't change or *do* something, all that I valued would be lost. This further alienated me by affecting my relationship with Trish and the kids.

What I wanted was for someone to comfort me and soften the feelings and fears that I was enduring. All the time I kept thinking 'My God, life is not bad. This is nothing compared to what some people go through,' and I felt really guilty that I couldn't handle this change in my life. I'd always handled everything else. Trish didn't give me what I *wanted* but she *did* give me what I needed – encouragement to confront and work through my feelings, rather than run away from them. So what did I do? I did what most men do when they are emotionally troubled or challenged. I looked for practical and immediate solutions to the pain. For me, this meant finding a highly paid and influential job. The problem was that all the opportunities for me career-wise were in London, a two-hour commute away.

So, it came down to a choice. Commit myself to a career that would mean less time with Trish and the children, but reclaim the security and familiarity of an identity defined by a job, or, explore my feelings and look for a new and less job-oriented identity. With a lot of encouragement from Trish I chose the latter. We did a lot of talking, often heated, about me and her message to me was 'Tough it out…see where it takes you, but don't run back to what you know best.' It seemed uncaring and hard at the time but it was the right advice. I actually saw a therapist a few times – a first for me – and it helped me check out the direction I was going to take. As all this unfolded, I was gradually becoming more settled here and had even managed to get a video membership card! A symbol, for me, of the first solid connection with the place I lived in.

Things worked out for me and, after using my skills as an unpaid volunteer with a local charity for a time, I found a great job (actually, the job found me) that had less status than what I was used to, but was eminently more fulfilling because it didn't jeopardise life with my family, which, after all, was the reason I had moved in the first place. Without Trish's encouragement I wouldn't have taken this path, I wouldn't know who I am today and I would certainly have less to contribute to this book. Oh, and by the way, any village cricket teams in need of a demon Aussie fast bowler, please get in touch!

Billie

I can tell when Pappy's down 'cos he's really grumpy and he takes all his anger out on me, mainly, not Madi! For instance, I'll come through the door from school and I'll say, 'Hello' and instead of saying 'Hello' back, he'll just growl at me to do my jobs or something. I wish I could think 'Oh-oh' and just stay clear, but all I do is just argue and then it gets worse and worse and in the end I have to do ten times more that what I would have had to do before. A real bummer! That's what he was like when we first came to England. But I was only eight so there's not a lot that I can remember.

Sometimes when Pappy's grumpy, it rubs off on Mum (or vice versa) and it seems like they're both looking for me to slip up. Then it makes me grumpy and I take it out on my little sister Madi. In a way, even though I'm cross with Mum and Pappy, I'm just as bad as they are!

Mum is always full-on whether she's happy or sad. When she's happy she's always joking around, farting freely and attempting to sing along with the songs on the radio and sounding like a wolfhound. When I do something wrong and she's in one of her happy moods, she just tells me off in a space of two minutes maximum. I probably listen more when she does that. But when she's down and I do something wrong, she'll give me a full-on nagging session for about ten minutes, and then she'll keep on and on about it for the rest of the day!

Another thing she does is to rush out to the shops, spend loads of money on things like potpourri and flowers and then for the rest of the day, she rushes around arranging them, until each twig is in the perfect position. If I talk to her, she doesn't listen and cuts me off halfway through, barking, 'I'm not interested, Billie! I'm not interested, Billie! You've come at the wrong time.' And then the next day, when she's meant to be picking me up from a school rounders match, she suddenly turns around and says, 'What rounders match? You never told me anything about a rounders match.' I know I've told her, but she was in one of her hyperactive moods, and was too engrossed in flower- arranging or newspaper-reading to hear me.

Sometimes when I'm upset, I exaggerate it slightly, to try and make Mummy and Pappy notice me more. I mope around and I talk in a quieter voice, which is unusual for me. And if they still don't notice me, I sometimes complain of headaches. But then I just get sent to bed early. If I tell Mum I need to talk to her, she comes into my room around bedtime and we have a chat. It makes me feel so much better. Same with Pappy. Depression is when someone is very, very sad. I know Mum lives with depression and it doesn't make much of a difference to me. She has good days and bad days, but that's just who she is.

Dr Terri's thoughts...

This might sound a little strange, but depression is one of my favourite subjects. There are two reasons for this. First, it is the one issue that affects all of us at some point in our lives. Although not everybody will suffer from a long-term episode of clinical depression, we all have moods and emotions that constantly change and vary over time. If you think about it, emotions are never static. You can wake up in the morning, the sun is shining, and you feel fairly happy and content, and then you go in to work and realise that you have to face a huge problem. Bang! Your feelings and mood change because you have just been informed that, say, you are going to be made redundant, leaving you feeling confused and worried about your future. So we all have the potential to get down for a period of time, even if it is over something as simple as that 'Monday morning' feeling.

Second, since depression is about emotions and moods, we all have to manage them constantly. Feeling down is often portrayed as something negative or bad. But when you think about it, emotions are an excellent tracking system for us to monitor how we are getting along in life. Some theories actually portray emotion as an early warning system that lets us know when we need to change the way we are doing things in our day-to-day lives. I am not saying that depression is great and that we should enjoy it! Far from it, but what I *am* saying is that when we are feeling down we do need to ask *why*, so that we can then begin to do something about it. And if the negative feelings actually help to identify something which isn't doing you any good, then that in itself can be positive. Think about the point Trisha got to before her emotions stopped her dead in her tracks.

To summarise, then, perhaps the most significant thing about depression is that it is about people and the way they feel, and affects most of us to a varying degree from time to time. In fact, it is often called the 'common cold' of mental health. The figures for the number of people in the UK who suffer from clinical depression range from 15 to 20 per cent. However, everyone in the population will feel low occassionally, which is normal, and if we ask ourselves *why* we can become much more self-aware and better at regulating our feelings and reactions to life stressors.

What is Depression?

Depression is a subjective state that can range from feeling really negative or not happy, to a completely flat, painful nothingness. It is a very personal state, and its causes are usually individualistic and personal, although there are certain characteristics, or symptoms, of this negative-feeling state that people will share. As I have already said, everyone feels down from time to time. It's only when this feeling persists for at least two weeks, accompanied by several other symptoms, that you may be heading for a more serious period of depression. The symptoms to watch out for include a complete loss of interest in your children/partner or personal forms of enjoyment, loss of appetite, feeling really fatigued, having a sense of worthlessness, seeing everything in a negative light, and ruminating on the negative things in your life. If you are depressed, you will constantly think about something in a negative way, over and over again, which will only serve to reinforce and prolong your negative feelings.

Depression does affect people differently however, with, for example, some people losing their appetites, while others eat more and more; some feeling completely flat and unable to move, while others become very irritable and unsettled. Trisha found that she couldn't sit still and had too much energy, and then, while in hospital, became afraid to move or speak. Basically, if you are depressed to the extent that it is more than a normal *downer*, you will eventually be unable to function in the way that you would normally in your day-to-day life, and this will in turn affect your family functioning. That's the time to get some professional help. And don't feel bad about it, it can happen to any one of us: men, women and children – think about Peter's experience when he had given up his job in Australia and wasn't working in England for a while. No one is exempt – susceptibility will depend on what is happening in an individual's life, their coping mechanisms, how stretched they are, and the kind of support network they have from friends and family.

Children, too, can become depressed, and again this will manifest differently according to the child or young person's personality and emotional style. One child may become very quiet and withdrawn, while another may become excessively irritable or angry. Again, Trisha kept a diary as a teenager and looks back at times when she can now identify how depressed she felt.

The Causes of Depression: Chicken or Egg?

Let's consider the *causes* of depression a little further. There is a consensus of opinion that depression is the result of both *exogenous* (external/outside influences) and *endogenous* (internal/chemical) factors, although it can be difficult to establish which comes first. Put simply, you may experience an event or situation that proves to be very stressful and challenging in terms of your ability to cope. This is an *exogenous* event. A typical example could be breaking up with your partner/lover – something many of us will have experienced at some point in our lives. Think about Trisha's experience, and the triggers to her breakdown: the post-natal illness of her second daughter, coping with a failing relationship, the discovery of her husband's infidelity, and then the final decision to end the relationship.

Then comes the *endogenous*, or internal factor; the biochemical changes in your brain. Basically, stressful events activate various branches of the nervous system, to release chemicals within the body. So, once you have started to feel down and continue to be exposed to ongoing stress, over time your biochemistry becomes unbalanced and set in a way that can make it difficult for you to move away from your negative feelings. Bingo: a longer-term episode of feeling depressed. Once you are in this position, you will need some help to get you back on top.

I would like to reflect on Trisha's experiences a little more in view of what I've written about so far, to help you start to recognise and think about depression in the context of everyday life. Firstly, as we know from what Trisha has told us, her childhood was difficult for her in many ways, and she had some psychological baggage from that period, which affected the way she thought and behaved in her earlier adulthood. Secondly, she also suffered some very traumatic life events during her teens: witnessing the schoolgirl being hit by the train at the station and the associated feelings of guilt, and, of course, the sexual assault. In her account, Trisha talks about how she developed a pattern of dealing with difficult issues in a very unhealthy way by either burying her head in the sand to avoid conflict at all cost, or working herself almost to the point of madness so that she didn't have the time to stop and think about her problems. Very significantly, Trisha also states that avoiding conflict and working in overdrive caused her to direct her anger inwards, which is very destructive. In Western culture anger is often seen as the one emotion that women should not outwardly express, despite the fact that it is a perfectly legitimate emotion for them to have from time to time. The problem is that when we suppress strong emotion, it has a tendency to surface somewhere else, as with Trisha's self-destructive behaviour. All of this, coupled with Trisha's years of failing relationships, excessive workload, the loss of her sister, having children and discovering her husband was having an affair, are the *exogenous*/external life events. The *endogenous* or internal aspect of her depression was an interactive ongoing part of it all, becoming really evident when she was sitting in her hospital room not being able to speak or move.

The Day-to-Day Effects of Depression

When you are depressed, you will see and frame everything in your day-to-day life as negative without even thinking about it. This can even apply to seemingly trivial situations. Here's an example: if you are held up in a traffic jam, you'll think 'I am so useless, I can't even get anywhere on time because I am so bad at everything,' when actually the reality of the situation is that everyone else on the road is in the same jam, and so will be late too. It isn't your fault – purely circumstance – yet you will attribute it to yourself. You may also tend to overgeneralise, with statements such as 'I never get anything right' when, again, that isn't true at all. Guilt is one kind of emotion that is commonly experienced by people when they become depressed, and people often fall in to the trap of thinking 'I feel so guilty that I must have done something wrong, I am such a bad person'.

People also commonly discount the positives in their life, such as any achievements they attain. For example, someone may have worked hard to pass an exam, get a promotion, or organise the day and keep a tidy house, yet will think 'Well, that's nothing, I am useless because that is easy, anyone can do that.' In summary, you will essentially be reacting to, and thinking about, everything you do as negative to the extent that it becomes your automatic or normal way of thinking.

How to Deal with Depression

If you think you might be seriously depressed you should immediately seek help from your GP, who will point you in the right direction for help. There are various forms of drugs available, which your GP can prescribe, and depending on how you feel, this may be a relevant short-term option. Most importantly (in my biased opinion) there are talking treatments or talking therapies. It is vital to think about *why* you may be depressed, and obtaining some form of counselling or therapy may help you to identify the possible answers to this. I am a firm believer in not merely relieving symptoms, but in treating or addressing the cause of the depression as well. In terms of treatment for depression, remember that your emotions are not static, which is good news! Over time you *will* begin to feel differently, even though at the time you are so depressed you may think things are never going to get better.

More on the Talking Therapies

Trisha had a lot of psychotherapy after her breakdown, which she identifies as being the key factor in helping her to get her life back on track. Not only did it help her to get going again, but it also helped her to become more self-aware, and to change the patterns of her behaviour that had previously been dangerous. She also began to change the way she viewed men, which helped her to make a better choice when it came to husband no. 3.

Cognitive behavioural therapy (the type of therapy she opted for) is specifically designed to help you challenge your automatic negative way of thinking by getting you to see and acknowledge the evidence that your life does contain positive elements; also, that your life is not static, and that for some of the day, even if it is only two minutes at first, you will have found a little enjoyment somewhere in something.

Trisha started out by realising that there was a massively important reason to live: she was a mother and her babies needed her (big plus). Second, the child psychiatrist worked very hard with Trisha and Billie to get them both to be able to see that life wasn't all blue stars (evidence that not every minute of every day is negative). The chart idea that Trisha referred to is fantastic because it was visual and meant that Billie, as a child, could really understand it. It was also a great way of getting Trisha and Billie to begin to talk about things.

Finally, any form of active *diversion* such as exercise or another form of hobby or activity at a time when you are depressed can be very helpful in providing some relief to depression. Trisha found that exercise was a great way to find relief, and has since kept it up as a means of regulating her moods.

Conclusion

There are only a couple of things left for me to say here. First, that depression is something you should never be ashamed of. It is the common cold of mental health, and you wouldn't feel ashamed if you had a cold or the 'flu, would you? The main thing is to get some help to support you (or the affected member of your family) through it, and when you do come out on top, you will be much wiser about yourself and your own mental health needs. Just look at how enriched Trisha and Peter's lives have become as a result of their experiences. Second, depression can often be the build-up of many stressful issues, and it can take time and effort on your part to work through it. You will need help and support to do this, and talking therapies are excellent for this purpose.

Finally, when I refer to talking therapies there are many practitioners with different titles. Lots of professional therapists use an integrative approach to their work, which literally means they use a variety of techniques ranging from cognitive behavioural to psychotherapeutic theoretical techniques. Some practitioners also use family therapy techniques, as was the case with the child psychiatrist who worked with Trisha and Billie simultaneously. The key thing to bear in mind is that you should only see a practitioner who is trained (or under supervised accredited training) and registered on the relevant professional practitioner database/register (see Chapter 10 for useful contacts).

Quiz

Depressed Debbie is a married, 34-year-old woman with two young children. When Debbie was young her parents divorced and she stayed with her mother and an elder brother. Her mother went through a turbulent, emotionally unstable period while adjusting to single parent life. During this time she sought emotional support from Debbie. At the time, this made Debbie feel as if she was her mother's confidante (she was feeling very grown up at 15 years of age), and she was always described by her mother and others as a 'good, responsible girl'. However, she has recently been experiencing periods of feeling overwhelmed and out of control in her adult life. Debbie is working full-time, while looking after two young children and trying to maintain a relationship with her husband, who is extremely loving and supportive of her. She is also involved in several local activities, such as a tennis and squash club and a running club, is studying part-time through the Open University, and runs a professional development group at work in her lunchtime. She is a very caring person and so frequently has friends phoning her up for advice on their personal problems, and she simply can't say no to helping anybody out when asked for a favour.

Depressed, Debbie has started to eat less and less, suffers from feeling excessively tired all of the time. At the same time she can't sleep, so she tosses and turns most of the night in bed. She is not interested in sex any more because she is too tired and too preoccupied with feeling useless and guilty. Also she no longer speaks to her husband unless he speaks first, and she does not take any interest in her children (whom she adores). Debbie now constantly thinks about herself as a complete failure because she believes that she does everything badly.

Your Contribution:

1) Make a list of all aspects or factors in Debbie's life that you identify as being positive, then write a separate list for *yourself*. Write down every positive thing you can think of that applies to your life. Include even the seemingly little things that you really appreciate or enjoy, such as having coffee in the garden in the morning on a weekend before getting dressed (that's my pleasure). Basically, anything that is actually nice or positive in some way for you.

2) What do you think is happening in Debbie's life at thistime, and how is depression affecting her?

3) What effect is her changing behaviour beginning to have on her family?

4) Finally I want you to keep a self-monitoring diary for the next couple of days. It would be great if you could do it for a whole week. It doesn't have to be fancy, just some rough notes on paper. Note down how you feel when you get up in the morning, then at various times through the day. Make a special note of any things or events during the day which trigger change in your moods and feelings, both positive and negative. Also note changes in your moods and feelings over time. If you can keep a self-monitoring diary for a few days, a week or even longer, have a look at your notes and see if you can begin to identify any patterns in your natural mood rhythms. Is there anything which particularly lifts your feelings in a positive direction, and if so, try doing more of it when you are feeling down.

Again, as I always remind you at the end of each chapter, ask yourself if there is anything that you have now realised is really positive about your life or self, and you need to do more of? Or is there something you may wish to consider changing?

Top Tips

1) Do everything in your power *not* to *suffer* with depression. Learn to *live* with it as you would have to if you had diabetes or asthma.

2) Get active: every scientific trial going suggests that exercise does wonders to improve everything, from feeling a bit annoyed to menopausal depression and even serious long-term clinical depression. So hop to it!

3) Serious physical illnesses are often accompanied by feelings of depression, so if you or a loved one is about to have surgery, bear that in mind.

4) Depression in one person can affect the whole family, *if* it's allowed to. Talk to loved ones about what the depressed person is dealing with. Get literature for both children and adults from mental health organisations (see Chapter 10, page 334).

5) When things get really bad, focus on keeping your vital organs going with food and sleep and basics, because when the fog lifts, you want your body well enough to feel the sunshine.

6) Never take a suicide threat anything but seriously. If you feel someone's crying 'Wolf' know that the person feels desperate enough about something to do that in the first place. Call in help immediately.

7) Keep moving! Keep breathing!

Case Study

The Cast
Stephen (27 years old)
Amanda (27 years old) – his partner

The story so far...
Amanda and Stephen have been together for eight years, and have two children. Amanda is 5 ft. 6, and 18 stone. She is very unhappy about her body image and because she has been teased in the past, won't leave the house. She has become fully dependent on Stephen and won't go anywhere without him. At one time Stephen persuaded her to leave the house once a day, but this didn't last very long, and now she won't go anywhere without him. Amanda admits that she has become very possessive of Stephen, and hates the fact that he has to go to work every day – it makes her very angry. If she could get him to work from home, she would. Her insecurity has made her jealous and suspicious, and she has been checking Stephen's phone for messages from other women. Unconfident, she won't let Stephen see her naked and says that sex with him is like a chore. Significantly, Amanda's mother died some time ago and this has had a massive impact on her.

Stephen is happily married, finds Amanda very attractive, and says that he has no problem with her weight. Her insecurity, however, puts a strain on their relationship. He has to go everywhere with her and is left to do everything for the kids. He is aware that they only have sex because she feels guilty. He finds Amanda's paranoia upsetting.

Help!

This is a good illustration of the complex factors that can contribute to someone becoming depressed to the extent that they lose their confidence, and lock themselves away from the outside world. Firstly, Amanda is overweight; secondly, the death of her mother has had a serious effect on her. The loss of a mother is an extremely distressing event, because it often leads people to question their existence and mortality. After all, one's mother has always been there physically (regardless of whether a person has had a good relationship with her). The loss of some-one close can often trigger feelings of depression and hopeless-ness, because it signals a time of huge emotional adjustment. Did Amanda begin eating more as a form of comfort to compensate for her grief? I would suspect that food has definitely provided some kind of psychological function in Amanda's life.

Stephen says that he doesn't have a problem with Amanda's weight, and is very supportive and encouraging of her. However, her weight *does* cause her a problem. Amanda has very low self-esteem and refuses to go out or expose her body to her partner. She doesn't feel at all sexy (sex being a chore rather than some-thing pleasurable). Her weight may not even be the primary cause of her depression, but is now most certainly a contributing factor, and is preventing her from enjoying her relationship with Stephen. Unfortunately, comfort eating and weight gain can become a vicious cycle. The more depressed you feel, the more you eat and gain weight, which in turn makes you even unhap-pier about yourself, and so you eat more.

It seems that Stephen has been assuming that Amanda's weight was the only reason for her depression, but he has now since realised that grief may also be playing a key part in her current emotional state. As I have suggested earlier in this chapter, a good way forward would be for Amanda to enlist some professional help. From here she could explore her feelings more in a supportive, constructive way, so that eventually she can begin to recognise the good and positive things in her life and feel empowered by herself.

Chapter Eight

Fit for Life

Trisha

We're breaking the pattern of the rest of the book here. This time I'm kicking off instead of Terri, though she'll be adding her thoughts later. This chapter is about how to work together as a family to survive the game of life. So here goes.

Let's say life is the big game; your family is your team, and every player has their own strengths and weaknesses, including you. I class you, or you and your partner, as the manager/coach.

If you, as manager/coach, and your team don't have a clue about how to talk to each other, arguments will be the order of the game. If every team member is at each other's throats, the fact is there's a good chance your team will break up and everyone will go their own way, with some players choosing to lose contact with others. Your team members may decide they've had such poor leadership or lack of understanding from the management and coach, that they'll distance themselves from you, act out your worst fears to draw attention to their unhappiness or put all their emotional energy into creating a team of their own. A bully as a team boss will in turn create team members who either go on to be bullies themselves or spend a lot of their lives being too weak to do anything but sit on the sidelines and opt out of the game altogether. If, on the other hand, the management is too sheepish and wishy-washy, the team will end up running the show, deciding which games they'll turn up for and sticking two fingers up at every referee they ever come across, tearing up the rule book until they're sent to the sin bin.

Finally, if you, the manager/coach, do a lousy job and the players know no better, then when they go on to set up their own teams, they'll unwittingly pass on a whole load of bad habits or downright destructive behaviour to another little generation of players. But, put in time, energy, enthusiasm and thought to telling and encouraging your team about what'll make them *feel* victorious, and the chances are very heavily stacked in favour of them doing you and, more importantly, *themselves* proud. First, though, a word of warning about the type of management and coaching that is either doomed to failure or your being rightfully labelled 'Chief Hypocrite'…

'Don't do as I do – Do as I say!' Whoever came up with this idiotically stupid, lazy, opt-out phrase needs a red card shoved up their you-know-what. Unless you belong to the Hitler, Stalin or Idi Amin school of how to be loved by instilling fear, forget it.

How many parents have I had on my show, angry that their teenager is smoking? Their evidence? 'Well, the damned child keeps nicking my fags!' Startling fact no.1. If you don't want your child to smoke, don't smoke yourself (best-case scenario) or, as my father did when he used to smoke, make sure you very rarely smoke anywhere near your kids, i.e. so they never see you puffing away.

Here's another one: 'My child's hugely overweight and doesn't exercise!' wails a parent, who (you've guessed it) could be describing themselves. I tell the parent it's a great opportunity for them to change their eating and exercise habits and, Abracadabra, they'll see a magical change in their kids and the rest of the family.

I'm not Miss Ain't-I-Always-Wonderful on this score either. I used to find myself nagging Billie about being too critical of her little sister until Peter pointed out the glaring fact that I had head-in-sand-like overlooked. I can be pretty critical myself. I still have to work hard to unlearn a habit that caused so much pain to me in childhood when my father was like that with me. Ah, yes, like any coach, you've got to take great care not to unintentionally hand down bad habits to your team. So, how do you manage and coach your team into being as ready as possible to go out onto the world pitch and score happiness?

Okay, we've come up with a few tactics you can use to get your team up to speed. The way this will work is that I'll kick off with the key area we're focusing on, and Peter will chip in on anything he feels strongly about. Billie gets to have her say at the end. The subjects we're covering aren't in any particular order, and what they're designed to do is to promote a fair, responsible, respectful, communicative, more balanced family training session, which should get your team well on the way to get the most out of the game (i.e. life). It's not meant to be a comprehensive list of everything you can do to get your team fit for life, but we reckon it's a pretty good basis for future training sessions!

Players' Rights

What are we talking about here? Well, think of this as being about a family members' Bill of Rights. I'll comment on the ones I work at maintaining in our household and Peter has firm views on other rights he often has to remind me of.

I firmly believe that each family member has the right to an abuse-free existence, but I'm not naïve enough to think that's the way it is. However, if you instil in your loved ones that it's their right *not* to be abused by *anyone* in *any way*, you're doing a lot to help them establish that there are lines no one should cross. When I talk about abuse here, I mean sexual, emotional and physical abuse. Obviously, if you constantly use put-down, belittling language (even in jest) when you're frustrated or angry with either your children or your partner, you're going to get absolutely nowhere telling your kids they should never let anyone hit them or call them names. If you are the very person who is stamping all over their rights, realise you are paving the way for them to go through life allowing anyone or everyone else to do the same. Likewise, if you're in a relationship where you allow your partner to hit you or put you down, you can tell your children they shouldn't let someone do the same to them till you're blue in the face, but it won't make a blind bit of difference. In a few years' time, despite your words, there's a massive chance you will have given your children a future of being abused. Either that or you'll end up with offspring who at some level are angry with you for putting up with a continuous abuse of your rights, and they, as kids, having to witness it.

My daughters' Australian school had a great way of encouraging children to have abuse-free lives. From the age of three, they drummed this into them: 'This is my body and I am in charge of it. It is precious. No one is allowed to hold or touch me in a way that makes me feel bad.' Thus, once, when someone close to us draped herself round Billie when she was three, in an attempt to give her a big sloppy kiss, she was taken aback by Billie pushing her away and saying, 'Hey, this is my body and I'm the boss of it. What you're doing doesn't feel good, so stop!' I explained to this poor well-meaning person that Billie's ability and strength to actually say what she truly felt instead of grinning and bearing it would be the very same learned characteristics that would go a long way to ward off less well-meaning physical attention throughout her life.

Every family member has a right to be respected, and not sworn at, cruelly labelled, or teased mercilessly. That's emotional abuse in its crudest form, which is why we go into more detail about it in Chapter 5 (page 145). Even if 'only done as a joke', trust me, constant name-calling, either by a parent or by a sibling, will cut deep and the 'labelled' child will grow up believing that they really are a 'total idiot' or a 'lard-ass'. In other words, 'labelling' someone will eat away at their self-esteem and if you do it to your partner, you are trudging slowly and surely towards separation. I'm not saying that criticism is to be avoided, because that extreme can be damaging in other ways. Rather, you need to label the *behaviour*, rather than the person, i.e. 'That was a really evil thing to do to your brother,' as opposed to, 'You're a really evil child.'

As far as swearing goes, if you don't want certain words to be used in your household, then don't use them yourself. I tell the girls that I don't care what language they may hear or be tempted to use in their outside world, but I reserve the right not to have to hear it in my house. Home should be a sanctuary from that kind of stuff. I also try to come up with alternative ways the girls could express themselves and constantly refer to non-stop swearing as Ape Man's last resort! Relying on swearing to make a point makes only one point: you haven't got the brains and imagination to come up with anything else. In the same breath I tell them I *know* they're way better than that.

Which brings us to the right I'll simply call 'esteem'. If criticism is a part of life, then so, too, should praise and we don't do it enough. Try introducing the right everyone in your family has to be congratulated on the things they do happily or well, or good behaviour. It balances up the fact that words of criticism always seem to sound so much louder, and does wonders for the self-esteem. Just putting up school paintings and certificates is a good way of praising effort.

Another, less obvious way of bolstering a family member's self-esteem is to take time to seek them out, sit quietly and talk to them about what's happening in their lives, when there *isn't* some huge problem to be dealt with. It's great for a child (or partner, for that matter) to be told, 'Hey, I know I've/you've been busy recently, but I've really been looking forward to catching up with you.'

And there's another right. We all need to be listened to. A good manager/coach does a lot to encourage team members to voice their opinions and feelings, but the flip side of this is that the results can sometimes make uncomfortable hearing. Remember, however, the volcano that lets off a little bit of steam often is far less scary than the one that appears to be inactive, then goes off with an almighty, fire-spitting explosion. The best way to listen is with your ears and *eyes*. When talking to a guest on the show, I pick up just as much by watching their eyes, hands and body language as I do from listening to what (and *how*) they talk about their lives.

In an ideal world, we should have the right to *feel* loved. I say *feel*, because there are many of us who may have *heard*, either directly or indirectly, that a parent loves us. You know, Mum says, 'I know he never says it or shows it, but Daddy *does* love you, you know, really.' Yeah, yeah, so Daddy had a tough upbringing where no one showed anyone any love. So, hey, Daddy, what about sparing the next generation the heartache you felt as a boy? Even if it does make you a feel a little awkward at first? A wooden hug is better than zero physical contact with your kids, isn't it?

Feeling loved is also about not being neglected, physically or emotionally, and if that's a legacy you're passing down to your children and you're struggling with how to change things because of your past, check out Chapter 10 for help. Bravo for recognising the fact – now do something about it!

Peter

One of the most important rights in any family is to be able to exercise some control over space. This might be a child's bedroom, a parent's bedroom or some other important space. In our family, the kids are very private about their bedrooms; they each have numerous signs on the door telling us to 'keep out', 'enter and die', 'parent-free zone'. It's really healthy to want private space and also to seek to exercise control over how that space looks, how tidy (or not) it is and who can come and go in it. Generally, we try and respect this by knocking and waiting for permission before we enter the girls' bedrooms. However, there is a fine line here we insist on – namely, the space must be respected and kept clean and looked after. Occasionally, when rooms get too untidy we need to override the privacy thing but we explain the reasons for this. In our case, we exercise privacy over our bedroom. The kids have to knock before coming in and, if the door is closed, then they can only knock in an emergency.

There are also other areas around the house that have become the unofficial property or domain of one particular family member. For me, it's the study and, of course, the shed. For Trish, it's the kitchen (for reasons of warmth and newspaper-reading rather than because of any traditional stereotypes) and the formal sitting-room (she doesn't use this space much but somehow she knows it's hers!). The kids have their bedrooms and a shared playroom.

Encouraging each other to exercise and express the need for privacy also makes for greater mutual understanding when it comes to living together. In addition to privacy, we recognise a number of other universal rights in our family. They are the rights to:

- *be angry*
- *be alone*
- *be embarrassing*
- *not act your age (something Trish excels at!)*
- *demand attention by passing wind (ditto!)*
- *not laugh at my jokes*
- *not like one another (for a while)*
- *be respected*
- *be held responsible*

These last two are very important. Trish and I are very similar in the sense that we believe that it is more important to let the children (and each other) make a decision that suits them (even if we disagree) as long as the consequences are known and met if things don't work out. We don't compel the children to do jobs around the house. We help them identify the benefits and the risks and to determine for themselves how much they want to contribute. As parents, we, in turn, determine how much we will give in response to their effort. So, if Billie can't be bothered to help me one day, then there is a fair chance I might be too tired to bother helping her the next. This might seem a little unforgiving to many parents but it keeps us sane, teaches the value of contribution, affords the power to make decisions but also to reap the consequences – good and bad.

Trisha

So, to stay with the sports team analogy, you could sum up each member's rights like this:

- **P**rivacy
- **L**ove & being **L**istened to
- **A**buse-free
- **Y**outh
- **E**steem
- **R**espect & Responsibility

Home Turf (*or how the state of your practice pitch affects how your team plays in the Big League!*)
A typical Saturday. The television's blaring in one room, a radio in another. Two kids are having an argument that could challenge Armageddon. The dog's barking, hubby's hammering and you're screaming 'Tea-time!' up the stairs. Ever despair at the almost constant full-on, full-bore noise in your household? The children don't seem to bother with talking; they're far more into shouting and screaming. Doors aren't shut, they're slammed. When you want peace and quiet, you have to holler for it... Hey, wait a minute!

Using our example of the sports team, as managers/coaches, the adults in the household hold the key to the state of the pitch: chaotic surroundings, chaotic play and even more chaotic communication. That's not to say a house should be as quiet as a church.

Let me give you an example of how seriously I take the 'family setting'. Back in my days in Australian television, I did a story on a woman who specialised in colour therapy. I have to admit, I was pretty sceptical at first – until we looked at her work in two widely contrasting scenarios: prisons and fast food chains. Where violent offenders were housed, she'd recommended calming pastel colours, and for the fast food chains, she'd selected vibrant jarring colours. This last idea was pretty nifty. Coupled with the high hard seats you had to perch on while seated at the too-narrow counters, it made burger-eaters wolf their food as fast as possible and get out. If you think about it, it makes perfect sense. Making them comfortable would've meant people hanging around for too long so that others would have to be turned away. Aha, so why not apply this colour and comfort psychology to your house?

Rather than using any old colour when decorating, I give a lot of thought to what each room is to be used for and who I want in there. When the girls saw my newly decorated sienna-coloured 'posh' room complete with elaborately ornate curtains, they reacted with 'Yuck!' Success. Their playroom, on the other hand, is sunshine yellow with multi-coloured curtains; upbeat and fun. Their bedrooms are decorated in calming colours, so I find that when they want to go a bit wild, they tend to move into the play-room, which is designed to be as messy as you like – you can just shut the door! Our bedroom is deep crimson and looks like a Middle Eastern bordello, complete with red lights. It oozes sex appeal. Guess why?!

I like the centre of the house to be the kitchen. That way, whoever's cooking is doing it with people around, talking about their day and discussing problems. It's a great way of combining eating and socialising and actively works against people sitting by themselves and paying little attention to what they're eating. Some rooms are designed to be tidy and their very layout dictates that. Others, such as the family room, are designed to be dishevelled so people know it's okay to relax and not sweat the small stuff there. If you give every room a very different feel, you can create different climates: quiet, thinking spaces, family talking places or time-to-let-off steam places. Yep, I'm a firm believer in thinking before you pick up the paintbrush.

If most of your house is like a tip, save your breath when it comes to telling junior to tidy up his room or pick up his clothes. I'm into a 'clear-up-as-you-go' thing, not just for the kids, but for myself too. So much easier than having to devote whole days to cleaning up.

I'm also a firm believer in only having one television in a central place. But then I'm a believer in taking the opportunity to watch the box with family members, especially kids, whenever possible. Commenting on the latest soapy plot is a great way of gauging what your kids think about a wide range of subjects, from teenage pregnancy to drugs and violence. Yes, having one television can cause friction when it comes to choosing who watches what, but you can also use those discussions as an opportunity for bargaining and compromise.

And so to noise. Kids learn by example. If you have the radio on while you're vacuuming and shouting above the lot, you're training your household into thinking that's the way it has to be. Get used to checking how many decibels are being pumped out and get into the habit of going upstairs, knocking on doors and chatting quietly, rather than screeching orders like a banshee. As I said (or if I didn't, I should have), a well thought-out pitch will breed more considerate play.

Peter

It's all about compromise, really. In many families it seems that parents do most of the compromising. In our family it is far more equitable: we try to teach the kids that we are all entitled to the same quality of life and living conditions, that we all have a role to play in achieving this and that, at times, we all have to forgo something in favour of someone else.

This might mean setting a limit on when the kids can watch television or play on the computer. This is because we want to encourage them to play creatively, to use their imagination, rather than someone else's imagination reflected in a computer programme. It's also because Trish and I recognise that we need kid-free space and kid-free time. We need the opportunity to just be adults rather than parents. For us, this is a central part of our relationship – we ensure that we have this space and time for our relationship and to practise being adults with each other. This might sound corny but sometimes we forget about our own, and our partner's, identity as we get consumed by parenting. It is really important to remind yourself, and be reminded, about the person you are and the person you are with – even if this means sending the kids to bed early. It won't seem fair to them but, then again, neither is having to pick them up at the school disco at 11 o'clock at night – it's all about compromise and being honest with each other about our needs.

Trisha

Teamwork and Telling It Like It Is

On the subject of rights, I passionately believe that children have a *right* to have rules. I've lost count of the number of troubled young people I see on my show, who desperately wish their parent/s would give them rules and guidelines and stick to them. If life is a highway, it's a hell of a lot easier to know where you're going if there are signs and signals to obey. Roundabouts would be bedlam without everyone knowing whom to give way to. And if you're travelling down life's highway in a convoy, it makes the journey a lot less traumatic if everyone knows which route to take and works together in getting to the destination.

And so it is with the family team. Teamwork needs a framework of rules. Every sport has them. And if, as the managers/coaches of the team you haven't sat down and *actively* worked out what these family rules are going to be, not only will you start clashing with the children when you make things up as you go along, but you and your partner will set yourselves up for endless arguments. It's so easy to play one management team off against each other if neither of them knows what's in the other one's rule book! 'Dad, Mum said I'm allowed to watch this 15+ video.' Father lets 13-year-old kid watch it. Mother interrupts and switches off television halfway through. Child has tantrum at mother. Mother has tantrum at father. *Kaboom!* If only the management team had had a chat about appropriate films, videos and television for each child to start with and then kept updating those rules as the kids got older. Like a coach, the best way to get the rules across is to gather the team together when a subject arises (say, after the unholy row about who watches what video) and for both parents to lay down the law. Naturally, rules will differ for each family member, because of age, ability etc., and you will invariably hear the whinge, 'But that's not fair!' Whereupon I quickly point out that there's no hard-and-fast rule that says everything always has to be fair. Fairness is all about family equity. Here's a story that illustrates this: a row of apples hangs from a tree. All the apples are the same distance above the ground. There are six kids, ranging from two to four feet in height, and each one wants an apple. Let's make it fair, and put some boxes under the tree so they can reach an apple. Er, so are the boxes all going to be the same height? No. Fairness is about each family member being given the opportunity to achieve the apple of opportunity, so some people will need more of a leg up than others.

Teamwork is all about everyone giving something as well as taking. Now this notion may well stun your kids when put to them. They often confuse being a child with having the God-given right to be no-strings-attached recipients of love, every penny you can spare, you as taxi service, party arranger, toy-, computer- and mobile phone buyer and as food and comfort provider. Peter and I feel it's vital to teach children from the start that they're expected to put in more than cute smiles and cheekiness. So, our girls have 'jobs' with terms and conditions. There is no such thing as pocket money for pocket money's sake in our house. Billie and Madi have to earn every penny. Madi has to empty the dishwasher four mornings a week and, in summer months, feed the fish in the garden ponds. Billie is expected to keep the numerous feed trays filled for the wild birds in our large country garden. No jobs, no pocket money. Under the rules of the game, if a job is persistently not done, your job (and the money that goes with it) is offered to another person, i.e. you get the sack, just like in the real world. As I write this, Peter and Billie have had a number of heated negotiations about her failing to do her job. Her argument is that, it being winter, she doesn't want to venture into a darkened garden even though parts of the garden are floodlit and she can use a torch. We pointed out that when she has friends over, they love screaming around the darkened garden, with torches. I also alerted her to the fact that, like Madi, she could do her job before going to school. But, no, she's dug her heels in, won't do it and isn't getting paid. The next step is that she'll get fired and lose the means to make money. We shall see…

If you have doubts about the notion of children having to earn their money, consider this. Recent research has found that the wealthier the family, the less money they give their children as pocket money and the more likely it is that it'll have to be earned. It seems that those who've had a tough childhood hand out more, no strings attached. But which group of children is learning bargaining powers and financial responsibility? Which group is learning the respect and importance of earning its own money, and which group is being given the message that living on handouts (and, later the dole) that you don't have to do anything to get is okay? On a personal note, eight-year-old Madi just bought her very own CD and, boy, is there a difference in the way she handles it and sings along with it in comparison to those CDs she's received as gifts. When we sing along to Destiny's Child's hit song, 'Independent Woman' (lyrics along the lines of 'The house I live in, I bought it. The car I'm driving, I bought it. The ring I'm wearing, I bought it – I depend on me when I want it?'), my girls have the fledgling stirrings that will prevent them from ending up in a bad relationship purely because they are financially dependent on some man.

Peter

I am a great believer in honesty, even if it hurts. In our family we tell it like it is. We don't make up silly little excuses when one of us annoys another one – we are honest and direct. This attitude is reflected in the concepts of teamwork and democracy.

While we all have rights we do not have equal influence. The fact is that some members of our family (Trish and I) contribute much more than others. We will tell our children that they have rights, that communication and honesty are good and that they will always be heard and respected but that doesn't mean they will always be right or be allowed to have the final say.

Trish is far more into negotiation than I am. She will argue a point with Billie for ages, going over and over her rationale and reasons for a decision. I agree with the principle of this, but the reality is that kids usually work out the reasons for parental actions early on and that negotiation is often just a process of trying to overturn a decision rather than increasing any understanding of it. In our family, I place a clear limit on how much negotiation I am willing to have. This often makes me appear harsh or unreasonable, but there is a limit – and in our family it is the parents who determine what that limit is.

I often say 'when you are an equal contributor, you can have equal influence', until then, we can discuss stuff but the parents have the final word. In many respects this is like a good team. There needs to be an identified leader, someone with a little more authority than everyone else. This person might be the manager, the coach, or a combination of the two. The managers/coaches respect the rights of their players to have a view, recognise that this view will be based on a unique perspective, and may even be open to negotiation and debate, but, ultimately, when a decision has to be made, they make it.

Trisha

Talk

I'm not going to rabbit on about the importance of communication: that's a given. But, knowing that it's got to happen and working out the realities of when and how it does are two quite different things. A few observations: with children, the more surreptitious (okay, sly) you are about how and when you talk to them, the better. And if you only rock up for a chat when the poo hits the air-conditioning, every time you approach – even if it's only to moan about the weather – they're going to flinch and start with the selective deafness stuff!

So, regular chats. When? For feedback on how they feel about sex, drugs, rock and roll, etc., you can't do much better than watching music videos on MTV together and discussing the lyrics afterwards, or watching soapies together and doing the same, as long as you start out by talking about the singer/character's stance before you breeze into talking about their feelings.

Want to talk about what and when they eat? 'Hey, give us a hand in the supermarket will you?' is where that conversation could start. Checking out new products and nutritional contents written on the backs of packets is a good opportunity to bring up too stodgy/junk foody/too restricted etc. chats. Walking the dog or going for an after-Sunday-lunch stroll is another great setting for a chat because it offers a change of scenery, which is good for putting touchy subjects into a neutral setting. This walk and talk option is particularly brilliant when trying to talk to girls with premenstrual tension and stroppy boys, by the way. With younger kids, you can play Cowboys and Indians, Star Trek, whatever. Them seeing you play can break down any reticence to talk. People who are fun are *soooo* much easier to chat to.

What I'm saying is, be creative in picking your time and place for a chat. Also, watch your guise. Is this the kind of friendly chat where what you're really doing is finding out their line of thinking on contentious issues? Is this a laying-down-the-law chat? (The children's bedrooms are not the best places for this, by the way. Don't sully their rest and retreat place with too much of the heavy stuff.) Or is this an 'explaining' type of chat (quiet walks and garden settings are a good idea here)? I'm a big fan of at least one big sit-down-together-around the dinner table a week, for a good old family discussion on whatever comes up. It's a great way to gauge who thinks what about which situation – politics, family, gossip, morals…any subject where you can encourage even the youngest family member to have their say as well as encouraging those with rusty listening skills to polish them up a bit.

Creativity

Back in the days of Australian single mum-dom I took Billie skiing in nearby New Zealand. She wasn't yet five. She'd had a hard time over her father and I splitting and, as children do, had that awful feeling that she was powerless and that big things would always conquer her. After she'd had numerous private skiing lessons, I took her up the mountain to an easy slope. If she fell over I insisted she got up on her own, even if she cried or screamed. I explained I wouldn't always be there to help her up and she needed to know how to look after herself. She thought I was a monster parent for threatening to ski off down the hill without her if she didn't stop the tears and put her energy into getting up, but I tell you what. When she'd managed to ski down that great big mountain all on her own and I turned her round to look high up into that edifice of snow, she beamed. 'See', I said, 'Little you, who thought you'd never make it! Little you who thought the big things would always win – you just skied all the way down that great big mountain all on your own! And if you can do that when you thought you couldn't – think what else you can do.' Sure I was making it up as I went along, but that bit of creative problem-solving really worked. In fact, eight years later, it still works…

A Sense of Humour

This is so important in our family. To give my father his due, he *did* pass his great sense of humour and love of the ridiculous on to me. He could be quite John Cleese-ish when I was growing up and had an infectious laugh I couldn't get enough of. Someone staying with us recently remarked at what a fabulous sense of humour our whole family had. Others I know call our family zany because of the fact that we're not afraid to have a laugh, and to hell with what bystanders may think.

I write a weekly diary-type magazine column and, again, readers say they love the tales of our humour-filled household. I think a lot of this comes from our Aussie background. Amongst our friends there it was okay for parents to act the idiot in front of the kids for a laugh. Being mates is virtually all about having a laugh, even if it's sometimes at your own expense. But humour is a great tool to use in a whole lot of ways: teaching your kids something you want them to remember, bringing a dragging argument to an end, making a point, or just showing your kids that you're human.

Examples? I have a massive problem with all those fairy tales and their helpless-princess-being-saved-by-dashing-prince lines. There's no way I want my daughters waiting for some man to liberate/take care of them, etc. Nevertheless, a few years ago, Madi was on at me to tell her one of these happily-ever-after bedtime stories. So, finally, I gave in and told her a hybrid Cinderella/Rapunzel/Sleeping Beauty one and ended it like this:

> ME (*in hushed tones*): *The prince gazed upon the sleeping princess, and was struck by her beauty. He knew instantly that he was in love with her. Slowly he lowered his lips to her crimson lips...*
>
> (*By this time Madi's eyes were wide with wonderment at the prospect of yet another broad being rescued by Mr Beefcake!*)
>
> ME: *Then, just as their lips met, the prince jumped up over the princess and farted in her face. You can bet that woke her up!*

I then fell about laughing, as did Madi. When she asked why I'd changed the ending, I told her that if you go into something with your eyes closed like our pal Sleeping Beauty, sooner or later you'll wake up to the nasty smell of a rotting relationship. She's never forgotten that little homily!

Often in the middle of a way-too-lengthy negotiation with the kids, when I'm well aware that the whole thing is a stalling tactic so they won't have to tidy up/do one of their chores or whatever, I'm well known to suddenly go into a Dalek-type voice and start towards the girls like a mad robot, screeching, 'You will comply or you will be destroyed!' Amidst much laughter, the girls give up and do what they're meant to. Sometimes I'll tell them I'm fed up with being a mother and from now on I am Superchicken. From then on I'll talk in sentences of clucks and pretend to fly from room to room. Or we have opera sessions where we have to sing everything we want to say. When the girls were younger, we'd have 'Who can tidy away the most toys?' races, with me providing a manic commentary. I actually had the girls looking forward to tidying up after themselves.

Cliché time: Laughter is the best medicine. A spoonful of sugar makes the medicine go down. Laugh and the whole world (or family) laughs with you.

Warning: The first sign of a family sliding into problems is a family that either rarely laughs together or stops laughing together.

Looking after the Locker Room

Teaching your team values is an important one. For instance:

- **What things cost.** *Working for pocket money goes some way towards this.*
- **The value of family pets.** *Feeding and grooming them; taking the dog for a walk helps teach them this.*
- **Property.** *This means looking after not only their own stuff, but other people's property too. If they lose a brother's CD, they do jobs and earn the money to replace it. They spray paint someone's wall? You take them to the hardware store, make them pay for cleaning materials and clean up the graffiti themselves.*
- **The value of elderly family members.** *Don't run grandparents down in front of the children. Let kids spend time with them and get into the habit of phoning them regularly.*
- **Respect for a family member's disability.** *Read through information on the disability together as a family. Encourage siblings to push wheelchairs and do your utmost to play up the disabled person's abilities by not allowing any feelings of guilt or pity to take over and make you mollycoddle them.*
- **Faith.** *This is a tricky one. I let the girls know what I believe and we often discuss faith. But then I encourage them to explore, learn about and appreciate all other faiths. I love the Ba'hai faith's message that all beliefs are equal and basically different versions of the same thing. Faith should be something to draw the members of humankind together, not drive them apart.*

Every team has its own values, but unless these are demonstrated and discussed, your players are more likely to take the mickey than play fairly and give respect in order to earn it in return.

I am NOT the Centre of the Universe

Some parents go overboard on this one and do what I call the 'Starving Children in Africa' thing at every opportunity. Beware of trotting out the line, 'Remember, there are people far worse off than you,' every time someone confides in you about a problem that is clearly causing them great angst. This can backfire, because what can happen is that you create a climate where people bury their true feelings of hurt and put up with something quite damaging in the belief that just because Mbele of the Kalahari, or Steve, who's just lost a million on the Futures Exchange, is having a hell of a time, they have no right to feel their own pain. Sure, the person will shut up about the pain they're feeling, but don't be fooled. Suppressing pain and dealing with it are two totally different things, with totally different outcomes – and guess which one leads to depression, lack of self-worth and often physical illness?

No, this is more about helping loved ones recognise that bad things aren't necessarily happening *because* of them. Someone snapping angrily at them may hurt their feelings, but is it about them or is it because the Snapper has seconds before shut their finger in the door and therefore would've snapped at whoever came along next, be it the Queen of England or your little Johnny? I guess it's about getting children to ask why things happen and why things have happened, while realising it's not always about or in reaction to them. Sort of… Don't take everything too personally…

Yellow Card/Red Card

There's more about conflict in Chapter 6 (page 169), but here are a few pointers on why it's important that your children learn how to handle it. Who are the people who are the most terrified of conflict and will go to any lengths to avoid it? The people I'm talking about will put up with being treated atrociously because they're frightened of the friction that'll be caused if they say, 'Stop, no more!' or become human Welcome mats because they bend over backwards so much to avoid conflict that they end up lying flat on the floor and somebody takes this as a signal to wipe their muddy boots on them.

Who are these people? Often, they're adults who've witnessed unresolved and scary verbal or physical violence as children. That may not come as a surprise, but what if I told you that there are just as many human doormats and head-in-sand cases who are like that because, 'My parents never argued.' These people may even describe their childhoods as 'happy', so why the fear of conflict? Because, animals that we are, we're very good at picking up on an atmosphere of simmering and unspoken resentment and anger and it can be every bit as emotionally poisonous as uncontrolled continuous outbursts where one person cowers, the other thunders and nothing ever gets worked out.

So, do I think it's bad for a child to sometimes witness their parents arguing? No, providing they also see the parents making up. The message is loud and clear: arguing and conflict are not the end of life as we know it. They're just necessary bumps on the road of understanding. Conflict can be used positively and constructively, as long as there are basic rules about how it's done and what's acceptable and what's not.

Balancing the Ball

The emphasis these days seems to be on having to be a super-every-thing. Just check out the magazine titles in the newsagents. How to be a super-looking super cook, supermum, super lover, super slim babe who's a dab hand at interior design and a green-fingered goddess in the garden on the side... Bah! Then there are all these flipping television types telling you how they've got it all... Like, what do *they* know about real life? Oops! Hang on, that's *me* on the front of that magazine. So how come if I've supposedly got it all, I feel so washed out and panicky about wasting time in the newsagents' when I've only got half an hour before I have to pick up the kids from school? There is no way I'm going to get round the supermarket in that time, let alone get to the bank.

On my three television studio days, I tend to either walk the dog or do the school run first. Then I go to work and do two shows in front of a live audience, back to back and without a lunch break. I leave work at six or seven in the evening and slot straight back into the usual timetable. These days we have a housekeeper and gardener who come three times a week. Before you sigh and think, 'Hey, the lucky cow's living a *Hello!* maga-zine life' in pre-dosh days, back in Australia, all housework was done by me. I still do a fair bit and Peter does a lot of gardening, plus we're both very hands-on parents.

Even though I'm a lucky little clown these days, the juggling act can still get me wound up enough for weekly bitching sessions with my girlfriend Lou. 'Yeah, well, how can the husband expect me to concentrate on kissing him and being the attentive wifey, plus talking about his day when I'm up to my eyeballs cooking, Mum's on the phone and I'm trying to unpack the shopping before the frozen stuff melts all over the kitchen floor?' 'Oh, look, why not just stick TAXI on the car and have done with it? I have to dash to Billie's singing lesson, pop into work while she's there. Then I have to dash back to pick Madi up from Club.'

Those are a few of the day-to-day whinges. On top of that, though, there's the issue of how I put all the little pieces that go to make up Trisha into the Big Picture. There's Me the Mother, Me the Lover, Me the Worker, Me the Housewife, Me the Woman, Me the Mate, Me the Public Person, Me the Private Person, Me the Parent and Me the Child.

A major source of conflict is that having been in the public eye for the last 15 years, I've grown to be quite wary of *why* people want to meet me. I've been burned too many times in the past by those claiming friendship, inviting me along to their parties or drinks down the pub. Excited at meeting new people, I'd turn up and quickly realise that the whole 'do' had been promoted as a 'Come and Meet Trisha Goddard Off the Telly'. I'd spend the whole evening being asked things like what was it like to be famous? Which celebs did I know? What were they really like? 'Just sign this to my little brother before I join the queue to have my photo taken with you.' I'd be seething with resentment and kicking myself that I'd been too naïve to see the trap I'd walked into.

So when Peter tells me to just come along to this or that, my guard is up. Peter's been 'had' before and I often think he's far too trusting of people. He gets cross when I start giving him the third degree about who's invited us to what and why. 'You're okay about going to television awards nights, though. There are loads of television types who do the "I *love* your show" stuff and if you don't mind when *they* do it, why make a fuss when people who've invited us out do it?' he says. I try to explain that television types make no pretence of wanting to be friends. They don't ask what it's like to be a star and all of that stuff which makes me want to throw up. At television bashes, I'm playing 'Trisha' and we all know the rules. Pose for the camera and get a free meal and a bit of publicity for the show. But when I'm being the real me, Mrs Gianfrancesco, why should I have to perform? That's why I like hanging out with the mums at school. To them I'm Madi and Billie's mummy with the unpronounceable surname. End of story. Their burning questions consist of whether Madi wants to come over to play with Harriet and do they have to wear school uniform for the day trip to the farm? The mothers see me as another one of them: flaws, warts, no make-up and all.

I'm far more ruthless when it comes to juggling my role of mother with people's reaction to the day job and I go into 'kill mode' when anybody attempts to push aside/interrupt/ talk over or interrogate my bambinas. However, I can see that my natural suspicion of people's motives gets in the way of Peter wanting to increase our social circles. He moans that if I was just any old wife, we could pop down to any scraggy little eatery for a quick bite or nip into any old nightclub for a bit of a bop. Nigh impossible. The stares, comments and constant interruptions mean that we tend to stick to the same tried and trusted member-only places that we both get bored with. Being Trisha has both its ups and its downs.

But I digress. What I'm really harping on about is that feeling that everyone seems to want a piece of your bottom, and, hey, they want it right now. That feeling that whichever way you play it, you just can't win. The children are playing up and need help with their homework at the same time as the dog needs feeding; your mother hasn't quite grasped the fact that you're grown-up with your own children and is laying some guilt trip on you down the phone. As always she times it to coincide with the exact second you're about to deliver that killer line during an argument with your husband, and I'll bet all this happens about 15 seconds after you open that letter you just *know* is from the bank and you're already feeling the first pangs of indigestion.

As I've discovered, there are no hard-and-fast rules about how to juggle the different roles we all have in life. But one thing is for sure, if you keep your wits about you, a fellow team member is bound to point out when you're hogging a particular ball. So the next time a loved one whinges, 'I hardly see you these days', or 'You're always at work', instead of immediately becoming defensive, sit down and draw a circle on a bit of paper. Then divide the circle up into all the different bits you're juggling, so that the more time you're giving to one part of your life, the bigger that portion of the circle is. Now ask the 'I want more of your time' whinger to do the same. You'll probably find that your diagrams will look pretty similar (even if the big bits of their circle aren't in the same areas as yours). You'll soon see which parts of your life are taking over. Ah, but what about the line, 'I need to work this much to support my family'? Well, hey, emotional poverty will wipe out a relationship much faster than financial poverty.

The other thing is that some people deliberately stack one part of their lives so that they can bury their heads in the sand to avoid the reality of another. We've all seen it – the new dad who suddenly starts working all hours going under the guise that he needs to increase his work time by 50 per cent in order to cover the costs of a ten-pound tot. It wouldn't be that he feels helpless and confused about the new addition, would it? Surely it's not about the fact that having always been Number One with his woman, he suddenly feels shut out and alienated and how's he meant to bring up the subject of sex and cuddles when it's plain the new mum feels so wrecked? So it's always a good idea to check out why part of your life (or your partner or children's lives) is so constantly and heavily dominated by one particular thing, be it work, eating, going out or staying down the pub. In the words of the Game, if one player is constantly hogging a ball, run up and tackle them about it!

Peter

It is not easy being married to a famous person. Undoubtedly, it has its advantages and most people would not understand when I say that I wish Trish could enjoy the success without the fame. It means we cannot enjoy the same spontaneity as many other couples. We can't just go out to a club to dance or to a small restaurant without being prepared to entertain the interest of many fans.

The other issue, which Trish has also touched on, is the problem of being involved in two very different worlds, and constantly juggling the two. For example, there is the world of my job as the manager of a mental health charity, where I am surrounded every day by very disadvantaged and poor people who have perhaps the lowest status in our society. By contrast, when I enter the television world with Trish, it is typically comfortable, prestigious and we are surrounded by wealthy and prominent people. It all seems a little unreal at times. One of the things I love most about Trish is that she is real. She would genuinely rather spend time with a person that I might deal with, or a single mum, than in the company of starlets. This enables us to enter the television world with a healthy dose of cynicism and to act as guests in this élite club rather than regular members.

Reality Check: I am the husband of a famous television star. I have to balance my need for normality against the reality of having vicarious fame. I have to balance my new identity against the one I gave up when we moved. I need to balance the various roles in my life, including that of manager, father, husband, handbag, lover, friend and incompetent handyman. I have to be all these things within a family that gives me love, security and constant humour. More than anything, I have to juggle the sense that I have it all worked out against the reality that I have so much more to learn about being me.

Trisha

Fit Teams Score Well

Before you roll your eyes, thinking this is where I do my preacher act about food and fitness, wait up! First, I want to blow a few stupid myths out of the water. Here's something I hear ad nauseam from audience members on my show, usually when we're doing a show about overweight people and their moaning partners. Someone always says to the disgruntled 'she's not the woman I married' hubby, 'Hey, mate. You should love her whatever she looks like. It's not what's on the outside that matters. It's what's on the inside.' Utter, utter tosh! If that's so, if we really shouldn't be bothered about what we look like on the outside, would someone please kindly explain the presence of mirrors? Peacocks have plumes of magnificent feathers, certain baboons have bright red bottoms – every animal preens and wants to take pride in their appearance and that of their mate, and we human animals are no different. Sorry, but I've seen a lot of relationships that could best be described as brother/sister passionless numbers, where at least one partner has long ago given up caring that his or her partner looks like something they wouldn't ordinarily touch with a bargepole. Those relationships are about complacency and opting out, in the head-in-sand belief that a lack of personal hygiene or not giving a damn about appearances doesn't bother them. Get real!

Let's look at exercise and diet from another angle. As a partner I feel you need to make sure you're 'fit' enough for your partner to fancy – you know, the very thing that helped get you two together in the first place. If you don't take pride in your appearance, why the hell should your partner? You need to be fit enough to feel confident and able in the bedroom department. You need to be fit enough to be a hands-on parent. Being fit makes you feel good about yourself, which in turn gives you bags of self-esteem, which in turn makes you attractive to yourself, your partner and your children…and don't think that what the kids think doesn't matter. Ask every hugely overweight parent about what it feels like when their children get teased about Mum or Dad's size. Okay, in an ideal world it shouldn't happen. But when it does, the kid's attention is then drawn to the fact that Mum/Dad is always too knackered to play/run/visit the funfair and is constantly moaning about how they look and feel down.

As for food, here's the choice. You can either eat for energy or lethargy. I have an idea that Peter and I see this differently (understatement!). I don't actually subscribe to the stuff-what-you-want-when-you-want school of thought. In the Western world, I see denying yourself when it comes to stodge as a good thing. But then I can still remember the part of my childhood that I spent in East Africa, when there was considerably less food than everybody needed, rather than an abundance of self-indulgent rubbish! I don't mean never having this or never eating that, I despise using the word 'treat' about any sort of food. What are we? Performing dogs or seals in that we do something 'good' and get 'treated' with 'bad food'? Daft. Peter's idea of healthy eating and mine differ hugely. But it pays to remember that when he first moved in with me, he immediately lost three stones. No diet. I helped him discover that you can do exciting foody things with fresh veg, fruit and seafood and that fat people don't eat breakfast.

All food is equal in my book. No treats. Some foods are necessary and some are blatantly not. I've got myself into never ever buying or having in the house food I don't intend my family members to eat. Does it work? Billie once stayed at a friend's and came back shocked. 'Mum, we were given pizza and chips for tea. Yuck! No vegetables or greenery, just a plate-ful of stodge.' Case proved, M'lud. My kids know about the five food groups and are into them, purely by what *I* buy and what *I* eat. Madi does grocery shopping with me and I swear that at eight years of age she can spot and avoid fatty mince from a million miles away. She has fun looking for the leanest portion in the supermarket fridge!

I buy low-fat crisps every three months or so, and that's it. I constantly try cooking and finding new foodstuffs, even though I haven't eaten meat since 1980. It's usually trial-and-error, but, what the heck, it keeps the kids' tastebuds on their toes. I always have a huge bowl of fresh fruit in the kitchen and the girls know they can help themselves at any time. Poor Peter still struggles to come to terms with fruit and I must admit I nag him about vegetables. But I'm not shy in pointing it out if he's stacking on the weight. My message being, yes, I'll always love him, but I fancy him far more when he's not too overweight and sluggish.

It's not all one way. I never *assume* Peter will fancy me. I put a bit of effort into looking good for him, and not just when we go out. While working in the Middle East, I came to understand something about Arab women. Sure, some may veil themselves in public, which leads sceptics to wonder why they buy all those gorgeous outfits in Harrods. I mean, who's going to see them? Their men, that's who. Maybe it's a hangover from harem days when a woman had to compete with other women for her shared husband's time, but I take a leaf out of their book, and I enjoy it. Taking care of myself and knowing and feeling I look good is confidence and sexiness boost Number One!

And what about that exercise word? I'll beat Peter to this and admit I'm pretty obsessed in that way. I love the way I look right now. I love that people gasp in surprise when they hear I'm 45 – and I aim to keep it that way for as long as I can. But, as someone who lives with depression, I've discovered that, as scientific studies have shown, working out does more for the mind than medication on its own ever can. I love weight-training too – especially as a means of burning off premenstrual tension.

I've also discovered the more muscle you have, the more you can eat without gaining a pound. That's why I don't believe in self-denial when it comes to food. Two points here. (1) I've re-trained my brain to enjoy the healthy stuff and not be so turned on by the unhealthy and (2) because I'm very muscular, if I indulge, my body burns the excess calories off very quickly. For the first time in my life, I have to work hard at *not* losing weight, which happens if I miss as much as one meal. Having once tipped the scales at almost 13 stones, trust me, that's a miracle!

How to get the kids active? Get them into the garden or park. Good 'lure' stuff: kites, water cannons and pistols in summer, all those funny fly-through-the-air-toys, a dog, a football, Barbie dolls in toy cars on a string, bikes, scooters, twigs for guns while playing Cowboys and Indians or Star Trek and Aliens. Yep, it's the leading by example thing again. Trust me, unless you're a total dragon, kids will usually jump at spending time with parents making a twit of themselves and getting dirty and playing.

Peter

This is probably the one bit of this book where Trish and I part ways. Look, you can't argue with most of what she says. Only last night, she thrust a newspaper article under my nose telling me about 15 ways to extend my lifespan and, yep, it is all probably true. However, living a long life is not my only motivation. I also want to live well. Don't get me wrong – life is great and I have no desire for it to end any time soon, but I have a real problem with the whole philosophy that the purpose of life is to make it as 'long and healthy' as possible. I strongly believe that along the way it has to be challenging, stimulating and, if need be, unhealthy and indulgent at times.

First, though, I have to say that I am immensely proud of my wife's commitment to *her* health. When we met she was pretty overweight but she is now slim, fit and strong. She looks better now than when we first met. She is like the woman in the Special K breakfast cereal ad. I fancy the pants off her and she works hard to ensure this.

It's very true when Trish says that I am a bit irresponsible at times with my own health. I don't eat as much fruit and veggies as I should, I neglect minor health problems, I have trouble maintaining a regular pattern of exercise (although I am sporty!) and I probably should listen more to the amazing health facts that she presents me with every second day. But, the reality is that I don't, and here's why.

I don't think I have an unhealthy lifestyle. I don't smoke, hardly drink, exercise more than most guys I know, eat low-calorie, low-fat food most of the time (or, at least, whenever Trish is around) but I also want to *not* do those things sometimes. I love pasta, for example – I could eat it five days a week. I am happiest when I eat pasta. If I eat it as much as I want then I know I would get hugely overweight...so...I eat it once a week. However, for someone as regimented and obsessive about their diet as Trish, this is weakness. And I think that's sad. A little indulgence, a little variation from a routine is a good thing. As a result, I can really enjoy food rather than just seeing it as a means to life extension.

My message here is to all you guys who like a pint or a curry or a bit of laziness. It's all right, but don't make it the only way you live. Balance it with some good stuff. You'll recognise the good stuff – basically, it's anything that your wife nags you about. My message to Trish is....hey, I'm a passionate man...I'm more bocconcini than broccoli! Understand that, chill out, stop nagging with the health message and maybe I'll hear more.

Trisha

Surviving the Scrum

In my years as a Mental Health Advisor, one thing came up again and again. How come some people can literally go through hell and come out the other side with an 'onwards and upwards' approach, while others are crushed forever by something so minor the rest of us probably wouldn't give it the time of day? Take mental illness and its distorting effects out of the picture and the answer to the riddle of what makes some stronger while others fall apart is this: resilience. The dictionary definition of 'resilience', roughly, is recovering from setbacks and springing back into shape after you've been squished!

Let's pull resilience apart and see what it's made up of.

People who are resilient have these qualities:

- **They are built on a bedrock of optimism:** *they see the glass as half full rather than half empty.*
- **They learn from change and adapt to it,** *instead of running and hiding from it and seeing any sort of change as a bad and scary thing.*
- **They stick at things:** *they come from the school of 'If at first you don't succeed, try, try, try again'.*
- **They don't make the mistake of thinking they're the centre of the universe:** *if someone growls and doesn't bother to say Good Morning to them, they realise it's probably not that Mr Grumpy hates/despises them; it's about Mr Grumpy being fed up with his own lot. He's probably totally unaware of anybody else.*
- **They're creative** *in their approach to problems.*
- **They have a well-developed sense of humour** *and they realise they don't have to take themselves too seriously all the time.*

So how do you go about instilling this resilience thing in your team?

First, by promoting optimism in them: as I've said already (see page 66), when I was a kid, every morning, my mum went out of her way to greet us with the cheeriest, happiest 'Good Morning'. It's amazing how something as seemingly simple as this can arm a child with a sense of optimism. That morning greeting told me, Life is fantastic! Today's another adventure! Let's get up and go. Come to think of it, it's exactly what a coach does with his team before the big game. He fills the guys with the spirit of success: 'We can do it! Get out there and do your best! I *know* you can do it.'

When I was going through what I call my dark days, as a struggling single mum fresh out of psychiatric hospital, optimism was bloody hard. But I achieved it with music and power-walking. Walking as fast as you can without breaking into a run – or, in fact, any kind of brisk repetitive exercise, creates a chemical version of optimism by producing endorphins in the brain that trigger a high. While walking, I used to listen to tapes of the most uplifting songs and music I could find; to this day, Jamiroquai's 'Return of The Space Cowboy' means a hell of a lot to me. In my mind it was about having been 'out there and out of it' in hospital – a bit like being in Outer Space. Songs have helped me in so many ways. The Isley Brothers' 'Who's that Lady?' allowed me to daydream about what people would say about me when I came back from the scrapheap they might have thought I was consigned to. Bill Withers' song 'Lovely Day' was another one. I even called my television production company 'C'est La Vie' after Robbie Neville's hit of that name. In that song he sang the lines that got me through absolute pits of self-pity: 'When you're down, there's just one way to go (Up!)' So, what with the thump, thump, thump of my steps and the uplifting music, I worked at putting myself into an 'I can make it' frame of mind. Note: If you get into this kind of 'mood manipulation' just make sure the music's not so loud you're unaware of traffic and keeping yourself safe! But, let's not forget, years before, my mother had helped sow the seeds of optimism that all this was just re-awakening.

I used to play uplifting music with personal meanings in the car on school runs and sing along with a then four-year-old Billie; songs like the one from The LightHouse Family with lyrics about how, 'There was a time when we didn't think we would make it through the night, but now we are together you and me.' We truly believed we were singing about our successful battle through the bad times and felt proud that nights of teary cuddles had turned into days of laughter. Even singing 'Always Look on the Bright Side of Life' over and over again in silly voices and fits of giggles did it for us back then.

But all hail to cheery 'Good Mornings' and 'Good Nights' said in a tone of voice that conveys the absolute buzz of life, bad stuff and all!

Learning from Change and Adapting to It

Looking back at what I've been through in life, let's be honest here. Yours truly often changed at a pace that would be hard put to challenge a snail! See Chapter 9 (page 302) for more on this but for now here's what I mean by learning from change and adapting to it.

Let's say you always travel on the motorway. You've timed your business trip meticulously. Then you find the motorway's shut. Cursing because you'll be late thanks to this, you're forced to take the winding, single-lane B road. Hey, it takes you along the coast! And there's fabulous scenery. Look, if you're going to be late anyway, why not stop at this roadside café and call ahead? Wow! This café is so quaint and what brilliant cream teas. Next, you're travelling through a forest. Just smell that pine!

Usually when you arrive at your hotel, you're so stressed after a few hours on the motorway that you head straight for the bar, have one too many and start the next day's work with a hangover. This time, though, all that scenery and greenery seems to have soothed your soul. You feel really laid back and after one drink, you turn in for the best night's sleep ever. The next day, you're so refreshed you knock 'em dead at the conference. People want to do business with you because you seem to be the only one who's not jittery and frantic. You look like someone in control.

> **Lesson:** The motorway may be good for time, but it's bad for stress and ultimately, *not that good for business*.
>
> **You adapt:** Stuff the motorway. You make a point of leaving earlier and always taking the coast road.

What's the saying? 'Every cloud has a silver lining.' Life has taught me that sometimes you go through situations that make you weep and wonder why you stay with it. The answer will come. Probably not now, but in years to come. But there'll be a time when you'll realise that there was a point to the things that have happened in your past, no matter how bad they've seemed. When my kid sister died, I raged at God. Why? Why? Why? Then it came to me. She was gone. It was traumatic. We who remembered her could make her death a dark and destructive thing. Or we could make good come of it. To fall apart in guilt and self-loathing would be to forever taint her memory with those negative feelings. To make good flow from it would mean that, we, her family, and people who didn't even know her felt her passing had some meaning; that it could make life better. So I dedicated ten years of my life to working to improve mental health services. I did fund-raising for Schizophrenia Australia in Winnie's name. People often thank me for my involvement in mental health issues. They should thank my sister and her passing.

I remind the girls that dinosaurs didn't have what it took to adapt to their ever-changing world, and where are they now? As the above section on optimism shows, we did a lot of adapting and changing after my divorce. I had to change the very way I parented. That's when I first used the 'team' approach with the girls, emphasising how we all needed each other to pitch in and to keep an eye on each other. Every time something good comes out of something my children initially thought was bad, I point it out to them. Peter and I also work hard to get them to think about how they can adapt to the unexpected. You don't even have to use real-life things to do this. Playing 'What if?' is a good one for getting them to think about dealing with change.

When we suddenly uprooted from Australia and arrived in chilly England, day-to-day life was all about adapting to new stuff. Occasionally, I remind Billie about how she never thought she'd fit into her new school. Here she is, four years on, with a close bunch of friends and loving schooldays. She's to be praised for sticking with it and adapting to a massive change in her life.

Coping with Loss

Sometimes we lose a team member. I've always said we should be issued with a T-shirt at some stage in our lives saying 'No one Gets Out of Here Alive!' Death is a fact of life – as is losing. It's how we cope with it that counts. Elsewhere, I've talked about how I dealt with my younger sister's suicide (see pages 9, 30, 217), but how do you explain the death of a loved one to younger players? Your first opportunity might be the death of a much-loved pet, as it was with Billie. In Australia we had a gorgeous big old cat called Henry who through illness had to be put down. Billie was about seven at the time and we decided to take her to the vet with us. It has to be said, we had a brilliant vet who added to the explanations Peter and I had given of what would happen. He explained to Billie that Henry would feel no pain and that it would be like drifting off to sleep with him.

Billie held Henry in her arms while the vet gave him the injection and kept talking to us all the time. 'See...he's drifting off now.' The vet even left us alone with Henry for a while and helped us put him back in his travel box to take home. There, Peter dug a hole in the back garden while Billie hammered a cross from a couple of pieces of wood. We had a ceremony and Billie and I hugged and cried together and talked about daft things Henry had done in the past and laughed.

It's worth taking on board the fact that children who live with farm animals and see their birth and passing as everyday things usually cope with natural death a lot better than city kids, who are far-removed from even where pork and beef really come from. It's important for a child to be talked to and not excluded on the grounds of age. I think it's also important for a child to see the grief of others. We in the West may 'tut' at that but, remember, in other cultures, death is marked by following the coffin accompanied by wailing and overt mourning. In some cultures, admittedly, kids might be a bit freaked out at parents going to that extreme, but I feel it's important for them to see Mum or Dad showing some emotion.

I don't recall seeing my mother cry when my grandmother died. As she'd always lived in the West Indies, I'd never even met her and yet when Mum got the news that Grandmother had passed away, I went to school that day and fell apart during school assembly. When I wailed to a concerned teacher about my loss, she commiserated with me. The teacher was then stunned when in response to her 'What was your grandmother like?' I answered I'd never even met her! I remember feeling I was crying on my mother's behalf. Maybe Mum has cried, but like so many of her generation, not in front of me.

Death isn't the only form of loss. Divorce is another. Children cope with it according to the degree of acrimony, sadness, conflict and other factors involved, like whether they're the only child or not and also the child's basic personality and age. Thus, as a tiny baby, Madi has no recollection of my splitting up with her natural father while Billie was four, and has a few, traumatic, albeit patchy memories and what I call mis-memories. Billie was so affected, not only by the split, but by my rapidly deteriorating mental health and exhaustion, that I did something I'll always be grateful for: taking her to see an eminent child psychiatrist.

I remember a parent of one of her school friends suggesting I was 'stigmatising' my daughter for doing this. She, too, was also going through a messy divorce and thought I was over-reacting to Billie's distress. Years later, I met up with this mum again. She'd had years of trouble with her son, and things were still pretty bad with her ex because of his behaviour, and she turned to me and said, 'How I wish I'd involved a shrink like you did.' I'm not saying that every kid who goes through the stress of divorce (or, for that matter, death) needs professional help, but it's folly to struggle on if the child's behaviour becomes extreme and stays that way even when things become less fraught. Billie didn't warm to her psychiatrist, but he acted as an independent voice for her at court custody hearings and nipped a lot of destructive things happening in the bud. He had her draw pictures and act out stories with a doll's house, and interpreted her reactions so that we knew what was happening for her. It often comes as a cold bucket of water to the partner who is leaving.

By the way, evidence shows that walking out on your partner is far less destructive to a child than the effects of affairs and infidelity, with both partners staying together. Partners who play around are usually focusing more on the anatomy that helped make the child in the first place than the poor little person who's trying to make sense of it all – and, yes, they work it out! If you know you're about to separate, at least one, if not, ideally, both parents, need to sit down and talk it through with the children. Kids are usually focused on what's going to happen to them, understandably. There are a number of good books, web sites and organisations that can give you a lot of advice in doing this (see Chapter 10, page 332, for information).

At any time of loss, it's hard not to be so wrapped up in yourself that you almost let the team members struggle on on their own. But if you do that rugby scrum-type thing and hunker down together, you see a lot more of what's going on. Of course that also means allowing the team members to see what's happening with you and I don't think you should be shy of doing that in a measured way.

The most powerful thing the team can see is the manager/coach being angry, upset, teary or woeful about a loss and then seeing that same person struggle and eventually come out the other side, even if it is with help. The message, then, is that loss is part of life, so the important thing is to find a way through the initial pain, and get back to celebrating life again. You know, the old triumph over adversity thing?

Peter

There are, of course, many types of loss. Our reaction to it, however, tends to follow a familiar pattern, regardless of the cause as we try to re-establish order, fill a void or adjust to a new set of circumstances. For men, and increasingly many women, the loss of a job is a particularly difficult situation to deal with.

Men are programmed to provide and our identities are often closely linked to this social role. For men, the loss of a job can mean an undermining of identity, embarrassment and a change in social standing. I know from experience that it can be extremely awkward when you are out of work – even when, as in my case, it is by choice. In our first year in the UK, when I wasn't at work, the one question I dreaded more than any was 'What do you do?'

I was never comfortable with the answer that I was a house husband or a consultant – both were accurate descriptions of what I was doing with my time but carried little social value with the people I met.

I learnt that work provides us with income, an opportunity to maintain or aspire to a certain lifestyle, a chance to express our abilities, a social currency and, most importantly, a definition of who we are. Losing this can be extremely difficult. The difficulty is compounded when people find it hard to regain work or have to do something at a lower level. A lot of personal adjustment is needed here. Only recently, Trish and I were discussing this with some friends of ours who have just opened a business and are working their butts off. It's interesting for us that we have had a bit of a role-reversal that we are now comfortable with and it's Trish rather than me who carries our family's expectation to provide.

As in all things in life, there is a balance to be struck between the things that we value highly. Take work. While it's important, it is not the be all and end all and by understanding the value of a job in the broader context of our life we will be better able to deal with the inevitable change and loss that is associated with not working. Hopefully, by now, you will have a sense of our perpetual struggle as individuals and a family to find this elusive balance.

Trisha

If At First You Don't Succeed…

…Try, try, try again. And if you're still getting nowhere, stop, take stock. There must be a better way of doing it. If you get nowhere because you're walking into a brick wall, try going over it. Too high? Then try going round it. There's no sign the wall is going to end? Then tunnel under it. You've been digging for hours, but the wall's foundations go down forever? Hmmm. Let's stand back and think about this. Talk it over with people who've scaled more than a few walls in their time. What? Someone's got a ladder? And someone else is willing to hold it at the bottom? Bingo! Mum taught me this.

'There's no such word as "can't"' is a good one to tell the kids. Your team needs to see you set an example in the not giving up without a fight stakes. Obviously, though, you'll have to balance this up with teaching them that there's also a time to walk away, if only to build up energy and expertise in re-tackling a problem.

Sticking at it can be taught from babyhood and those early days of trying to build towers of bricks. When your little one gets frustrated because the bricks keep falling down, it's easy to introduce the subject by saying, 'Hey, why don't we try building them another way?' Keep it light, and laugh when they all fall down again. Try another way – singing a 'build up the bricks' type silly song. What you're doing is showing your child that trying different ways to do things can be fun. Naturally, baby gets a huge hug and a 'well done for sticking at it' when the tower is finally built.

Playing to Win

The message here isn't actually that winning is everything. When the girls get their school reports, we make it very clear that what we're looking for is evidence that they've given a subject their best shot and as a result there has been an improvement compared to the teacher's comments and marks last term.

Winning is more about getting your team to better themselves at every opportunity. After all, improvement is not only about personal growth, it also gives people goals and a sense of achievement in their lives. No matter if your child has poor reading skills. They can still win by steadily improving those skills to the point where, say, they can read a page of a comic, or work out which prize is being offered on the back of a breakfast cereal box. I hate to sound like a broken record here, but the best way to show your team this is to lead by example. No, you don't have to have the fitness of an athlete or the figure of a model, but losing a few pounds and getting yourself fit enough to compete in the Mummy or Daddy race at the next school sports and not come last like you did the previous year is a far more modest and achievable goal.

Occasionally I'll take the girls out jogging in the countryside with me. When they're puffed out and start to complain they simply can't go any farther, I get them to focus on a tree up ahead. 'You can make it to the tree. Tell yourself you can and you will.' (I got that one from my mum.) Then, when we get to the tree, I tell them how amazing they are and how they can make it down to the river. And they do. It's a basic lesson in goal-setting, then positive mind talk followed by achieving the aim and feeling justifiably proud about it. Four years ago I told my personal trainer there was no way he'd ever get me to run and he did the same thing with me. Minus three-and-a-half stones later, I love running through the woods every day, and often do 12-mile runs, no trouble. When I first ran that distance, I came home buzzing and breathless and told the family. The look of pride on their faces and their congratulations meant a hell of a lot to me. And to them, I suspect. If you put importance on bettering yourself, so will your team.

A Last Word on the Vast Importance of Resilience...

A psychiatrist once said to me, 'Trisha, so many dreadful things have happened to you. Is it scary when you look back?' 'No,' I said. 'What's more scary is thinking about who I'd be and where I'd be if all those dreadful things *hadn't* happened to me!' It took years, but I've finally learned what the band Bluezeum meant when they sang: 'If life is full of crumbs, make some appetisers and when life is full of shit, make some fertiliser.' I did. Then I went ahead and planted a whole lot of flowers in it with a lot of help...

You Gotta Have Faith....

To be honest, I totally forgot the power of faith until I started recalling Billie's visit to the child psychiatrist. This man was a professor and expert in child and adolescent matters who'd worked closely with courts both in Australia and Canada when it came to formulating issues like child access visits and the rights of the child in divorce cases. I was lucky to get to see him. On our first meeting, he sat me down to interview me about Billie, and one of his first questions has stuck with me ever since. 'Does the little girl believe in God?' I was taken aback. 'What's that got to do with anything?' I asked cautiously. 'Oh, it's just that in all my years of experience with thousands of troubled children, the ones that have a faith in a Greater Power always do so much better!' Naturally I wanted to know why. He explained:

'If a child has no sense of a Greater Power and sees Mummy and Daddy as being where the buck stops, when Mummy and Daddy are at each other's throats, preoccupied, depressed or angry, that child feels there's no greater power to take their problems to. When they believe in God, they have tangible hope in prayer, in the Big Guy Upstairs who ultimately can make Mummy and Daddy be nice/see sense/stop shouting or hitting each other – one day. In other words, their God gives them hope. They also have someone to get cross with, shake their fists at, and bargain with. Obviously, God will listen to them, however fed-up, teary, angry or incoherent they may be. They don't even feel they need to form full sentences for the higher power to look out for them. Suffer the Little Children and all that!'

As it happened, although I prefer not to align myself with any particular religion, I have a strong faith in a Higher Being and had always talked to Billie about it. If I went the whole hog I'd probably become a Ba'hai. (In a nutshell, they believe all faiths are equal and pretty much about the same thing, only with different prophets.) But the point was, here was this deeply scientific man basically telling me that he'd probably have far more success, far more quickly and more long lasting, if Billie believed that Mummy and Daddy weren't the final arbitrators when it came to her future happiness. And no, this psychiatrist wasn't a 'God-botherer' or a Born-Again anything.

There are studies that back up this psychiatrist's basic concept when it comes to recovery from illnesses, both mental and otherwise. I have an aunt who sat with me for hours when my sister was in intensive care, dying, back in the late 1980s. She helped re-fan the embers of my faith.

I saw Peter grapple with the death of his dear mother, at times pleading and wishing he could believe in something. There was nowhere for him to go, no higher Court of Appeal where he could take his suffering and my heart bled for him. Again, it reinforced my belief that it's important the girls believe there is a higher order than the fallible world of humankind. I encourage them to learn about every faith, just as my mother did with me. When living in the Middle East, I took the opportunity to delve deeply into Islam and was shocked to find how much rubbish about that faith is peddled in the West. I've also gone through years of looking at Judaism through an outraged fascination with Man's inhumanity to Man during the Holocaust.

Madi has inherited my fascination with faith – surprisingly, not through me. It was Peter she went to at the age of seven, saying that she wasn't sure about taking on this 'Christian-thing' lock, stock and barrel. Did Pappy know where she could discover what other faiths were about? Together they went on to the Internet and a strange thing happened. Peter, the non-believer-in-anything, had printed off a whole load of stuff about faiths for Madi and she'd come back saying she thought she might want to become a Ba'hai. I've been very careful not to name any particular faith to the girls, but maybe during our frequent discussions about the state of the world today, I've waxed lyrical about how faith should bring people together and not tear them apart. The Ba'hai faith is very practically and massively involved in peace movements the world over and the conflict resolution course I studied in Australia was also run by people of this faith.

Unless you pass on the ideals of faith to your child as a way of despising or belittling others, I can highly recommend it. In the process you get to teach them respect for other people's beliefs and never go on popular press versions of what people supposedly believe. Encourage them to explore where others are coming from. I'm not necessarily talking about getting heavily into the 'Organised Church' here. I'm talking about a tangible fear I and others involved in mental health and social policy have that we are breeding children who will worship some very, very scary and destructive 'gods': the gods of Fame, Money, Vanity and Me,me,me – unless you offer them something else to grab hold of. We all need something to believe in. Think long and hard about what you're teaching your team to put their faith in.

Billie

I like hanging out at home. Okay, sometimes when I've had a row with my parents or I'm just bored stiff, it's one of the last places I want to be. But generally it's a cool place to be. It's always warm and welcoming, and I have loads of things to do/play with. One thing I can't get over though is how we live in a reasonably big house, and I feel I have hardly any privacy. My bedroom door is plastered from top to bottom in 'Do Not Enter' and 'Do Not Disturb' signs, yet no one pays any attention. My parents walk in when ever they feel like it, and my sister isn't much better. It's really hard when I'm trying to talk on the phone and no matter where I try to escape someone is there. Okay, maybe I'm over-exaggerating, but we teenagers need our privacy! I mean, even now as I'm trying to write this my sister is trying to make me listen to one of her jokes! But it's not that bad. It's great when you come home from a stressful day at school and you can just chill out in front of the television.

Most of the time, the reason I get into trouble is because I try to negotiate everything. And I hate it when Pappy tells me that 'we are a family, not a democracy! I am an adult, I make the rules!'

No child tells their parents everything. In fact, I bet most kids my age would tell their parents less than a quarter of what happens in their lives, whether it's to do with school, or even involving a brother or sister. It makes me smile when Mum and Pappy think they know exactly what's going on, when they don't even know the half of it!

When I do talk to my parents, I find it easier to talk to Mum because if it's about something embarrassing she understands. I only talk to Pappy about stuff when I'm angry with Mum. He can be pretty understanding too. When either Mummy or Pappy are working long hours, I don't really think about it that much because

I'm so busy at school. It only hits me when I see them and I realise how much I've missed them. We usually have a cuddle then.

Mum keeps teaching me to be an independent woman. She tells me that I have to do well at school, so that when I'm older I don't have to rely on anyone. I know from her that women don't have to be all weak and girly-girly and that we are just as good (if not better at some things) than men!

When my school report comes in, Mum congratulates me on the subjects in which I've done well, but tells me to improve on the others. With Pappy, even if I've got As in loads of things, if I drop in a subject he wants to know why and tells me I need to improve.

I'm a member of Young Minds (the mental health charity) and I help man their stall at the National Mental Health Day Street Fair. At one time I worked with mental health service users to put together and perform in a play at my prep school. It was about the effects of bullying and it raised money. I got involved with Young Minds because both my parents work in the mental health area and I've seen my mum affected by mental health problems. I want to help people with mental health problems and I also want to show others that you don't have to be frightened of people going through a tough time. After all, my Mum wasn't that scary when she was ill!

I love skiing and rollerblading, which Mum taught me when I was about four years old. I also play rounders, netball, hockey, do cross-country running and athletics at my school. I'm on the school teams for those things. But I don't see them as exercise, I see them as fun. I'm quite a sporty person. Mum and I are the sporty ones of the family while Madi and Pappy have to be nagged to get active! Mum ensures that I have a healthy diet and eat at least five portions of fruit and veg every day. I see that as normal. But it does get a bit annoying that everything in our house is fat-free, low-calorie, semi-skimmed, etc. I couldn't get fat even if I wanted to!

Does our family laugh a lot? Yes, we're crazy! Mum does a mean chicken impression and I'm sure if she put her mind to it she could fart the alphabet! Mum's only good at being funny when she's not trying to be. When she tries to be funny, she cracks awful jokes she reads in the newspaper. Pappy has a good sense of humour. We watch *The Simpsons* with him on television. He's good at doing impressions, but he tells the worst jokes. Both my parents aren't afraid to have a laugh and make fools of themselves and us kids.

Dr Terri's thoughts...

There's a consensus of opinion these days that we've never had it so easy in a material sense. Kids are often thought of as being spoilt, with their PlayStations™, computers, designer clothes and music. Also, for women (a bit of feminism creeping in here) the message that's continually promoted these days is that we can have it all! My response to all this is, well, in part it's true. We do now have many wonderful material comforts available to us, and we also have more choices than ever. However, at the same time I also believe that life, and particularly family life, has become more challenging than ever in different ways. We are now often faced with too much choice, and our task can often be to limit the impact that materialism is having on our children. The latest issue is that of children and obesity. So much junk food is being targeted at young children, and, with the added pressures of modern life on parents, we can often go for the seemingly easy options with our kids. I call it the 'yes factor'. Similarly, when a child is playing up for something – be it food, a new toy, or a desire to continue playing long after bedtime – it can be easier to say 'yes' than to challenge and enforce boundaries. It is much harder and emotionally more demanding to engage with a child than to give in to them, because engaging means that you have to control your emotions when a child is being resistant to your parental requests.

Trisha, Peter and Billie have given you some really interesting tips to think about in terms of how they balance their lives. What I am going to advocate, which underlines their message, is getting the right *balance* for yourself and your family. That is the key challenge in life and it applies to most things you need, whether as individuals or within a family. If you have too much on your plate, whether it's food or the number of hours you devote to work, it can destroy the balance within yourself, and ultimately everything around you. I like Peter and Trisha's ongoing battle over broccoli and exercise. The point here is that Peter is right about balancing what is good for your health with having fun, and indulging a little here and there. If all you did was worry about your health in terms of every single thing you did and ate, then life wouldn't actually be much fun. Trisha is also right about trying to keep her family on the move, walking in the park, skating and eating a well-balanced diet. So, between them, they strike a good balance. Also, they teach their children the essential life-coping skills through honesty and example, but in a supportive way.

Role Models

Being a role model to the rest of your family, particularly your children, is very important because you have such an impact on forming their belief system. If you always encourage your children to eat a healthy diet, and set an example by also eating healthily yourself, then you are increasing the likelihood that your child(ren) will internalise this way of living into their adulthood.

Okay, they may also rebel for a while, but fundamentally they will be better equipped with the knowledge to make informed choices about things as they get older (I am talking about everything here, from diet to balanced beliefs on drug-taking, smoking, sex, education and work). If nothing else, your children will have a benchmark to gauge their choices against.

Set against everything that has been written so far, I want to ask you if you have any idea of how you find balance for yourself within your own life, apart from that of your family? How do you cope when stressed? Is there something special that you believe in, or, perhaps, a hobby that allows you to channel your energy? I have taken up horse riding lately to distract myself from work, and it is paying off because I engage in this with my son. What do *you* do? Think about how Trisha balances things for herself – she knows that the best form of mood management for her is exercise, and she thrives on it. So your challenge is to find out (if you don't know already), and then use, whatever helps you most to maintain some form of balance and perspective in your everyday life. This, in turn, will have a knock-on effect of balancing out the way you perceive and manage your family. Remember, gaining a balance may even mean that you see where more changes are necessary. Most important of all, though, is the message that if you don't get the balance with your emotional health right, then you are putting everything else around you at risk. Emotional balance (some people refer to it as 'mental wellbeing') is fundamental for a healthy lifestyle, and ultimately staying fit for life.

Relaxation

Finally, if you are someone who finds it difficult to deal with stress and don't always feel completely fit for life, and you don't yet have any coping strategies to help you, may I suggest that you try some basic relaxation. A good, simple relaxation technique is not rocket science, but can be one of the most effective ways of learning to cope with stress and anxiety (even panic attacks). If you experience underlying stress continuously, your body (nervous system) begins to wind itself up. After a while, it will become so charged up and jittery, that you may find it difficult to relax or sleep properly, even when very tired. If the underlying anxiety becomes prolonged and has no outlet, it can even lead to anxiety attacks. What relaxation does is to help the body and mind re-learn how to really *unwind* and let the nervous system rebalance itself. Once you can learn to let go, you will literally detach yourself from all worries and responsibilities and lose yourself in some wonderful neutral focus, even if it's only for half an hour.

There are two main forms of relaxation: mental and physical. There are also a wide range of different forms you can try. A good start might be to look at the various tapes on the market. Some consist of music, and others also talk you through a process of systematically relaxing the whole of your body and muscle groups, from your head down to your toes. If you have never tried out any form of relaxation technique before, a whole body relaxation tape is a good starting point. It will get you into the habit of focusing your mind, and building up the process, until you become more familiar with it.

Physical body relaxation technique ────────

1) Find a place where you are not going to be disturbed at all for the next 20–30 minutes. You need to be free from all noise, including telephones. Once you have found this space, get yourself into a comfortable position – sitting comfortably in a chair, say, or lying down with your arms laid gently by your sides.

2) Now close your eyes and take a few deep breaths. Breathe in slowly, holding your breath for a second, then breathe out. Repeat this, breathing from your whole diaphragm rather than your upper chest. Concentrate on your breathing consciously for a couple of minutes until you have gained full control of this.

3) While continuing to breathe in and out slowly, focus your mind on your head. Concentrating on your forehead, cheeks, eye muscles, jaws and tongue, firstly tense them up as much as possible (screw up your face as tightly as you can). Push your tongue into the roof of your mouth. Hold it all for several seconds, then relax all the muscles. Feel the tension flooding away. Repeat this once.

4) Now focus on your neck and shoulders. Again, tense them up as much as possible by drawing your shoulders up to your neck and holding it all tightly for a few seconds. Then let it all relax. Repeat once more.

5) Next, concentrate on your arms and hands. Tense up your arms and hands, clenching your fists tightly and holding for a few seconds. Then let your muscles relax. Repeat once.

6) Now focus on your stomach and buttocks, again tensing those muscles up as much as possible by clenching your buttocks tightly and pulling in your stomach. Hold it all tightly for a few seconds, and then release, letting all the tension go. Repeat once.

7) Now to your upper legs/thigh muscles. Tense first, hold and then let go. Repeat once.

8) Focus on your lower legs and feet. Tense up your muscles tightly, pushing your feet downward and screwing up your toes. Hold for a few seconds, then let it all go. Repeat once.

9) Now completely relax, keeping the breathing slow, comfortable and full. Concentrate on that feeling of weightlessness you may now be experiencing – no tension in your body. Feel it from the top of your head, right down through your toes and out the ends of your fingers... Stay like this for several minutes. You may even want to fall asleep at this point.

10) When you are ready, open your eyes and begin to re-orientate yourself back to whatever time of the day or evening it is. Slowly stretch and get up when you feel ready.

Top Tips

1) See your home as more than four walls and a roof. It's shelter, refuge, a place to nurture, be loved and learn about the Big World outside. Plan it as such.

2) Try to make sure everyone has a corner to call their own.

3) Your family is a team. Those not included and involved will feel left out and will eventually challenge a lot of what your team stands for.

4) Talk, talk and talk some more! Use the television, kids' drawings, walks, family meals, whatever…but be inventive when it comes to encouraging loved ones to talk…and *listen* when they do!

5) Have rules and let everyone know what they are. Ditto punishments and sanctions! Stick to both.

6) Keep an eye on balance. We all go through periods when work far outweighs everything else, but flag up when it goes on too long and starts to affect one or more family members.

7) Don't put people down or use name-calling. Look for good points rather than continually dwelling on the bad. Find every opportunity to *laugh*.

8) Make each person responsible for something in your household – a bedroom, a pet, a chore, etc.

9) Never shop on an empty stomach and don't put it in your shopping trolley if you don't want it in your mouth. Healthy eating starts in the supermarket.

10) Get your whole family to see being active as 'normal'. Er…that means you setting the example!

Case Study

Ted (46 years old)

Andy (32 years old)

The story so far...

Ted and Andy are brothers. Andy was extremely worried about Ted because he was so obese. It all started with Ted gradually putting on weight over a period of several years; each year Ted seemed to get larger. He would say to himself that he was happy being large, and didn't really care at all. However, deep down his weight played on his mind constantly. His sheer size prevented him from doing so many things and going places. Then one day Ted had a serious scare – a minor heart attack. This was the catalyst to him taking up the challenge of changing things for himself.

Ted bought himself a Walkman and started exercising by walking around the park. He found it hard at first, but kept it up until he was able to start jogging. He also completely changed his diet and has lost 12 stones by doing so! Ted says it was initially the most difficult thing he has ever had to face in his life, but he is now feeling fantastic. Andy is so amazed, relieved, and proud of his brother and is urging him to keep it up.

This case study is an amazing example of how a man decided to *challenge* and *change* the way he was in terms of his own fitness for life. He chose to start exercising by using a simple method and it paid off. He also completely changed his diet, which must have taken a lot of perseverance and difficult challenges. By changing two key things – his diet and taking regular exercise – Ted discovered a sure way of losing weight. In addition, he gained a lot of support to help him keep it up when the going got tough and continues to receive support from his brother. Support is vital if one is to keep up a changed behaviour without completely falling back into old ways. Now Ted must feel really fit compared to when he was 12 stones heavier! Ted shows us that despite it looking seemingly impossible to be able to turn things around – *change is possible*.

Chapter Nine

Choices and Changes

A Note from Dr Terri

Change is one of the most important elements of life. Without it, painful though it can sometimes be, we cannot grow and develop into mature adults, or achieve any kind of real happiness. Look at the way Trisha is now. She is successful, and lives a happy, fulfilled family life with Peter and her two children. But she didn't reach this point by accident. She had to work to get there, by making some tough decisions about the way her life was going.

As you've seen in Chapter 1 (page 2), Trisha didn't always necessarily make the best choices for herself, something she freely admits today. But although she had a rough time to start with, she began to learn from these difficult experiences and eventually realised that she could do something about her life, and shape the future direction she wanted it to go. Once she realised she could make these choices – even when things seemed awful – her life took on a new dimension. Trisha and Peter both had to choose to make some basic changes in the way they were living, which involved them both moving to England and changing the way they worked. Now they function extremely successfully – not only in their dual relationship as parents and partners, but also with the various pressures of their jobs and their other responsibilities.

The fundamental thing to remember is that even though upsets can occur, they don't necessarily have to have a totally negative effect on your life. It's the way you adapt to them that counts. Billie didn't have any choices available to her as a child when she had to move to England from the other side of the world. The change for her was learning to stand back and adapt to the new situation. She herself now admits that she was glad those things happened, because they forced her to change.

Trisha

Peter and I have been together ever since our first date, but I'm well aware that there's no way he would have ever fancied the woman I was before I took the decision to make some significant changes in my life. Okay, let me come clean here. It's not that I'm particularly heroic – it was the hell that my life was that forced me to make the changes and the choices that led to where

I am and what I have now: my job, the love of a good man, my sanity and a happy family.

I wouldn't have changed if it wasn't for the fact that I'd simply run out of choices. It's that way with many of us. Look at all the people who can *never* give up smoking, no matter how hard they try. Then they have a heart attack and, hey presto! Me? Smoke? Never! It was hardly rocket science. I quickly worked out that up until my breakdown, my choices had been killing me, emotionally, and there was a strong possibility that I'd finish myself off physically.

The only way you can start to realise you're not a victim, but that you are where you are because of the choices you've made, is to take stock. To take time and look back at where you've come from. Having done that, you again have a choice. Do you blame your bad choices on things that have happened in your past? If so, do you choose to allow those incidents or people who made your past a misery to have a hold over your future? Are they worth that? Do you choose to go along with the status quo (as far as family or a partner is concerned), no matter what emotional and physical damage is being done? Do you choose to start rewriting your future and that of your family tree? Can you see that good can come from bad? Or do you make the decision that it's all too hard? Whatever your choice, realising that you are the key to things changing or staying the same is absolutely vital.

On my show, I've heard countless battered women say they haven't got a choice. They stay in their abusive relationships because they are afraid, and are financially or emotionally dependent on the men who continuously beat them up. Basically, one day they reach the decision that they've literally had the ability to make any kind of choice – either mental or physical – drained out of them. Trace it back, though. There would have been a first time – a time when they might have been able to make those choices, even if that moment goes way back. I may not have found the research to back this up, but my experience tells me that a difficult early relationship with a significant male (brother, father-figure, etc) is often behind women becoming programmed to confuse love with being controlled emotionally or physically.

Think about your own background. Are you able to see destructive patterns in your life, and make conscious decisions to avoid them? Some people can do this, either on their own (or with the help of family and friends), or because they are forced into it by a life crisis, perhaps followed by therapy. Others go into total denial, preferring to hide behind obsessions or addictions, or stumbling blindly on, handing hurt from generation to generation. For most of us, however, things aren't quite that dramatic and it's simply a case of working out how we can improve on the status quo. Whatever the generation, the message is clear: improving the quality of life isn't about how many flash holidays you can afford, when and if you buy your own house or car or what designer clobber you wear. You can choose what your family life is like and what you want to pass on to the next generation of your family. The only thing you can bequeath, knowing the tax man can't get a cut, interest rates won't affect and the envious will have difficulty stealing…is the legacy of an ever-improving family.

Peter

There are all sorts of things that shape our abilities, values and, ultimately, our choices in life. Undoubtedly, these things include our unique abilities as a person, the support we get from those around us, the environment in which we live and the opportunities that we experience. I'm not going to get into the argument about whether opportunities are created or chanced upon, other than to say that, to some extent, we make our own luck and that 'fortune favours the brave'. I like the last quote because it captures a central theme in my life – namely, that when an opportunity exists it can be both good and bad. There will be inevitable upsides and downsides. But for me the key issue is whether you are willing to 'back yourself' and take a chance. Trish, the kids and I did this in relation to our move to the UK from Australia and, as you'll have seen by reading this book, the benefits seemed very remote intially but are gradually being realised now, although perhaps not in the way you would imagine.

One of the major influences on our abilities as adults is undoubtedly the experience and capabilities we develop though childhood and adolescence. These experiences determine our key characteristics as people, including our 'coping repertoire', values and aspirations. My own memories of growing up, while not unusual, are a constant source of explanation to my quirks as an adult. I also strongly believe in trusting your 'gut instinct' – it will usually be right. Somehow I knew that getting married to Trish was the right thing to do, just as I knew that coming over to England was the right thing to do. My philosophy is, back your instinct, be prepared for the worst-case scenario and then try to make it work. Whatever happens, life is full of challenge and change, and for Trish and I this is a feature that keeps life interesting, nurtures our love and maintains our curiosity in 'what could be' for us and our family.

Dr Terri's thoughts…

Change is one of the most challenging issues that any one of us can face in life. Trying to change something about ourselves that has become a familiar or long-standing way of coping or doing things can be very difficult. This is perfectly normal. We can often become over-attached to the way we do things because it makes us feel secure with the way we are, even when we are unhappy. Trisha raises a good example of this above (page 303) when she describes how some women remain in violent, abusive relationships for years, in which they are constantly beaten up by their partners. Many onlookers can't understand why they don't just leave. But for these women, leaving would mean having to face massive changes, so being in the only situation they know, however terrible, is more appealing than facing the unknown. They know how to be battered wives, because they know what it feels like. But they don't know what it might feel like to be away from this, which can be very scary indeed – changing things somehow seems so impossible. Many women in this situation, of course, feel they have no choice because of financial or other associated reasons. Ultimately, however, we *always* do have a choice. It's just that it can sometimes take a long time to feel brave enough to make it.

Let's take another example. Every time a child behaves badly, the parent shouts at him. This child becomes even more difficult, so the parent shouts even more. This is the classic sort of situation that always ends badly, with both child and parent being upset and no positive resolution to the problem. The parent is frustrated, and the child doesn't learn how to control his behaviour and may be confused. Ring any bells?

But what if *instead* of responding in this way, the parent chooses to calmly explain that until the child stops doing whatever it is he is engaged in, the parent will not speak to him? The parent then sticks to this and doesn't give in. Once this has happened several times, the child will begin to learn that the only way to get the parent's focused attention is by stopping or calming down. Then the parent can communicate with the child in a calmer way, explaining why his behaviour isn't acceptable. Bingo, something has changed here. Sounds easy, but in practice it is difficult to do. It can take a lot of planning and perseverance to change a habitual way of responding – in the heat of the moment it can be difficult to imagine that you will eventually get the desired result. So don't underestimate how difficult change can be. At the same time, don't forget that you do have choices and you can change many elements of the way you live your everyday life. As the two examples above show, some of the changes you face will be bigger than others. In essence, however, the process is the same.

The Cycle of Change

Let me explain further by using the ideas of two researchers, J.O. Prochaska and C.C. Diclemente who have studied this subject in detail. They talk about the different stages people may go through when trying to bring about change in their life: pre-contemplation, contemplation and action.

Let's take the example of someone who has been leading a very unhealthy lifestyle: eating chips and fast food, being overweight to the extent that it's likely to affect their health, taking no exercise, working under a lot of pressure, and not having any time for themselves or their family. At first this person may not think they need to change anything about themselves or the way they live, and so would be defined as being in *pre-contemplation*. However, although they may start out thinking they don't need to change anything, eventually something will act as a trigger to make them start thinking they *do* have a problem. It could be anything, from their partner saying they can't put up with things for much longer, to actually getting a physical symptom such as aches and pains. Suddenly, this person starts to realise they do have a problem after all, and begins to think about what they will have to change to improve their life. Now they are said to be in *contemplation*. The length of time they stay in this stage will vary – it could be a week, a month, or a year. Basically, there is no time limit – it will vary from person to person and their personal experiences and pressures.

During the period of contemplation, the person eventually becomes so uncomfortable with their situation that they will decide to do something, and so literally start engaging in change. In our example this would mean changing to a healthier diet or perhaps trying to lose weight. They might even start engaging in some form of exercise, or try to put some time aside to be with their partner and family, rather than working all the time. They are now said to be in *action*, and so have moved to the next stage of the process. For a while, the person may feel good about themselves – the fact that they have finally taken the decision to change, and are actively doing something about it. They may even feel a sense of control and achievement. However, keeping all this up over a period of time can be extremely difficult and if this person experiences any situation or event that is stressful, they may lapse back into their previous behaviour, maybe eating several bags of crisps, some chips and a couple of bars of chocolate. This is because they've known this kind of behaviour for so long that it feels familiar, providing them with a form of comfort and relief.

What happens next? Well, the person can either go into a full-blown relapse and return to their old ways of living, or they could go back into contemplation for a while. They may even go straight back into action. What they have learnt, though, is that it takes a lot of effort and perseverance to finally get to that desired place of long-term change, and that, for a while, maintaining something different can be difficult. However, it does become easier, and over time people can find they have changed into much healthier, happier individuals with more balance and perspective in their lives.

To summarise, change of any form can be really difficult to get used to at first, but it is definitely possible. One of the greatest hurdles may actually be in recognising that we *do* have choices. Once we have made a decision to change something, we then have to stick at it for a while before it becomes a more permanent way of living. Finally, we may have to go round this cycle several times before reaching that place of long-term change. So don't be put off – if at first you don't succeed, try, try and try again.

Trisha (again!)

As I write this, it's Christmas Eve 2002. Yesterday I turned 45. Tomorrow it's Christmas Day, and next week we all celebrate New Year. It's funny how this time of the year makes us reflect on the changes we need to make, whether they're about not stuffing ourselves silly with too much food, getting sloshed and ending up having yet another family row, or just coming up with the usual half-hearted New Year's resolutions about giving up smoking. All things are about making choices.

Sometimes birthdays can make us re-evaluate our lives, especially when we hit middle age. We can often get so confused and tangled up in feelings that time is running out for us, that we can feel like doing all sorts of outrageous things – running off with a toyboy, or floozy, say, buying a ridiculously expensive and powerful sports car, taking up clubbing or wearing leather trousers.

Mind you, that's more about regretting we didn't make life-changing decisions and choices earlier!

So, why wait for those artificial milestones? By now, we've given you quite a few things to think about and helped you realise stuff doesn't just happen to us all the time – that we're not victims waiting for the next sting in the tail, but are to a large extent masters and mistresses of our own destinies. Plus we have a massive say in the futures and destinies of our families and loved ones by engineering family life to promote happiness, positivity, well-being and better mental health. So, basically, this is your turn to do some work!

Dr Terri: How to Make Changes for Yourself

Now that you have read about Trisha and her family's choices and changes, and learnt more about the cycle of change, think about your own current situation and whether there's something you want to change. Have you ever stopped to think about where you are in life? Is there something you are not entirely happy with? Would you like to become more assertive; take up an educational course, say, or a hobby for relaxation; stop smoking; or improve your relationship with your children? Do you spend too much time working instead of being with your partner? Spend some time thinking about this and see if there is anything you can identify that you would like to change in some way.

There is an air of caution that goes with this. Trisha's experiences were pretty dramatic at times. It is true that out of terrible situations fruitful times can emerge. Sometimes it can take a crisis to bring about change – and that is exactly what happened to Trisha. But I am not suggesting that your need for change is, or should be, anything like that. If you are at crisis point, then seek help, support and advice before you start to undertake big steps – there are various contact numbers, addresses and website addresses in Chapter 10 (page 332). For most of us, however, the changes we need to make are small.

Quiz

1) Make a note of any area in your life (include family members) you feel needs change or improvement.

2) Spend some time thinking and trying to identify one small action that would take you a little bit closer to where you want to go – perhaps you want to spend more time with your children.

3) Set yourself a small goal of organising an activity that includes you and the children – it could even be something simple such as going for a walk together, or going to see a movie. Keep the following in mind:

- *If you focus on one small thing at a time, you'll increase your chances of success.*
- *Don't underestimate just how effective small changes can be – you may start something that you look back on in years to come with complete amazement.*
- *Don't forget – you do have a choice as to whether you do it or not! Good luck!*

Top Tips

1) If you feel like a victim, take responsibility for the outcomes of choices you've made. Choose not to make those choices again.

2) Instead of dwelling on blaming others or feeling guilty about the past, start listing the Changes you want to happen from now on and the Choices you need to make to get there.

3) Change the little things before you tackle major issues. In other words: learn to walk before you start training for running life's marathons!

4) Let children experience the full impact of their choices. Bailing them out every time will just set them up to continue making lousy choices as adults and blame everyone else but themselves.

5) There's no such thing as being in a relationship that totally stifles your freedom to make any of your own choices – you are still making a choice NOT to change your life and take the risk of going it alone.

Chapter Ten

Help

A Note from Dr Terri

Throughout this book we've talked about mental health and have shown that good mental health is a factor in determining how we deal with change, how we manage relationships, what we are like as parents and how we define ourselves. We've talked about the importance of looking after yourself mentally as well as physically and have touched on areas such as stress and depression. In all these discussions, we have given out one message loud and clear: that it is okay not to be coping, not to be effective or happy, as long as you make an effort to preserve and improve your mental health. In this chapter, we are going to look at some of the more common mental health problems, how to recognise them early and how to get outside help if your own ability to deal with things fails.

We'll start by getting Trisha's take on the subject of getting help followed by Peter's. Then Peter and I will talk about early warning signs to look out for, in terms of deciding whether you need help.

Trisha

If only when we needed help, we did what drowning people in movies do: shout 'Help! Somebody help me.' But the fact is, we don't. Instead, our needs come out in other ways: withdrawing, bullying, attacking, bouts of anger and depression, or being sexually promiscuous as a way of life – all ways of indicating that we're not coping.

But whether we're ready to accept help, or even want it, is another thing! Audience members on my show often suggest that a guest should have counselling when I haven't even brought the subject up. That's because I only suggest it when I can see somebody's ready or suitable for it. It's not the answer for everyone and for those who haven't reached their personal rock-bottom or self-awareness, it's a downright waste of time.

The obvious example for me was a guy who had half a bottle of brandy for breakfast, several cans of strong cider for lunch and spent the evening downing beer until he passed out. He never seemed drunk, didn't eat much and had a yellowish tinge to the eyes. And yet when his partner brought him on the show to try to drum home the fact that he had a drinking problem, he firmly stuck to his opinion that every hard-working man like himself (miraculously he was holding down a job as a furniture removal man) needed 'a few bevvies to unwind of a night time'. This was not a man crying for help, however much his partner wanted him to have it. His partner, by the way, was the daughter of an alcoholic who as a little girl had watched her father destroy himself and hadn't been able to help. So, there she was, eight-and-a-half months pregnant by an ex, in deep with our drinking friend after a couple of weeks and demanding that he give up drinking for 'me and the baby'. Oh, yes, she was due in about ten days! Who needed the help there? Correct! She did. I pointed out that she was going through the typical 'Let me help and save you' pattern that children of addicts often do over and over again in relationships.

We all go through what I somewhat cynically call the 'Land Rights for Gay Whales and Save the Planet' phase round about the age of 18, when we want to save everything and help everyone. That phase usually follows one of being so into 'me, me, me' that it's a refreshing change. But, gradually, we learn that not every person leaning out of a tower is a potential Rapunzel and not every guy with a sword is in danger of being eaten by a dragon without our help. She in the tower may just be sightseeing and deliberately stuck up there. He with the sword may simply be violent – and just as likely to run you through as he is to fight any mythical monster. But some, thanks to something wanting in our childhood, may be permanently stuck in knight in shining armour or Mother Teresa mode. Fine if you devote yourself to charity; a problem if you apply that criteria to every relationship. For one thing, knight and helpless maiden may seem very romantic at the beginning, but when she's dragging you under with her spending and is flimsy support when you lose your job or hit a crisis, that's when you start sneering at the very person you thought you could help merely by being there. Likewise, saving a drinker from himself may feel noble in the early days but isn't quite so romantic when you're sitting on bare floors because he's sold the sofa and carpets from under you and you can't afford Christmas presents for the kids.

In these situations, I find people would still rather focus on the partner who ostensibly needs help rather than the fact that they themselves may need help in not continually getting involved in trying to save the unsaveable. Many a family will spend energy on trying to get help for one child whose behaviour is seen to be wrecking everything, when the child is really like a pimple on a face. In other words, the child is the visible evidence of something in the *whole* family being not quite right, in the way that a pimple is the visible evidence of oily or unclean skin.

So how do you pass the 'It's okay to ask for help' message on to children without turning them into total wimps who give up and wheedle for help at the first signs of difficulty? It's a bit of a tightrope, I'm willing to concede, but there are ways of doing it.

I often look back on the days when Peter was acting in a parenting role for the very first time. When I first met him he was a totally single male – in every sense of the word. The thought of children hadn't even crossed his mind and yet he chose to get involved in a relationship where there was absolutely no question that the children were an extremely important part of the package. What blew me away was that he had no problem in asking a seven- and two-year-old for help. 'Right, girls,' he'd say. 'This is where you could tell me a fib, but I'm relying on you here. Would Mummy let you watch television at this time if she were here?' The amazing thing was that the girls were even more blown away than I was that a grown-up should ask for help and they'd give this sort of answer: 'Well, we'd like to watch this show, but Mummy would normally say we can't unless we'd put away our toys!' If ever a kid needed a lesson in it being okay to ask for help, it was amplified by the fact that such a big man was fine with asking such little girls for help and, like most decent human beings, they gave it, even when it probably wasn't the way to get exactly what they wanted!

In my days as a single parent, I often used the 'Help' line. As in, 'Hey, girls, I'm whacked! I'd really love your help in tidying up these toys. Let's see who can pick up the most things by the time I count to ten.' Then I'd congratulate two very-pleased-with-themselves little girls with, 'Wow! Thanks so much. You made things so much easier for Mummy. You guys helping me means that we can all cuddle down and read a story together now.' Worked a treat! Plus it seems it did a pretty good job in letting them know that not only was it okay to ask for help, but that helping out felt good.

It's obviously a different scenario when junior barely reads the homework assignment and then starts wheedling for help, i.e. 'Can you do this sum for me?' Then you have the opportunity to say, 'Well, let's see how I can help you to work it out yourself.' That's when you start sort of doing a 'Give Us a Clue' number and asking the child questions that will kick-start their reasoning powers. At the first sign of 'But I can't', and a shutting down of the listening skills, you do the gentle but firm, 'I believe you can. Let's not give up...' and when they figure it out, you do the 'Wow! I knew you could. How did you work that one out? I'm impressed!' Obviously, you won't remember, or will be too dog-tired, to do that every time, but make tackling the help issue this way the rule rather than the exception, and you'll be well on the way to helping your kids to really think about when to ask for help and when to have a jolly good try themselves first.

I'm a firm believer in never ridiculing children when they ask for help, even if you know your final answer will be a no. Making anyone embarrassed or constantly feel a failure for asking for help is setting them up for what I call the possibility of a future silent drowning: you know, they're silently sinking and you don't know about it until it's way too late.

Ultimately, in families where it's patently obvious that talking things through is the norm, and no one is routinely ridiculed, it's okay to voice opposition, anger, regret, happiness, a feeling of achievement and, equally, a feeling that you might be failing and that you need a bit of a life-line. If, on the other hand, a household is full of criticism, inconsistency, competition, sweeping problems under the carpet and being hung up on how neighbours, relatives and friends see you ('make a good impression…') family members could sink without trace or run away rather than ask for help. In those kind of families, asking for help or any other apparent symptom of not being able to cope in a situation, is seen as failure: if not by the parents, then by the children.

In extreme cases, these kind of families produce offspring who can use self-harm as a way of venting frustrated pain. Worse still, they can breed a member who, not having any idea of how to go about asking for help – and even if they did, would regard it as the ultimate failure – sees suicide as an option when it comes to escaping personal hell.

I'm not saying that families where there is a 'needing help=shame' culture are the only ones to have members displaying this distress, but think about it. It happens in families where, for instance, there is sexual abuse and the child is intimidated into not telling, or if they do a parent can't bear to hear it or denies it. How do these children ask Mummy or Daddy for help in this kind of situation? It happens where there is drug or alcohol abuse and the child needs help because the very people who he or she expects to help them through life are…totally helpless. And at the opposite end of the spectrum, it happens in families where pride, academic success and a good name is all – if you can't cut it and failure means to be cast out, again, how do you ask Mummy or Daddy for help? Well, maybe in cases like this you ask *someone* for help. You rob a bank, take drugs and become helpless, you get pregnant really young and then all those nice doctors and midwives show you attention and help you, or you fight everyone and anyone… It's then that you come to the notice of The System: police, social services, etc. Don't even start me on how we all like to point the finger at these services and say it's totally up to them to help people. Hey, check out your own backyard first, eh?

How good are you at asking for help when you can't cope? How good are you at spotting when your nearest and dearest are crying out for help, not disdain, anger or your putting in more hours at the office?

As I've said elsewhere in this book, I am one of those people who has to be backed into the tiniest of corners or two inches off rock-bottom before it occurs to me that I need help! Some would say I'm a typical eldest child – we think we have the answer to everything and can be lousy at owning up to anything but success. But I'd like to think I'm getting better at asking for help. Family therapy has shown me that I can *live with* my tendency for depressive moods, rather than *suffering from* it by asking my family for help in spotting signs and symptoms I may miss. And poo of poos, that means asking for help.

Peter and I recently did an interview for a magazine where the journalist asked, among other things, what really annoyed us about each other. Peter jokily mentioned flatulence, which embarrassed me no end, but certainly didn't shock me. After the laughter died down, he said that what really got to him was basically my reluctance to admit to my more negative moods – that when I felt upset or down, I hid it. I don't know why (okay, I do!) but I immediately associated this with my reticence to put my hand up and admit that I'm out of my depth, whether it's with work, juggling school runs, organising the Sunday roast, planning a holiday, or writing this book! Basically, what I tend to do is to send out smoke signals cunningly disguised as the Smell of Burning Martyr! But instead of coming over all flustered, snappy and saintly, what I *should* be doing is saying, 'I need a bit of help here.'

During my tough times, help has often come from surprising places. After spending time in the psychiatric hospital following my breakdown in 1994, some of the people who helped me the most were people who'd been through bouts of severe mental illness themselves. I also received help from various people I had helped over the years, so you can see why I believe that every little act of help you can give someone will ultimately come back to you. Naturally, you have to realise that you can't help every person you come across who is in strife. But we all find ourselves in situations where a spur-of-the-moment use of a contact, exchange of information, or even a smile, can be just the help someone needs to turn their lives around. If you're of a queasy disposition, get the sick bag out now, but when people ask why I do the sort of show I do (and remember, I did a similar kind of show for a number of years Down Under) I quote those who threw me the lifeline of a little bit of help here and there and gave me the backing and strength to be where I am today. My job on the show gets communities (i.e., the audience) together to suggest solutions and point out realities and the result is often that those who want help have access to it. We have two full-time counsellors, Ricky and Jackie, working with us, and Peter visits the office to talk to our researchers and producers about mental health matters. We refer people on to mental health organisations, further education and literacy programmes such as the government's Learn Direct, as well as parenting initiatives and other helplines and groups (see page 332). Even the show's website is linked to them (www.angliatv.com/trisha). The show satisfies the mental health activist part of me, but hey, I'm not a total fairy godmother – it also satisfies my joy of working with people and in television.

Staying involved with these groups, The Ashcroft Project (a Norfolk group supporting women with mental health needs) and the mental health charity MIND helps keep me real and in touch with serious and pertinent issues. Doing the school run and living in the middle of the countryside, surrounded by a loving family and a mad shaggy dog, helps me keep the sanity I once fought so hard to hang on to! Nice destination if you can get there... But what if you need help?

So what stops us asking for it? What has stopped me in the past? As I describe earlier, fear of being a failure, for one. So many women fear the label 'bad mother' and the accompanying threat of the People Who Will Take Your Kids Away if you fail. That myth of the perfect mother and the supposed bogeyman role of social services has done more to corner mothers with dangerous parenting practices than anything else (cue soapbox – it's time for a campaign to dispel those destructive myths). It's also one of the major reasons I decided to get involved when Home-Start was set up in my home town of Norwich. A charitable organisation, Home-Start trains parents to be volunteers who can support families where parenting skills have been damaged – usually because the adults have their own histories of abuse and neglect and have basically never really known what having loving parents is all about. Some parents simply need help getting through a bad patch.

Single mothers and fathers are often particularly bad at asking for help, for a combination of reasons. The right-wing tabloids have done a fabulous job in convincing us all that should your relationship collapse, your husband/wife die or run off with a younger model, or should you leave him after he/she abuses you, then the ultimate cherry on the cake awaits you: your children are supposedly destined to become illiterate, pregnant vandals with low IQs and a tendency to rob old ladies and end up on the dole.

And if you're in this kind of situation and you ask for help, it of course only fans the flames of their arguments. See? You're not coping! Single parents who *are* coping get that 'hero' label and are rightly proud of their success. So proud and self-sufficient that they see asking for help when they're going through a shaky patch as an admittance of failure. Hey, guys: Superman and Superwoman have been felled by Kryptonite!

To those outside looking in, I have one word... Understand; to the right-wing tabloids, two words – only one of them printable; to those sliding down the drain with their head held high and their will to live crumbling, I say, What's worse? Being 'right' or biting the bullet and doing what you need to do to keep your little team happy and functioning? Luckily, the stigma of getting help is lessening somewhat in many areas.

The major area where it's not happening is with mental health problems, and even then there's a pecking order. For example, it's easier to get help for eating disorders if you're a woman than if you're a man – if you can get help at all. It's easier to get help if you're too thin than if you're way too fat. It's much easier to get help if you've been abused as a child than it is if you feel you could become a child abuser because of your own traumatic past, and so on.

Some kids with depression are marginally easier to get help for than others. The mere mention of a personality disorder can be enough to send your local psychiatrists on a permanent holiday if they'll see you at all, and heaven forbid if your mental health problem comes hand-in-hand with drug and/or alcohol abuse, self-harm, or a long criminal record! Help in the mental health area is where Peter really comes into his own. He's gained an international reputation in his expertise in user-friendly mental health services, so let me hand over to him...

Peter

Mental health problems are very common. About one in four of us will need to get professional help for a mental health problem at some point in our lives. Think about that. Imagine your last family get-together, football game or trip to the pub. Imagine all of the people who are, or will be affected, by a mental health problem at some point in time. It's a lot of people and for most of us getting help will be associated with fear, embarrassment and shame. For many of us with mental health problems, this will be enough to prevent us from doing anything until things get out of hand. There are other reasons, too, that explain why it is often hard to take that first step.

Ignorance and denial are powerful factors that prevent us from doing the things we need to do in order to be mentally healthy. If we get a runny nose, blocked sinuses, headache, aches and pains, we recognise this as a cold or the 'flu and take steps to stop it from getting worse. But what if those symptoms were lethargy, negativity, sadness, poor sleep and loss of appetite? Would we be capable of recognising that we were suffering from stress/depression and then doing something about it? Probably not. There is generally a very poor level of awareness when it comes to the early warning signs of a mental health problem.

This is in part because there are all sorts of reasons why we don't want to admit our mental health is poor, so we make excuses. 'I'm overworked, stressed out, burnt out and all I need to do is relax and it will all get better.' Well, sometimes this is true and sometimes it isn't. If we could recognise the early signs, put words to feelings and be prompted to take action at a certain point then we would minimise the impact of these problems.

Dr Terri and Peter's thoughts...

This is not meant to be a manual for the diagnosis of mental health problems but it will help you be alert for the signs that something unhealthy may be going on and that maybe it's time to do something about it. We're just going to focus on two main areas: stress and depression, because they represent the more common experiences and they share some common early warning signs.

The first thing you have to do before you start worrying about your behaviour, or someone else's, is to first think – What is normal for them? What are they usually like? Is this problem usually present? As a general rule, you should be more worried if what you are feeling in yourself or seeing in someone else represents a change to their normal character or behaviour.

Stress and Depression

Most of us can easily identify with the experience of feeling 'stressed'. In fact, without stress, our lives would feel incredibly mundane, predictable, safe and unfulfilling. Stress usually arises when there is a risk of imminent change or challenge such as a looming exam, a job interview, moving house or a relationship starting or ending. The less control we feel over this imminent change the more likely it is to be stressful.

Stress is a normal part of our human experience and it physically helps us to prepare for, and overcome, perceived threats. When we feel the common symptoms of stress such as a rapid heartbeat, sweating, being extra alert, we are actually increasing our ability to identify and respond to the threat. The reality, though, is that for much of our usual life experience, being hyper-alert is not the best state to be in when trying to deal with the issue at hand. This is why so much emphasis is placed on calming down, 'chilling out' or unwinding. For most of us, for most of the time, stress is a useful or easy-to-manage experience that will not cause any significant problems. However, the symptoms of stress can sometimes become distressing, affecting our ability to carry on with everyday life and, for many people, developing into serious mental health problems.

Conditions such as obsessive compulsive disorder, anxiety disorders, sexual dysfunction and phobias are all strongly linked to stress. In addition, when we are stressed our bodies are constantly working harder and this in itself can make us vulnerable to physical illnesses such as the common cold or other infections.

We covered depression in detail in Chapter 7 (see page 191) so this is by way of being a round-up. At some point in our lives, we will all suffer with depression to some degree. It's normal, once in a while, to feel a bit low or down – say, when you have had time off work and then have to go back, or if a relationship is coming to an end and it is emotionally very draining. This is all part of the normal course of life, and you can eventually feel quite down as a result for a while. But it is the extent of the effects of depression on our ability to carry out daily activities, such as being a parent, working, eating, talking, enjoying sex and so on, that matters. It's when you feel down and that feeling of painful flatness/nothingness persists for at least two weeks, accompanied by several other factors, that you may be heading for a more serious period of depression. Somehow, suddenly you can't seem to shake this negative feeling off and you get no respite from it. This is important to bear in mind with other family members as well as for yourself.

So, how do you know when stress is having a negative effect or when you are depressed, rather than simply feeling down? Well, as with many mental health problems, the first thing you'll notice are changes in behaviour and thinking. Once again, you need to make sure you understand these changes in the context of 'what's normal' for yourself or the person you care about. Specifically, you should be alert to the following:

- **Disturbed sleep patterns.** When stress is involved (particularly when it relates to a deep-rooted cause that won't go away), this usually means finding it hard to get to sleep and lying awake at night, worrying...searching for that magical solution to make it all better. In the case of depression, it can sometimes have the opposite effect – sleeping to excess, and feeling totally lethargic and lifeless.
- **Digestive problems**, including nausea, stomach pain, constipation, diarrhoea.
- **A loss or increase in appetite.** When we're stressed we often don't find time to eat, and this in itself can lead to a vicious circle – the less we eat, the less we want to eat. Depression can have the effect of making us feel so flat that food no longer feels important. Both stress and depression can also have the totally opposite effect of making us eat more than usual, often relying on fast, junk food, or so-called 'comfort eating'. Either way, your body won't be getting the nutrients it needs.
- **Poor concentration.** When we are really stressed or

depressed our thinking can become affected. The combination of being pre-occupied with worry, feeling tired from lack of or inadequate sleep and being undernourished in terms of diet can manifest as poor concentration, a reduced ability to solve problems and less creativity.

- **Mood changes.** Unresolved stress can cause significant mood changes, making us irritable, easily frustrated and defensive, or, alternatively, quiet, withdrawn and unusually passive. Moods are a key area when it comes to depression, and are quite different from feelings. A feeling is something temporary – about a specific person, event or situation. Moods are overall states that can last over a longer period of time, infiltrating our general awareness. When we are depressed, our overall mood becomes very negative, which is experienced as a sense of overwhelming flatness or nothingness, to the point of not being able to feel anything at all. The negative thoughts can in turn lead to us blaming ourselves for things, even when they're patently not our fault.

- **A loss of interest in sex** – from exhaustion, preoccupation with worry, or an ability to take any interest in life or any form of pleasure.

Now, imagine the combined effects of all these factors, and you will see that they can all lead to a vicious circle – not enough sleep or good food, compounded by an impaired ability to actually solve the problem, and the cycle goes on, eventually making us lose sight of what was stressing/depressing us in the first place – *unless* we do something about it.

Here are some useful tips for controlling stress and depression in your life.

Reduce stimulants: Drink less coffee and increase your water intake.

Write it down: List the sources and causes of your stress (so you don't lose touch with them later). If you are depressed, keep a mood diary to increase your self-awareness. The more you become aware of the peaks and troughs in your mood rhythms, the more likely you will be able to identify which aspects, events, situations or people impact on you in both positive and negative ways. Then you can begin trying out activities and strategies to try and change the way you are feeling. Write down every time you enjoy something. Also write down everything you can think of that is positive about yourself and/or your life. You might need a bit of help in identifying some of these things if you are feeling depressed, but there will almost certainly be something about you which is positive – even if it's realising that you had a good night's sleep last evening!

Do relaxing stuff: Quiet walks, massage, aromatherapy, hot baths.

Get out of bed! If you find yourself lying in bed worrying, then get up, put the lights on, sit in a hard chair...do the opposite of sleeping...*until* you feel sleepy. Then go to bed and try to sleep again.

Try diversion strategies: Try out some physical activity that will take your mind off the way you are feeling. You may not actually feel like doing this, but force yourself to go swimming or jogging. After a short while you may be amazed at the effect this can have on your mood. Also, try out some mental diversion tactics, such as going to an evening class that you have to get mentally involved in or concentrate on in some way. Take your mind off the way you are feeling for a little while.

Top Tips

1) **Get to know yourself.** Become familiar with what's normal for you so that you can easily recognise when things are becoming unfamiliar. Educate others about what is the 'normal you' so that they too can recognise change and compare it against their usual expectations of you.

2) **Tell someone.** The one thing that usually helps more than anything else is to tell someone, get it off your chest, share your distress or worry. Sometimes the most difficult and draining part of experiencing a mental health problem is the energy that goes into keeping it a secret. The minute you tell someone you will feel better...just make sure it's someone you can trust.

3) **Getting your sleep right.** We cannot overestimate the importance of sleep. It is a basic human requirement and we all vary in terms of how much we need and when. Try the following to get your sleep back to normal: exercise, hot baths before bedtime, warm milk and honey, standing naked in front of an open fridge door (sounds crazy, I know, but next time you are lying awake in bed and can't get to sleep, try it. Open the fridge door and stand there until you are really cold. Then get back into your bed which will now feel warm and cosy – you'll drift off – trust us, it works!), relaxation exercises and, if all else fails, medication.

4) Get outside. We all exist in a community, an environment and a world. For many people with mental health problems there is a tendency to withdraw away from the world and to stay indoors avoiding people. Try and fight this, even if all you do is set yourself one task a day that involves going outside.

5) Be with others. Seek the company of the people you trust. They might just be your greatest asset. They can be kind and supportive but also help give you an objective assessment of whether you are getting better. For all sorts of reasons, we often lose our sense of scale and sense of self when our mental health is poor – others don't and we need them to help re-establish the right perspectives.

6) Eat well. Try and keep your eating habits normal. Try not to eat less or more. Indulge yourself a bit if you need the comfort of nice food or treats but don't go overboard. Be strict about mealtimes and always eat something. Avoid drinking lots of coffee (try peppermint tea), pasta and bread. These foods will slow you down and increase the feelings of withdrawal. Your body may seem sluggish but often there is a lot of anxiety underneath and this uses up lots of fuel – keep eating as healthily as possible.

7) Keep moving. Don't give up. Try and keep involved with your normal activities. You don't have to enjoy them but you do need to keep doing stuff, whether it's work, leisure, pleasure or study. Just keep doing something...if you stop moving you'll drown.

8) Have a goal. Set yourself a goal every day. It doesn't matter what it is as long as it is achievable and you do it.

When you achieve it, pat yourself on your back – it won't have been easy! It might be going for a walk, playing with the children, eating a healthy meal – whatever.

9) **Treat yourself.** Remind yourself that you are a unique person with valuable qualities, potential and a right to feel good about yourself. Reward yourself regularly. It's okay to feel good and you may need to celebrate those times by indulging yourself. Just make sure you can afford it and that you can recall it when things don't seem so good.

10) **Learn.** Treat all experience as positive. Sometimes the hardest of times are ultimately the most rewarding and valuable in our lives – but only if we learn the lessons to help us avoid the cause in future, and, if not, to recognise the problems earlier and if not, to get help sooner. I am a great believer that 'what doesn't kill you makes you stronger'. This is because we can learn from the experience but only if our eyes are open to it.

Getting Outside Help

If these strategies don't work, you may need to seek out some form of help. As Trisha has said earlier in this chapter, help can take so many different forms. You may find it helpful, for instance, to be around people who you know are generally upbeat and positive. Or it might be that a smile you get from your neighbour every day at a certain time challenges your thinking. However, it may be that the only way to make sure things don't get worse is to ask for professional help. We cannot impress enough that asking is a sign of strength. It may be a question of learning how to literally re-train your thoughts, challenging negative thoughts to start recognising the positives in life again. This will take time and may only come from outside. There are many organisations that can help you to set this process into motion. Some are listed below.

Helplines

There are many free and confidential telephone helplines that can help you determine what is going on, how serious it is and what you should be doing about it. We have identified several below that are well regarded and cost no more than a local call, regardless of where you are in the UK.

MIND Infoline　　**08457 660 163**
Run by the mental health charity MIND and staffed between 9am and 5pm Monday to Friday. They can give you information and support on a whole range of mental health issues.

Saneline　　**08457 678 000**
Run by the mental health charity Sane and staffed by trained volunteers between 12pm and 2am. They can offer support and

information on mental health issues, current treatments and the mental health system.

Samaritans   **08457 909 090**

Long-established charity supporting people who feel suicidal or despairing. This helpline is available 24 hours a day, seven days a week and costs no more than a local call. They can also be contacted via email (jo@samaritans.org).

Websites

Online mental health support is becoming increasingly available. This can range from information on common mental health issues, to interaction with a support person via email, interactive self-help programmes and even online counselling. The list below is just a starting point for exploring all the help that is available on the Internet.

www.mind.org.uk
mental health charity; lots of useful information

www.sane.org.uk
mental health charity; easy-to-use site

www.samaritans.org
charity; interactive help

www.mindbodysoul.gov.uk
aimed at young people; tons of useful information

www.mentalhealth.org.uk
charity; excellent information on where to get help

www.bbc.co.uk/health
BBC health site with a very good mental health section

www.depressionalliance.org
charity; good information on depression and self-help

www.bullying.co.uk
great website for help with bullying

www.forparentsbyparents.com
USA, everything to help with parenting

Useful Organisations

We can't hope to give you a comprehensive listing of organisations, but here are some that we have found useful for dealing with the problems encountered by people on the show. Even if they are not in your area, they will be able to point you in the direction to similar organisations near where you live.

The Ashcroft Project

14 Bridewell Street
Wymondham
Norfolk NR8 0AR
tel: 01953 605191
email: TheAshcroftProject@care4free.net
This Norfolk-based group aims to provide specialist care and rehabilitation for women with severe mental health needs. It offers residential and respite services and a supported housing scheme.

Barnardos
Tanners Lane
Barkinside
Ilford
Essex IG6 1QG
tel: 020 8550 8822
fax: 020 8551 6870
website: www.barnados.org.uk
A good source of information and books on subject like children and bereavement, sexual abuse, mental health, teenage pregnancy, etc.
National Offices:
Northern Ireland
    542–544 Upper Newtownards Road
    Belfast BT4 3HE
    tel: 028 9067 2366
Scotland
    235 Corstrophine Road
    Edinburgh EH12 7AR
    tel: 0131 334 9893
Cymru
    11–15 Columbus Walk
    Brigantine Place
    Atlantic Wharf
    Cardiff CF10 4BZ
    tel: 029 2049 3387
Regional Offices:
London East Anglia & South East
    Tanners Lane
    Barkinside
    Ilford

Essex IG6 1QG
tel: 020 8551 0011

Midlands
Brooklands
Great Cornbow
Halesowen
West Midlands B63 3AB
tel: 0121 550 5271

South West
Unit 19
Easton Business Centre
Felix Road
Easton
Bristol BS5 0HE
tel: 0117 941 5841

North West
7 Lineside Close
Liverpool L25 2UD
tel: 0151 488 1100

North East
Orchard House
Fenwick Terrace
Jesmond
Newcastle Upon Tyne NE2 2JQ
tel: 0191 281 5024

Yorkshire
"Four Gables"
Clarence Road
Horsforth, Leeds
West Yorkshire LS18 4LB
tel: 0113 258 2115

The British Association for Counselling and Psychotherapy
BACP House
35–37 Albert Street
Rugby CV21 2SG
website: www.bacp.co.uk

The British Psychological Society
St. Andrews House
48 Princess Road East
Leicester LE1 7DR
website: www.bps.org.uk

Home-Start
2 Salisbury Road
Leicester LE1 7QR
tel: 0116 233 9955
fax: 0116 233 0232
Originally set up in Leicester in 1973, Home-Start is a charitable organisation that aims to help families who find themselves unable to cope with caring for their children – say, because of poverty, ill-health or mental health problems.

Learn Direct
tel: 0800 100 901
website: www.learndirect.co.uk
This government-funded organisation offers high quality online learning on a wide range of subjects, from languages to mathematics to computer and business skills.

Sure Start
Level 2, Caston House, Tothill Street
London SW1H 9NA
tel: 020 7273 4830
fax: 020 7273 5182
email: sure.start@dfee.gov.uk
A government-funded organisation that works with parents, parents-to-be and children to promote the physical, intellectual and social development of babies and young children, especially those who are disadvantaged.

Children and Bereavement
Childhood bereavement network
National Children's Bureau
8 Wakley Street
London EC1V 7QE
tel: 020 7843 6000
fax: 020 7278 9512
website: www.ncb.org.uk
Launched in 2001 to act as resource for anyone who comes into contact with bereaved children, e.g. parents, friends, teachers, doctors, school and community nurses.

Children and Divorce
www.NetDoctor.co.uk
www.ivillage.co.uk
Two of many website with advice on talking to children about a family break-up.

GPs

For most of us, the starting point in addressing our health concerns, is our GP. Unfortunately however, when it comes to mental health, people report a wide variation in the quality of understanding and support received from their GP. This probably reflects the fact that mental health problems are harder to talk about, more difficult to diagnose and hence take longer consultations – a commodity that many GPs feel is compromised by the demand for their services. Nevertheless, mental health concerns are legitimate and you deserve to be listened to, to be understood and, wherever possible, to be given a range of options for treatment.

If you have a problem with stress or depression, don't ever settle for medication alone unless you are taking steps to identify and address the cause. Always ask your GP for information on possible side-effects and advice on other ways of resolving your problems.

Conclusion

A final note from Trisha:
A chance to be a star…in your family's future!

If you genuinely want to annoy me, mention 'pity' when hearing about my past. If you *really* want to upset me, call me lucky. I know that the luckiest things that have happened to me are my experiences, good and bad – and I continue to work damned hard to use what I've learned from those experiences to make my life, and my family's life, worthwhile.

When people see me in the flesh, they always comment on how I'm smaller, more shy, more 'ordinary' than the Trisha they see on television. They're right. Given the combined talents of a team of lighting specialists, a make-up lady, someone who dresses you, a personal assistant, a publicity department, etc, you too would give the impression that you're bigger and brighter, completely confident and totally in control. But underneath, you'd still have the hopes and fears that a studio makeover couldn't fix. Well, that applies to me, too. As you've no doubt gathered by now, I've had to deal with many major challenges in my life, a lot of them far from positive. Challenges that have impacted not just on me, but on my family. And if I can deal with these challenges, if I can make the major changes necessary for my life, for my family's survival (albeit with a struggle), so can you.

I truly believe that the most powerful changes we can make are for the good of our children, and their children's children. Each and every one of us has the power to help them become a little bit happier or, at the very least, that little less troubled. It takes courage, but we have the power to change a culture of criticism to a culture of praise. We can realise that a proud family history of so-called success might be hiding emotional failure. Success should be defined not just as academic or financial achievement, but as personal happiness. And it's the duty of parents to pass this message to their kids, to break a cycle of harsh, demanding and unjust social expectations. Mums of daughters can, through becoming role models, teach their daughters that 'security' doesn't mean hooking up with the first man with a regular income: it means developing a sense of true self-reliance, of personal identity. Fathers can teach sons that being a 'real man' has got precious little to do with how many beers you can sink, women you can pull or partners you can control.

Not many of us will achieve the kind of fame that changes the world. But we can be a shining star in our own family, and help to mould, in a positive way, the destiny of our children.

I still have to look up the recipe for a good roast turkey at Christmas. I still need to get help when my computer starts mucking up. Every so often I have to dig out the handbook on my car. On weekends I check out the latest fashions and where to buy them. I still trawl through the local real estate pages, even though we own our house. I love learning about the latest lifestyle stuff. Peter reads up on boys' toys, takes time to track down cricket scores and do a bit of research on holiday destinations and prices. This all takes a lot of effort. But don't think we're resting on our laurels when it comes to parenting. Family survival needs just as much – if not more! – time and energy devoted to research, discussion and planning as all these other day-to-day things. When dealing in family matters you have to be patient, open-minded, understanding, resilient and focused. And if that's the only thing you've got out of this book…yippee!!

ALSO AVAILABLE FROM VERMILION

Birth and Beyond	0091856949	£17.99
I Can Handle It!	0091857473	£6.99
The New Contented Little Baby Book	0091882338	£9.99
Toddler Taming Tips	0091889677	£5.99

FREE POSTAGE AND PACKING
Overseas customers allow £2.00 per paperback

ORDER:

By phone: 01624 677237

By post: Random House Books
c/o Bookpost
PO Box 29
Douglas
Isle of Man IM991BQ

By fax: 01624 670923

By email: bookshop@enterprise.net

Cheques (payable to Bookpost) and credit cards accepted

Prices and availability subject to change without notice.
Allow 28 days for delivery.
When placing your order, please mention if you do not
wish to receive any additional information.

www.randomhouse.co.uk